Primitive M

Louis Figuier

Alpha Editions

This edition published in 2024

ISBN 9789362096692

Design and Setting By

Alpha Editions
www.alphaedis.com

Email - info@alphaedis.com

As per information held with us this book is in Public Domain.
This book is a reproduction of an important historical work.
Alpha Editions uses the best technology to reproduce historical work
in the same manner it was first published to preserve its original nature.
Any marks or number seen are left intentionally to preserve.

Contents

PREFACE TO THE ENGLISH EDITION. ....- 1 -

PRIMITIVE MAN. ....- 3 -

FOOTNOTES: ....- 20 -

CHAPTER I. ....- 22 -

CHAPTER II. ....- 35 -

CHAPTER III. ....- 54 -

FOOTNOTE: ....- 73 -

CHAPTER IV. ....- 74 -

CHAPTER I. ....- 85 -

FOOTNOTES: .... - 136 -

CHAPTER I. .... - 137 -

FOOTNOTES: .... - 140 -

CHAPTER II. .... - 142 -

FOOTNOTES: .... - 218 -

CHAPTER III. .... - 219 -

FOOTNOTES: .... - 239 -

I. THE BRONZE EPOCH. .... - 240 -

CHAPTER I. .... - 241 -

FOOTNOTES: .... - 249 -

- CHAPTER II. — 250 —
- FOOTNOTES: — 260 —
- CHAPTER III. — 261 —
- CHAPTER IV. — 266 —
- FOOTNOTES: — 273 —
- CHAPTER V. — 274 —
- CHAPTER VI. — 316 —
- FOOTNOTE: — 333 —
- CHAPTER VII. — 334 —
- FOOTNOTE: — 357 —
- CHAPTER VIII. — 358 —
- FOOTNOTE: — 367 —
- II. The Iron Epoch. — 368 —
- CHAPTER I. — 369 —
- FOOTNOTES: — 382 —
- CHAPTER II. — 383 —
- FOOTNOTE: — 417 —
- PRIMITIVE MAN IN AMERICA. — 418 —
- CONCLUSION. — 425 —

PREFACE TO THE ENGLISH EDITION.

THE Editor of the English translation of 'L'Homme Primitif,' has not deemed it necessary to reproduce the original Preface, in which M. Figuier states his purpose in offering a new work on pre-historic archæology to the French public, already acquainted in translation with the works on the subject by Sir Charles Lyell and Sir John Lubbock. Now that the book has taken its position in France, it is only needful to point out its claims to the attention of English readers.

The important art of placing scientific knowledge, and especially new discoveries and topics of present controversy, within easy reach of educated readers not versed in their strictly technical details, is one which has for years been carried to remarkable perfection in France, in no small measure through the labours and example of M. Figuier himself. The present volume, one of his series, takes up the subject of Pre-historic Man, beginning with the remotely ancient stages of human life belonging to the Drift-Beds, Bone-Caves, and Shell-Heaps, passing on through the higher levels of the Stone Age, through the succeeding Bronze Age, and into those lower ranges of the Iron Age in which civilisation, raised to a comparatively high development, passes from the hands of the antiquary into those of the historian. The Author's object has been to give within the limits of a volume, and dispensing with the fatiguing enumeration of details required in special memoirs, an outline sufficient to afford a reasonable working acquaintance with the facts and arguments of the science to such as cannot pursue it further, and to serve as a starting-ground for those who will follow it up in the more minute researches of Nilsson, Keller, Lartet, Christy, Lubbock, Mortillet, Desor, Troyon, Gastaldi, and others.

The value of the work to English archæologists, however, is not merely that of a clear popular manual; pre-historic archæology, worked as it has been in several countries, takes in each its proper local colour, and brings forward its proper local evidence. It is true that much of its material is used as common property by scientific men at large. But, for instance, where an English writer in describing the ancient cave-men would dwell especially on the relics from the caves of Devon and Somerset as worked by Falconer and Pengelly, a French writer would take his data more amply from the explorations of caves of the south of France by De Vibraye, Garrigou, and Filhol—where the English teacher would select his specimens from the

Christy or the Blackmore Museum, the French teacher would have recourse to the Musée de Saint-Germain. Thus far, the English student has in Figuier's 'Primitive Man' not a work simply incorporated from familiar materials, but to a great extent bringing forward evidence not readily accessible, or quite new to him.

Some corrections and alterations have been made in the English edition. The illustrations are those of the original work; the facsimiles of pre-historic objects have been in great part drawn expressly for it, and contribute to its strictly scientific value; the page illustrations representing scenes of primitive life, which are by another hand, may seem somewhat fanciful, yet, setting aside the Raffaelesque idealism of their style, it will be found on examination that they are in the main justified by that soundest evidence, the actual discovery of the objects of which they represent the use.

The solid distinctness of this evidence from actual relics of pre-historic life is one of the reasons which have contributed to the extraordinary interest which pre-historic archæology has excited in an age averse to vague speculation, but singularly appreciative of arguments conducted by strict reasoning on facts. The study of this modern science has supplied a fundamental element to the general theory of civilisation, while, as has been the case with geology, its bearing on various points of theological criticism has at once conduced to its active investigation, and drawn to it the most eager popular attention. Thus, in bringing forward a new work on 'Primitive Man,' there is happily no need of insisting on the importance of its subject-matter, or of attempting to force unappreciated knowledge on an unwilling public. It is only necessary to attest its filling an open place in the literature of pre-historic archæology.

E. B. T.

PRIMITIVE MAN.

INTRODUCTION.

FORTY years have scarcely elapsed since scientific men first began to attribute to the human race an antiquity more remote than that which is assigned to them by history and tradition. Down to a comparatively recent time, the appearance of primitive man was not dated back beyond a period of 6000 to 7000 years. This historical chronology was a little unsettled by the researches made among various eastern nations—the Chinese, the Egyptians, and the Indians. The *savants* who studied these ancient systems of civilisation found themselves unable to limit them to the 6000 years of the standard chronology, and extended back for some thousands of years the antiquity of the eastern races.

This idea, however, never made its way beyond the narrow circle of oriental scholars, and did nothing towards any alteration in the general opinion, which allowed only 6000 years since the creation of the human species.

This opinion was confirmed, and, to some extent, rendered sacred by an erroneous interpretation of Holy Writ. It was thought that the Old Testament stated that man was created 6000 years ago. Now, the fact is, nothing of the kind can be found in the Book of Genesis. It is only the commentators and the compilers of chronological systems who have put forward this date as that of the first appearance of the human race. M. Édouard Lartet, who was called, in 1869, to the chair of palæontology in the Museum of Natural History of Paris, reminds us, in the following passage taken from one of his elegant dissertations, that it is the chronologists alone who have propounded this idea, and that they have, in this respect, very wrongly interpreted the statements of the Bible:

"In *Genesis*," says M. Lartet, "no date can be found which sets a limit to the time at which primitive mankind may have made its first appearance. Chronologists, however, for fifteen centuries have been endeavouring to make Biblical facts fall in with the preconcerted arrangements of their systems. Thus, we find that more than 140 opinions have been brought forward as to the date of the creation alone, and that, between the varying extremes, there is a difference of 3194 years—a difference which only applies to the period between the commencement of the world and the birth of Jesus Christ. This disagreement turns chiefly on those portions of the interval which are in closest proximity to the creation.

"From the moment when it becomes a recognised fact that the origin of mankind is a question independent of all subordination to dogma, this question will assume its proper position as a scientific thesis, and will be accessible to any kind of discussion, and capable, in every point of view, of receiving the solution which best harmonises with the known facts and experimental demonstrations." [1]

Thus, we must not assume that the authority of Holy Writ is in any way questioned by those labours which aim at seeking the real epoch of man's first appearance on the earth.

In corroboration of M. Lartet's statement, we must call to mind that the Catholic church, which has raised to the rank of dogma so many unimportant facts, has never desired to treat in this way the idea that man was created only 6000 years ago.

There is, therefore, no need for surprise when we learn that certain members of the Catholic clergy have devoted themselves with energy to the study of pre-historic man. Mgr. Meignan, Bishop of Châlons-sur-Marne, is one of the best-informed men in France as respects this new science; he cultivates it with the utmost zeal, and his personal researches have added much to the sum of our knowledge of this question. Under the title of 'Le Monde et l'Homme Primitif selon la Bible,'[2] the learned Bishop of Châlons-sur-Marne published, in 1869, a voluminous work, in which, taking up the subjects discussed by Marcel de Serres in his "Cosmogonie de Moïse, comparée aux Faits Géologiques,"[3] and enlarging upon the facts which science has recently acquired as to the subject of primitive man, he seeks to establish the coincidence of all these data with the records of Revelation.

M. l'Abbé Lambert has recently published a work on 'L'Homme Primitif et la Bible,'[4] in which he proves that the discoveries of modern science concerning the antiquity of man are in no way opposed to the records of Revelation in the Book of Moses.

Lastly, it is a member of the clerical body, M. l'Abbé Bourgeois, who, more a royalist than the king—that is, more advanced in his views than most contemporary geologists—is in favour of tracing back to the tertiary epoch the earliest date of the existence of man. We shall have to impugn this somewhat exaggerated opinion, which, indeed, we only quote here for the sake of proving that the theological scruples which so long arrested the progress of inquiry with regard to primitive man, have now disappeared, in consequence of the perfect independence of this question in relation to catholic dogma being evidently shown.

Thanks to the mutual support which has been afforded by the three sister-sciences—geology, palæontology, and archæology,—thanks to the happy combinations which these sciences have presented to the efforts of men animated with an ardent zeal for the investigation of the truth;—and thanks, lastly, to the unbounded interest which attaches to this subject, the result has been that the limits which had been so long attributed to the existence of the human species have been extraordinarily extended, and the date of the first appearance of man has been carried back to the night of the darkest ages. The mind, it may well be said, recoils dismayed when it undertakes the computation of the thousands of years which have elapsed since the creation of man.

But, it will naturally be asked, on what grounds do you base this assertion? What evidence do you bring forward, and what are the elements of your proof?

In the following paragraphs we give some of the principal means of examination and study which have directed the efforts of *savants* in this class of investigation, and have enabled them to create a science of the antiquity of the human species.

If man existed at any very remote epoch, he must have left traces of his presence in the spots which he inhabited and on the soil which he trod under his feet. However savage his state may be assumed to have been, primitive man must have possessed some implements of fishing and hunting—some weapons wherewith to strike down any prey which was stronger or more agile than himself. All human beings have been in possession of some scrap of clothing; and they have had at their command certain implements more or less rough in their character, be they only a shell in which to draw water or a tool for cleaving wood and constructing some place of shelter, a knife to cut their food, and a lump of stone to break the bones of the animals which served for their nutriment. Never has man existed who was not in possession of some kind of defensive weapon. These implements and these weapons have been patiently sought for, and they have also been found. They have been found in certain strata of the earth, the age of which is known by geologists; some of these strata precede and others are subsequent to the cataclysm of the European deluge of the quaternary epoch.

The fact has thus been proved that a race of men lived upon the earth at the epoch settled by the geological age of these strata—that is, during the quaternary epoch.

When this class of evidence of man's presence—that is, the vestiges of his primitive industry—fails us, a state of things, however, which comparatively seldom occurs, his existence is sometimes revealed by the presence of human bones buried in the earth and preserved through long ages by means of the deposits of calcareous salts which have petrified or rather *fossilised* them. Sometimes, in fact, the remains of human bones have been found in quaternary rocks, which are, consequently, considerably anterior to those of the present geological epoch.

This means of proof is, however, more difficult to bring forward than the preceding class of evidence; because human bones are very liable to decay when they are buried at shallow depths, and require for any length of preservation a concurrence of circumstances which is but rarely met with; because also the tribes of primitive man often burnt their dead bodies; and, lastly, because the human race then formed but a very scanty population.

Another excellent proof, which demonstrates the existence of man at a geological epoch anterior to the present era, is to be deduced from the intermixture of human bones with those of antediluvian animals. It is evident that if we meet with the bones of the mammoth, the cave-bear, the cave-tiger, &c.,—animals which lived only in the quaternary epoch and are now extinct—in conjunction with the bones of man or the relics of his industry, such as weapons, implements, utensils, &c., we can assert with some degree of certainty that our species was contemporaneous with the above-named animals. Now this intermixture has often been met with under the ground in caves, or deeply buried in the earth.

These form the various kinds of proof which have been made use of to establish the fact of man's presence upon the earth during the quaternary epoch. We will now give a brief recital of the principal investigations which have contributed to the knowledge on which is based the newly-formed science which treats of the practical starting-point of mankind.

Palæontology, as a science, does not count more than half a century of existence. We scarcely seem, indeed, to have raised more than one corner of the veil which covers the relics of an extinct world; as yet, for instance, we know absolutely nothing of all that sleeps buried in the depths of the earth lying under the basin of the sea. It need not, therefore, afford any great ground for surprise that so long a time elapsed before human bones or the vestiges of the primitive industry of man were discovered in the quaternary rocks. This negative result, however, always constituted the chief objection against the very early origin of our species.

The errors and deceptions which were at first encountered tended perhaps to cool down the zeal of the earlier naturalists, and thus retarded the solution of the problem. It is a well-known story about the fossil salamander of the Œningen quarries, which, on the testimony of Scheuchzer, was styled in 1726, the "human witness of the deluge" (*homo diluvii testis*). In 1787, Peter Camper recognised the fact that this pretended *pre-Adamite* was nothing but a reptile; this discomfiture, which was a source of amusement to the whole of scientific Europe, was a real injury to the cause of antediluvian man. By the sovereign ascendancy of ridicule, his existence was henceforth relegated to the domain of fable.

The first step in advance was, however, taken in 1774. Some human bones, mingled with remains of the great bear and other species then unknown, were discovered by J. F. Esper, in the celebrated cavern of Gailenreuth, in Bavaria.

Even before this date, in the early part of the eighteenth century, Kemp, an Englishman, had found in London, by the side of elephants' teeth, a stone hatchet, similar to those which have been subsequently found in great numbers in various parts of the world. This hatchet was roughly sketched, and the design published in 1715. The original still exists in the collection at the British Museum.

In 1797, John Frere, an English archæologist, discovered at Hoxne, in Suffolk, under strata of quaternary rocks, some flint weapons, intermingled with bones of animals belonging to extinct species. Esper concluded that these weapons and the men who made them were anterior to the formation of the beds in which they were found.

According to M. Lartet, the honour of having been the first to proclaim the high antiquity of the human species must be attributed to Aimé Boué, a French geologist residing in Germany. In 1823, he found in the quaternary loam (loess) of the Valley of the Rhine some human bones which he presented to Cuvier and Brongniart as those of men who lived in the quaternary epoch.

In 1823, Dr. Buckland, the English geologist, published his 'Reliquiæ Diluvianæ,' a work which was principally devoted to a description of the Kirkdale Cave, in which the author combined all the facts then known which tended in favour of the co-existence of man and the antediluvian animals.

Cuvier, too, was not so indisposed as he is generally said to have been, to admit the existence of man in the quaternary epoch. In his work on 'Ossements Fossiles,' and his 'Discours sur les Révolutions du Globe,' the immortal naturalist discusses the pros and cons with regard to this question, and, notwithstanding the insufficiency of the data which were then forthcoming, he felt warranted in saying:—

"I am not inclined to conclude that man had no existence at all before the epoch of the great revolutions of the earth.... He might have inhabited certain districts of no great extent, whence, after these terrible events, he repeopled the world; perhaps, also, the spots where he abode were swallowed up, and his bones lie buried under the beds of the present seas."

The confident appeals which have been made to Cuvier's authority against the high antiquity of man are, therefore, not justified by the facts.

A second and more decisive step in advance was taken by the discovery of shaped flints and other implements belonging to primitive man, existing in diluvial beds.

In 1826, M. Tournal, of Narbonne, a French archæologist and geologist, published an account of the discoveries which he had made in a cave in the department of Aude, in which he found bones of the bison and reindeer fashioned by the hand of man, accompanied by the remains of edible shell-fish, which must have been brought there by men who had made their residence in this cave.

Three years afterwards, M. de Christol, of Montpellier, subsequently Professor in the University of Science of Grenoble, found human bones intimately mixed up with remains of the great bear, hyæna, rhinoceros, &c., in the caverns of Pondres and Souvignargues (Hérault). In the last of these caverns fragments of pottery formed a part of the relics.

All these striking facts were put together and discussed by Marcel de Serres, Professor in the University of Science at Montpellier, in his 'Essai sur les Cavernes.'

The two bone-caverns of Engis and Enghihoul (Belgium) have furnished proofs of the same kind. In 1833, Schmerling, a learned Belgian geologist, discovered in these caverns two human skulls, mixed with the teeth of the rhinoceros, elephant, bear, hyæna, &c. The human bones were rubbed and worn away like those of the animals. The bones of the latter presented, besides, traces of human workmanship. Lastly, as if no evidence should be wanting, flints chipped to form knives and arrow-heads were found in the same spot.

In connection with his laborious investigations, Schmerling published a work which is now much esteemed, and proves that the Belgian geologist well merited the title of being the founder of the science of the antiquity of man. In this work Schmerling describes and represents a vast quantity of objects which had been discovered in the caverns of Belgium, and introduced to notice the human skull which has since become so famous under the name of the *Engis skull*. But at that time scientific men of all countries were opposed to this class of ideas, and thus the discoveries of the Belgian geologist attracted no more attention than those of his French brethren who had brought forward facts of a similar nature.

In 1835, M. Joly, at that time Professor at the Lyceum of Montpellier—where I (the author) attended on his course of Natural History—now Professor in the Faculty of Sciences at Toulouse, found in the cave of Nabrigas (Lozère) the skull of a cave-bear, on which an arrow had left its evident traces. Close by was a fragment of pottery bearing the imprints of the fingers of the man who moulded it.

We may well be surprised that, in the face of all these previous discoveries, Boucher de Perthes, the ardent apostle in proclaiming the high antiquity of our species, should have met with so much opposition and incredulity; or that he should have had to strive against so much indifference, when, beginning with the year 1836, he began to maintain this idea in a series of communications addressed to the Société d'Emulation of Abbeville.

The horizontal strata of the quarternary beds, known under the name of *diluvial*, form banks of different shades and material, which place before our eyes in indelible characters the ancient history of our globe. The organic remains which are found in them are those of beings who were witnesses to the diluvial cataclysm, and perhaps preceded it by many ages.

"Therefore," says the prophet of Abbeville, "it is in these ruins of the old world, and in the deposits which have become his sole archives, that we must seek out the traditions of primitive man; and in default of coins and inscriptions we must rely on the rough stones which, in all their imperfection, prove the existence of man no less surely than all the glory of a Louvre."

Strong in this conviction, M. Boucher de Perthes devoted himself ardently to the search in the diluvial beds, either for the bony relics of man, or, at all events, for the material indications of his primitive industry. In the year 1838 he had the honour of submitting to the Société d'Emulation, at Abbeville, his first specimens of the antediluvian hatchet.

In the course of the year 1839, Boucher de Perthes took these hatchets to Paris and showed them to several members of the Institute. MM. Alexandre Brongniart, Flourens, Elie de Beaumont, Cordier, and Jomard, gave at first some encouragement to researches which promised to be so fruitful in results; but this favourable feeling was not destined to last long.

These rough specimens of wrought flint, in which Boucher de Perthes already recognised a kind of hatchet, presented very indistinct traces of chipping, and the angles were blunted; their flattened shape, too, differed from that of the polished hatchets, the only kind that were then known. It was certainly necessary to see with the eyes of faith in order to discern the traces of man's work. "I," says the Abbeville archæologist, "had these 'eyes of faith,' but no one shared them with me." He then made up his mind to seek for help in his labour, and trained workmen to dig in the diluvial beds. Before long he was able to collect, in the quarternary beds at Abbeville, twenty specimens of flint evidently wrought by the hand of man.

In 1842, the Geological Society of London received a communication from Mr. Godwin Austen, who had found in Kent's Hole various wrought objects, accompanied by animal remains, which must have remained there since the deluge.

In 1844, appeared Lund's observations on the caverns of Brazil.

Lund explored as many as 800 caves. In one of them, situated not far from the lake of Semidouro, he found the bones of no less than thirty individuals of the human species, showing a similar state of decomposition to that of the bones of animals which were along with them. Among these animals were an ape, various carnivora, rodents, pachyderms, sloths, &c. From these facts, Lund inferred that man must have been contemporaneous with the megatherium, the mylodon, &c., animals which characterised the quarternary epoch.

Nevertheless, M. Desnoyers, librarian of the Museum of Natural History at Paris, in a very learned article on 'Grottos and Caverns,' published in 1845 in the 'Dictionnaire Universel d'Histoire Naturelle,' still energetically expressed himself in opposition to the hypothesis of the high antiquity of man. But the discoveries continued to go on; and, at the present time, M. Desnoyers himself figures among the partisans of the antediluvian man. He has even gone beyond their opinions, as he forms one among those who would carry back to the tertiary epoch the earliest date of the appearance of our species.

In 1847, M'Enery found in Kent's Hole, a cavern in England, under a layer of stalagmite, the remains of men and antediluvian animals mingled together.

The year 1847 was also marked by the appearance of the first volume of the 'Antiquités Celtiques et Antédiluviennes,' by Boucher de Perthes; this contained about 1600 plates of the objects which had been discovered in the excavations which the author had caused to be made since the year 1836.

The strata at Abbeville, where Boucher de Perthes carried out his researches, belong to the quaternary epoch.

Dr. Rigollot, who had been for ten years one of the most decided opponents of the opinions of Boucher de Perthes, actually himself discovered in 1854 some wrought flints in the quaternary deposits at Saint

Acheul, near Amiens, and it was not long before he took his stand under the banner of the Abbeville archæologist.

The *fauna* of the Amiens deposits is similar to that of the Abbeville beds. The lower deposits of gravel, in which the wrought flints are met with, have been formed by fresh water, and have not undergone either alteration or disturbance. The flints wrought by the hand of man which have been found in them, have in all probability lain there since the epoch of the formation of these deposits—an epoch a little later than the diluvial period. The number of wrought flints which have been taken out of the Abbeville beds is really immense. At Menchecourt, in twenty years, about 100 well-characterised hatchets have been collected; at Saint Gilles twenty very rough, and as many well-made ones; at Moulin-Quignon 150 to 200 well-formed hatchets.

Similar relics of primitive industry have been found also in other localities. In 1853, M. Noulet discovered some in the Infernat Valley (Haute-Garonne); in 1858, the English geologists, Messrs. Prestwich, Falconer, Pengelly, &c., also found some in the lower strata of the Baumann cavern in the Hartz.

To the English geologists whose names we have just mentioned must be attributed the merit of having been the first to bring before the scientific world the due value of the labours of Boucher de Perthes, who had as yet been unsuccessful in obtaining any acceptation of his ideas in France. Dr. Falconer, Vice-president of the Geological Society in London, visited the department of the Somme, in order to study the beds and the objects found in them. After him, Messrs. Prestwich and Evans came three times to Abbeville in the year 1859. They all brought back to England a full conviction of the antiquity and intact state of the beds explored, and also of the existence of man before the deluge of the quaternary epoch.

In another journey, made in company with Messrs. Flower, Mylne, and Godwin Austen, Messrs. Prestwich, Falconer, and Evans were present at the digging out of human bones and flint hatchets from the quarries of St. Acheul. Lastly, Sir C. Lyell visited the spot, and the English geologist, who, up to that time, had opposed the idea of the existence of antediluvian man, was able to say, *Veni, vidi, victus fui!* At the meeting of the British Association, at Aberdeen, September the 15th, 1855, Sir C. Lyell declared himself to be in favour of the existence of quaternary man; and this declaration, made by the President of the Geological Society of London, added considerable weight to the new ideas.

M. Hébert, Professor of Geology at the Sorbonne, next took his stand under the same banner.

M. Albert Gaudry, another French geologist, made a statement to the Academy of Sciences, that he, too, had found flint hatchets, together with the teeth of horses and fossil oxen, in the beds of the Parisian *diluvium*.

During the same year, M. Gosse, the younger, explored the sand-pits of Grenelle and the avenue of La Mothe-Piquet in Paris, and obtained from them various flint implements, mingled with the bones of the mammoth, fossil ox, &c.

Facts of a similar character were established at Précy-sur-Oise, and in the diluvial deposits at Givry.

The Marquis de Vibraye, also, found in the cave of Arcy, various human bones, especially a piece of a jaw-bone, mixed with the bones of animals of extinct species.

In 1859, M. A. Fontan found in the cave of Massat (department of Ariége), not only utensils testifying to the former presence of man, but also human teeth mixed up with the remains of the great bear (*Ursus spelæus*), the fossil hyæna (*Hyæna spelæa*), and the cave-lion (*Felis spelæa*).

In 1861, M. A. Milne Edwards found in the cave of Lourdes (Tarn), certain relics of human industry by the side of the bones of fossil animals.

The valleys of the Oise and the Seine have also added their contingent to the supply of antediluvian remains. In the sand-pits in the environs of Paris, at Grenelle, Levallois-Perret, and Neuilly, several naturalists, including MM. Gosse, Martin, and Reboux, found numerous flint implements, associated, in certain cases, with the bones of the elephant and hippopotamus. In the valley of the Oise, at Précy, near Creil, MM. Peigné Delacour and Robert likewise collected a few hatchets.

Lastly, a considerable number of French departments, especially those of the north and centre, have been successfully explored. We may mention the departments of Pas-de-Calais, Aisne, Loire-et-Cher, Indre-et-Loire, Vienne, Allier, Yonne, Saône-et-Loire, Hérault, Tarn-et-Garonne, &c.

In England, too, discoveries were made of an equally valuable character. The movement which was commenced in France by Boucher de Perthes, spread in England with remarkable rapidity. In many directions excavations were made which produced excellent results.

In the gravel beds which lie near Bedford, Mr. Wyatt met with flints resembling the principal types of those of Amiens and Abbeville; they were found in company with the remains of the mammoth, rhinoceros, hippopotamus, ox, horse, and deer. Similar discoveries were made in Suffolk, Kent, Hertfordshire, Hampshire, Wiltshire, &c.

Some time after his return from Abbeville, Mr. Evans, going round the museum of the Society of Antiquaries in London, found in their rooms some specimens exactly similar to those in the collection of Boucher de Perthes. On making inquiries as to their origin, he found that they had been obtained from the gravel at Hoxne by Mr. Frere, who had collected them there, together with the bones of extinct animals, all of which he had presented to the museum, after having given a description of them in the 'Archæologia' of 1800, with this remark: ... "Fabricated and used by a people who had not the use of metals.... The situation in which these weapons were found may tempt us to refer them to a very remote period indeed, even beyond that of the present world."

Thus, even at the commencement of the present century, they were in possession, in England, of proofs of the co-existence of man with the great extinct pachyderms; but, owing to neglect of the subject, scarcely any attention had been paid to them.

We now come to the most remarkable and most characteristic discoveries of this class which have ever been made. We allude to the explorations made by M. Édouard Lartet, during the year 1860, in the curious pre-historic human burial-place at Aurignac (Haute-Garonne).

Going down the hill on the road leading from Aurignac, after proceeding about a mile, we come to the point where, on the other side of the dale, the ridge of the hill called *Fajoles* rises, not more than 65 feet above a rivulet. We then may notice, on the northern slope of this eminence, an escarpment of the rock, by the side of which there is a kind of niche about six feet deep, the arched opening of it facing towards the north-west. This little cave is situated forty-two feet above the rivulet. Below, the calcareous soil slopes down towards the stream.

The discovery of this hollow, which is now cleared out, was made entirely by chance. It was hidden by a mass of *débris* of rock and vegetable-earth which had crumbled down; it had, in fact, only been known as a rabbits' hole. In 1842, an excavating labourer, named Bonnemaison, took it into his head one day to thrust his arm into this hole, and out of it he drew forth a large bone. Being rather curious to search into the mystery, he made an excavation in the slope below the hole, and, after some hours' labour, came upon a slab of sandstone which closed up an arched opening. Behind the slab of stone, he discovered a hollow in which a quantity of human bones were stored up.

It was not long before the news of this discovery was spread far and wide. Crowds of curious visitors flocked to the spot, and many endeavoured to explain the origin of these human remains, the immense antiquity of which was attested by their excessive fragility. The old inhabitants of the locality took it into their heads to recall to recollection a band of coiners and robbers who, half a century before, had infested the country. This decidedly popular inquest and decision was judged perfectly satisfactory, and everyone agreed in declaring that the cavern which had just been brought to light was nothing but the retreat of these malefactors, who concealed all the traces of their crimes by hiding the bodies of their victims in this cave, which was known to these criminals only.

Doctor Amiel, Mayor of Aurignac, caused all these bones to be collected together, and they were buried in the parish cemetery. Nevertheless, before the re-inhumation was proceeded with, he recorded the fact that the skeletons were those of seventeen individuals of both sexes. In addition to these skeletons, there were also found in the cave a number of little discs, or flat rings, formed of the shell of a species of cockle (*cardium*). Flat rings altogether similar to these are not at all unfrequent in the necklaces and other ornaments of Assyrian antiquity found in Nineveh.

Eighteen years after this event, that is in 1860, M. Édouard Lartet paid a visit to Aurignac. All the details of the above-named discovery were related to him. After the long interval which had elapsed, no one, not even the grave-digger himself, could recollect the precise spot where these human remains had been buried in the village cemetery. These precious relics were therefore lost to science.

M. Lartet resolved, however, to set on foot some excavations in the cave from which they had been taken, and he soon found himself in possession of unhoped-for treasures. The floor of the cavern itself had remained intact, and was covered with a layer of "made ground" mixed with fragments of stone. Outside this same cave M. Lartet discovered a bed of ashes and charcoal, which, however, did not extend to the interior. This bed was covered with "made ground" of an ossiferous and vegetable character. Inside the cave, the ground contained bones of the bear, the fox, the reindeer, the bison, the horse, &c., all intermingled with numerous relics of human industry, such as implements made of stag or reindeer's-horn, carefully pointed at one end and bevelled off at the other—a pierced handle of reindeer's-horn—flint knives and weapons of different kinds; lastly, a canine-tooth of a bear, roughly carved in the shape of a bird's head and pierced with a hole, &c.

The excavations, having been carried to a lower level, brought to light the remains of the bear, the wild-cat, the cave-hyæna, the wolf, the mammoth, the horse, the stag, the reindeer, the ox, the rhinoceros, &c., &c. It was, in fact, a complete Noah's ark. These bones were all broken lengthwise, and some of them were carbonised. *Striæ* and notches were found on them, which could only have been made by cutting instruments.

M. Lartet, after long and patient investigations, came to the conclusion that the cave of Aurignac was a human burial-place, contemporary with the mammoth, the *Rhinocerus tichorhinus*, and other great mammals of the quarternary epoch.

The mode in which the long bones were broken shows that they had been cracked with a view of extracting the marrow; and the notches on them prove that the flesh had been cut off them with sharp instruments. The ashes point to the existence of a fire, in which some of these bones had been burnt. Men must have resorted to this cavern in order to fulfil certain funereal rites. The weapons and animals' bones must have been deposited there in virtue of some funereal dedication, of which numerous instances are found in Druidical or Celtic monuments and in Gallic tombs.

Such are the valuable discoveries, and such the new facts which were the result of the investigations made by M. Édouard Lartet in the cave of Aurignac. In point of fact, they left no doubt whatever as to the co-existence of man with the great antediluvian animals.

In 1862, Doctor Felix Garrigou, of Tarrascon, a distinguished geologist, published the results of the researches which he, in conjunction with MM. Rames and Filhol, had made in the caverns of Ariége. These explorers found the lower jaw-bones of the great bear, which, with their sharp and projecting canine-tooth, had been employed by man as an offensive weapon, almost in the same way as Samson used the jaw-bone of an ass in fighting with the Philistines.

"It was principally," says M. Garrigou, "in the caves of Lombrives, Lherm, Bouicheta, and Maz-d'Azil that we found the jaw-bones of the great bear and the cave-lion, which were acknowledged to have been wrought by the hand of man, not only by us, but also by the numerous French and English *savants* who examined them and asked for some of them to place in their collections. The number of these jaw-bones now reaches to more than a hundred. Furnished, as they are, with an immense canine-tooth, and carved so as to give greater facility for grasping them, they must have formed, when in a fresh state, formidable weapons in the hands of primitive man....

"These animals belong to species which are now extinct, and if their bones while still in a fresh state (since they were gnawed by hyænas) were used as weapons, man must have been contemporary with them."

In the cave of Bruniquel (Tarn-et-Garonne), which was visited in 1862 by MM. Garrigou and Filhol, and other *savants*, there were found, under a very hard osseous *breccia*, an ancient fire-hearth with ashes and charcoal, the broken and calcined bones of ruminants of various extinct species, flint flakes used as knives, facetted nuclei, and both triangular and quadrangular arrow-heads of great distinctness, utensils in stags' horn and bone—in short, everything which could prove the former presence of primitive man.

About three-quarters of a mile below the cave there was subsequently found, at a depth of about twenty feet, an osseous *breccia* similar to the first, and likewise containing broken bones and a series of ancient fire-hearths filled with ashes and objects of antediluvian industry. Bones, teeth, and flints were to be collected in bushels.

At the commencement of 1863, M. Garrigou presented to the Geological Society of France the objects which had been found in the caves of Lherm and Bouicheta, and the Abbé Bourgeois published some remarks on the wrought flints from the *diluvium* of Pont-levoy.

This, therefore, was the position of the question in respect to fossil man, when in 1863, the scientific world were made acquainted with the fact of the discovery of a human jaw-bone in the diluvial beds of Moulin-Quignon, near Abbeville. We will relate the circumstances attending this memorable discovery.

On the 23rd of March, 1863, an excavator who was working in the sand-quarries at Moulin-Quignon brought to Boucher de Perthes at Abbeville, a flint hatchet and a small fragment of bone which he had just picked up. Having cleaned off the earthy coat which covered it, Boucher de Perthes recognised this bone to be a human molar. He immediately visited the spot, and assured himself that the locality where these objects had been found was an argilo-ferruginous vein, impregnated with some colouring matter which appeared to contain organic remains. This layer formed a portion of a *virgin* bed, as it is called by geologists, that is, without any infiltration or secondary introduction.

On the 28th of March another excavator brought to Boucher de Perthes a second human tooth, remarking at the same time, "that something resembling a bone was just then to be seen in the sand." Boucher de Perthes immediately repaired to the spot, and in the presence of MM. Dimpré the elder and younger, and several members of the Abbeville *Société d'Emulation*, he personally extracted from the soil the half of a human lower jaw-bone, covered with an earthy crust. A few inches from this, a flint hatchet was discovered, covered with the same black patina as the jaw-bone. The level where it was found was about fifteen feet below the surface of the ground.

After this event was duly announced, a considerable number of geologists flocked to Abbeville, about the middle of the month of April. The Abbé Bourgeois, MM. Brady-Buteux, Carpenter, Falconer, &c., came one after the other, to verify the locality from which the human jaw-bone had been extracted. All were fully convinced of the intact state of the bed and the high antiquity of the bone which had been found.

Boucher de Perthes also discovered in the same bed of gravel two mammoth's teeth, and a certain number of wrought hatchets. Finally, he found among the bones which had been taken from the Menchecourt quarries in the early part of April, a fragment of another jaw-bone and six separate teeth, which were recognised by Dr. Falconer to be also human.

The jaw-bone found at Moulin-Quignon is very well preserved. It is rather small in size, and appears to have belonged to an aged individual of small stature. It does not possess that ferocious aspect which is noticed in the jaw-bones of certain of the existing human races. The obliquity of the molar-tooth may be explained by supposing some accident, for the molar which stood next had fallen out during the lifetime of the individual, leaving a gap which favoured the obliquity of the tooth which remained in the jaw. This peculiarity is found also in several of the human heads in the collection of the Museum of Natural History in Paris.

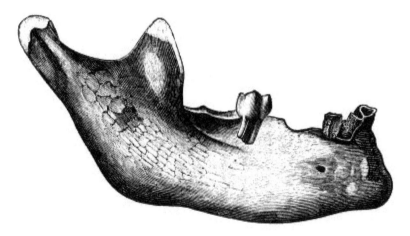

Fig. 1.—Human Jaw-bone found at Moulin-Quignon, near Abbeville, in 1863.

The jaw-bone of the man of Moulin-Quignon, which is represented here (fig. 1) in its natural size, and drawn from the object itself, which is preserved in the Anthropological Gallery of the Museum of Natural History of Paris, does not show any decided points of difference when compared with those of individuals of existing races.

The same conclusion was arrived at as the result of the comparative examination which was made of the jaw-bones found by MM. Lartet and De Vibraye in the caves of Aurignac and Arcy; the latter remains were studied by M. Quatrefages in conjunction with Pruner-Bey, formerly physician to the Viceroy of Egypt, and one of the most distinguished French anthropologists.

On the 20th of April, 1863, M. de Quatrefages announced to the institute the discovery which had been made by Boucher de Perthes, and he presented to the above-named learned body the interesting object itself, which had been sent from Abbeville.

When the news of this discovery arrived in England it produced no slight sensation.

Some of the English *savants* who had more specially devoted their attention to the study of this question, such as Messrs. Christy, Falconer, Carpenter, and Busk, went over to France, and in conjunction with Boucher de Perthes and several members of the Académie des Sciences of Paris, examined the exact locality in which the hatchets and the human jaw-bone had been found; they unanimously agreed in recognising the correctness of the conclusions arrived at by the indefatigable geologist of Abbeville.[5]

This discovery of the hatchets and the human jaw-bone in the quaternary beds of Moulin-Quignon completed the demonstration of an idea already supported by an important mass of evidence. Setting aside its own special value, this discovery, added to so many others, could not fail to carry conviction into most minds. From this time forth the doctrine of the high antiquity of the human race became an acknowledged idea in the scientific world.

Before closing our historical sketch, we shall have to ask, what was the precise geological epoch to which we shall have to carry back the date of man's first appearance on this our earth.

The beds which are anterior to the present period, the series of which forms the solid crust of our globe, have been divided, as is well known, into five groups, corresponding to the same number of periods of the physical development of the earth. These are in their order of age: the *primitive rocks*, the *transition rocks*, the *secondary rocks*, the *tertiary* and *quaternary rocks*. Each of these epochs must have embraced an immense lapse of time, since it has radically exhausted the generation both of animals and plants which was peculiar to it. Some idea may be formed of the extreme slowness with which organic creatures modify their character, when we take into consideration that our contemporary *fauna*, that is to say, the collection of animals of every country which belong to the geological period in which we exist, has undergone little, if any, alteration during the thousands of years that it has been in being.

Is it possible for us to date the appearance of the human race in those prodigiously-remote epochs which correspond with the primitive, the transition, or the secondary rocks? Evidently no! Is it possible, indeed, to fix this date in the epoch of the tertiary rocks? Some geologists have fancied that they could find traces of the presence of man in these tertiary rocks (the miocene and pliocene). But this is an opinion in which we, at least, cannot make up our minds to agree.

In 1863, M. Desnoyers found in the upper strata of the tertiary beds (pliocene) at Saint-Prest, in the department of Eure, certain bones belonging to various extinct animal species; among others those of an elephant (*Elephas meridionalis*), an animal which did not form a part of the quaternary *fauna*. On most of these bones he ascertained the existence of cuts, or notches, which, in his opinion, must have been produced by flint implements. These indications, according to M. Desnoyers, are signs of the existence of man in the tertiary epoch.

This opinion, however, Sir Charles Lyell hesitates to accept. Moreover, we could hardly depend upon an accident so insignificant as that of a few cuts or notches made upon a bone, in order to establish a fact so important as that of the high antiquity of man. We must also state that it is a matter of question whether the beds which contained these notched bones really belong to the tertiary group.

The beds which correspond to the quaternary epoch are, therefore, those in which we find unexceptionable evidence of the existence of man. Consequently, in the quaternary epoch which preceded the existing geological period, we must place the date of the first appearance of mankind upon the earth.

If the purpose is entertained of discussing, with any degree of certainty, the history of the earliest days of the human race—a subject which as yet is a difficult one—it is requisite that the long interval should be divided into a certain number of periods. The science of primitive man is one so recently entered upon, that those authors who have written upon the point can hardly be said to have properly discussed and agreed upon a rational scheme of classification. We shall, in this work, adopt the classification proposed by M. Édouard Lartet, which, too, has been adopted in that portion of the museum of Saint-Germain which is devoted to pre-historic antiquities. Following this course, we shall divide the history of primitive mankind into two great periods:

1st. The Stone Age;

2nd. The Metal Age.

These two principal periods must also be subdivided in the following mode. The "Stone Age" will embrace three epochs:

1st. The epoch of extinct animals (or of the great cave-bear and the mammoth).

2nd. The epoch of migrated existing animals (or the reindeer epoch).

3rd. The epoch of domesticated existing animals (or the polished-stone epoch).

The "Metal Age" may also be divided into two periods:

1st. The Bronze Epoch;

2nd. The Iron Epoch.

The following synoptical table will perhaps bring more clearly before the eyes of our readers this mode of classification, which has, at least, the merit of enabling us to make a clear and simple statement of the very incongruous facts which make up the history of primitive man:

THE STONE AGE.	1st. Epoch of extinct animals (or of the great bear and mammoth).
	2nd. Epoch of migrated existing animals (or the reindeer epoch).
	3rd. Epoch of domesticated existing animals (or the polished-stone epoch).
THE METAL AGE.	1st. The Bronze Epoch.
	2nd. The Iron Epoch.

FOOTNOTES:

[1] 'Nouvelles Recherches sur la Coexistence de l'Homme et des grands Mammifères Fossiles réputés charactéristiques de la dernière période Géologique,' by Éd. Lartet, 'Annales des Sciences Naturelles,' 4th ser. vol. xv. p. 256.

[2] 1 vol. 8vo., Paris, 1869; V. Palme.

[3] 2 vols. 12mo., 3rd edit., Paris, 1859; Lagny frères.

[4] Pamphlet, 8vo., Paris, 1869; Savy.

[5] It should rather have been said, that the ultimate and well-considered judgment of the English geologists was against the authenticity of the Moulin-Quignon jaw.—See Dr. Falconer's 'Palæontological Memoirs,' vol. ii. p. 610; and Sir C. Lyell's 'Antiquity of Man,' 3rd ed. p. 515. (Note to Eng. Trans.)

THE STONE AGE.

I.

The Epoch of Extinct Species of Animals; or, of the Great Bear and Mammoth.

CHAPTER I.

The earliest Men—The type of Man in the Epoch of Animals of extinct Species—Origin of Man—Refutation of the Theory which derives the Human Species from the Ape.

MAN must have lived during the time in which the last representatives of the ancient animal creation—the mammoth, the great bear, the cave-hyæna, the *Rhinoceros tichorinus*, &c.—were still in existence. It is this earliest period of man's history which we are now about to enter upon.

We have no knowledge of a precise nature with regard to man at the period of his first appearance on the globe. How did he appear upon the earth, and in what spot can we mark out the earliest traces of him? Did he first come into being in that part of the world which we now call Europe, or is it the fact that he made his way to this quarter of our hemisphere, having first seen the light on the great plateaux of Central Asia?

This latter opinion is the one generally accepted. In the work which will follow the present volume we shall see, when speaking of the various races of man, that the majority of naturalists admit nowadays one common centre of creation for all mankind. Man, no doubt, first came into being on the great plateaux of Central Asia, and thence was distributed over all the various habitable portions of our globe. The action of climate and the influences of the locality which he inhabited have, therefore, determined the formation of the different races—white, black, yellow, and red—which now exist with all their infinite subdivisions.

But there is another question which arises, to which it is necessary to give an immediate answer, for it has been and is incessantly agitated with a degree of vehemence which may be explained by the nature of the discussion being of so profoundly personal a character as regards all of us: Was man created by God complete in all parts, and is the human type independent of the type of the animals which existed before him? Or, on the contrary, are we compelled to admit that man, by insensible transformations, and gradual improvements and developments, is derived from some other animal species, and particularly that of the ape?

This latter opinion was maintained at the commencement of the present century by the French naturalist, de Lamarck, who laid down his views very plainly in his work entitled 'Philosophie Zoologique.' The same theory has again been taken up in our own time, and has been developed, with no small supply of facts on which it might appear to be based, by a number of scientific men, among whom we may mention Professor Carl Vogt in Switzerland, and Professor Huxley in England.

We strongly repudiate any doctrine of this kind. In endeavouring to establish the fact that man is nothing more than a developed and improved ape, an orang-outang or a gorilla, somewhat elevated in dignity, the arguments are confined to an appeal to anatomical considerations. The skull of the ape is compared with that of primitive man, and certain characteristics of analogy, more or less real, being found to exist between the two bony cases, the conclusion has been arrived at that there has been a gradual blending between the type of the ape and that of man.

We may observe, in the first place, that these analogies have been very much exaggerated, and that they fail to stand their ground in the face of a thorough examination of the facts. Only look at the skulls which have been found in the tombs belonging to the stone age, the so-called *Borreby skull* for instance—examine the human jaw-bone from Moulin-Quignon, the Meilen skull, &c., and you will be surprised to see that they differ very little in appearance from the skulls of existing man. One would really imagine, from what is said by the partisans of Lamarck's theory, that primitive man possessed the projecting jaw of the ape, or at least that of the negro. We are astonished, therefore, when we ascertain that, on the contrary, the skull of the man of the stone age is almost entirely similar in appearance to those of the existing Caucasian species. Special study is, indeed, required in order to distinguish one from the other.

If we place side by side the skull of a man belonging to the Stone Age, and the skulls of the principal apes of large size, these dissimilarities cannot fail to be obvious. No other elements of comparison, beyond merely looking at them, seem to be requisite to enable us to refute the doctrine of this debased origin of mankind.

The figure annexed represents the skull of a man belonging to the stone age, found in Denmark; to this skull, which is known by the name of the Borreby skull, we shall have to allude again in the course of the present work; fig. 3 represents the skull of a gorilla; fig. 4 that of an orang-outang; fig. 5 that of the *Cynocephalus* ape; fig. 6 that of the *Macacus*. Place the representation of the skull found in Denmark in juxtaposition with these ill-favoured animal masks, and then let the reader draw his own inference, without pre-occupying his mind with the allegations of certain anatomists imbued with contrary ideas.

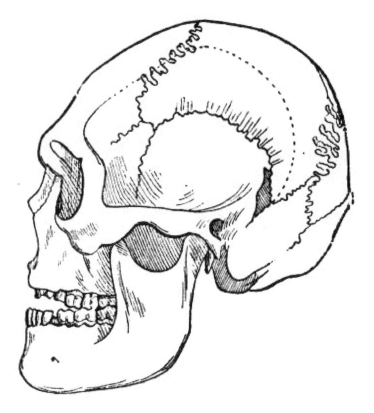

Fig. 2.—Skull of a Man belonging to the Stone Age (the *Borreby Skull*).

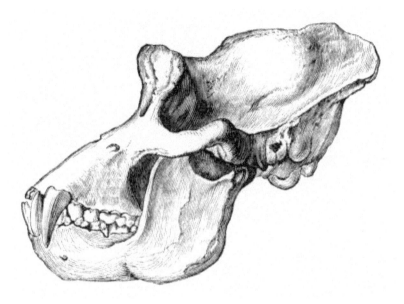

Fig. 3.—Skull of the Gorilla.

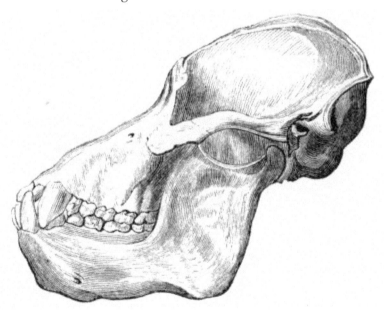

Fig. 4.—Skull of the Orang-Outang.

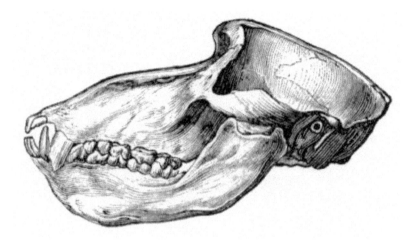

Fig. 5.—Skull of the Cynocephalus Ape.

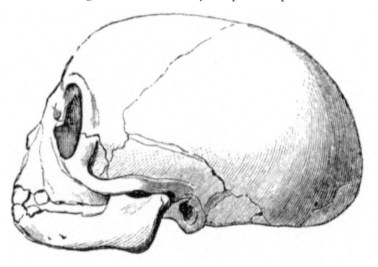

Fig. 6.—Skull of the *Macacus* Baboon.

Finding themselves beaten as regards the skulls, the advocates of transmutation next appeal to the bones. With this aim, they exhibit to us certain similarities of arrangement existing between the skeleton of the ape and that of primitive man. Such, for instance, is the longitudinal ridge which exists on the thigh-bone, which is as prominent in primitive man as in the ape. Such, also, is the fibula, which is very stout in primitive man, just as in the ape, but is rather slender in the man of the present period.

When we are fully aware how the form of the skeleton is modified by the kind of life which is led, in men just as in animals, we cannot be astonished at finding that certain organs assume a much higher development in those individuals who put them to frequent and violent use, than in others who leave these same organs in a state of comparative repose.

If it be a fact that the man of the epoch of the great bear and the mammoth had a more robust leg, and a more largely developed thigh-bone than most of the races of existing man, the reason simply is, that his savage life, which was spent in the midst of the wild beasts of the forest, compelled him to make violent exertions, which increased the size of these portions of his body.

Thus it is found that great walkers have a bulky calf, and persons leading a sedentary life have slender legs. These variations in the structure of the skeleton are owing, therefore, to nothing but a difference in the mode of life.

Why is it, however, that the skeleton is the only point taken into consideration when analogies are sought for between man and any species of animal? If equal investigation were given to other organs, we should arrive at a conclusion which would prove how unreasonable comparisons of this kind are. In fact, if man possesses the osseous structure of the ape, he has also the anatomical structure of many other animals, as far as regards several organs. Are not the viscera of the digestive system the same, and are they not organised on the same plan in man as in the carnivorous animals? As the result of this, would you say that man is derived from the tiger, that he is nothing but an improved and developed lion, a cat transmuted into a man? We may, however, just as plausibly draw this inference, unless we content ourselves with devoting our attention to the skeleton alone, which seems, indeed, to be the only part of the individual in which we are to interest ourselves, for what reason we know not.

But, in point of fact, this kind of anatomy is pitiable. Is there nothing in man but bones? Do the skeleton and the viscera make up the entire sum of the human being? What will you say, then, ye blind rhetoricians, about the faculty of intelligence as manifested in the gift of speech? Intelligence and speech, these are really the attributes which constitute man; these are the qualities which make him the most complete being in creation, and the most privileged of God's creatures. Show me an ape who can speak, and then I will agree with you in recognising it as a fact that man is nothing but an improved ape! Show me an ape who can make flint hatchets and arrow-heads, who can light a fire and cook his food, who, in short, can act like an intelligent creature—then, and then only, I am ready to confess that I am nothing more than an orang-outang revised and corrected.

It is not, however, our desire to speak of a question which has been the subject of so much controversy as that of the anatomical resemblance between the ape and the man without thoroughly entering into it; we have, indeed, no wish to shun the discussion of the point. On the present occasion, we shall appeal to the opinion of a *savant* perfectly qualified in such matters; we allude to M. de Quatrefages, Professor of Anthropology in the Museum of Natural History at Paris.

M. de Quatrefages, in his work entitled 'Rapport sur le Progrès de l'Anthropologie,' published in 1868, has entered rather fully into the question whether man is descended from the ape or not. He has summed up the contents of a multitude of contemporary works on this subject, and has laid down his opinion—the perfect impossibility, in an anatomical point of view, of this strange and repugnant genealogy.

The following extract from his work will be sufficient to make our readers acquainted with the ideas of the learned Professor of Anthropology with regard to the question which we are now considering:

"Man and apes in general," says M. de Quatrefages, "present a most striking contrast—a contrast on which Vicq-d'Azyr, Lawrence, and M. Serres have dwelt in detail for some considerable time past. The former is a *walking animal*, who walks upon his hind legs; all apes are *climbing animals*. The whole of the locomotive system in the two groups bears the stamp of these two very different intentions; the two types, in fact, are perfectly distinct.

"The very remarkable works of Duvernoy on the 'Gorilla,' and of MM. Gratiolet and Alix on the 'Chimpanzee,' have fully confirmed this result as regards the anthropomorphous apes—a result very important, from whatever point of view it is looked at, but of still greater value to any one who wishes to apply *logically* Darwin's idea. These recent investigations prove, in fact, that the ape type, however highly it may be developed, loses nothing of its fundamental character, and remains always perfectly distinct from the type of man; the latter, therefore, cannot have taken its rise from the former.

"Darwin's doctrine, when rationally adapted to the fact of the appearance of man, would lead us to the following results:

"We are acquainted with a large number of terms in the Simian series. We see it branching out into secondary series all leading up to anthropomorphous apes, which are not members of one and the same family, but corresponding superior *terms* of three distinct families (Gratiolet). In spite of the secondary modifications involved by the developments of the same natural qualities, the orang, the gorilla, and the chimpanzee remain none the less fundamentally mere *apes* and *climbers* (Duvernoy, Gratiolet, and Alix). Man, consequently, in whom everything shows that he is a *walker*, cannot belong to any one of these series; he can only be the higher term of a distinct series, the other representatives of which have disappeared, or, up to the present time, have evaded our search. Man and the anthropomorphous apes are the final terms of two series, which commence to diverge at the very latest as soon as the lowest of the apes appear upon the earth.

"This is really the way in which a true disciple of Darwin must reason, even if he solely took into account the *external morphological characteristics* and the *anatomical characteristics* which are the expression of the former in the adult animal.

"Will it be said that when the degree of organisation manifested in the anthropomorphous apes had been once arrived at, the organism underwent a new impulse and became adapted for walking? This would be, in fact, adding a fresh hypothesis, and its promoters would not be in a position to appeal to the organised gradation presented by the quadrumanous order as a whole on which stress is laid as leading to the conclusion against which I am contending: they would be completely outside *Darwin's theory*, on which these opinions claim to be based.

"Without going beyond these purely morphological considerations, we may place, side by side, for the sake of comparison, as was done by M. Pruner-Bey, the most striking general characteristics in man and in the anthropomorphous apes. As the result, we ascertain this general fact—that there exists 'an *inverse order* of the final term of development in the sensitive and vegetative apparatus, in the systems of locomotion and reproduction' (Pruner-Bey).

"In addition to this, this *inverse order* is equally exhibited in the series of phenomena of individual development.

"M. Pruner-Bey has shown that this is the case with a portion of the permanent teeth. M. Welker, in his curious studies of the sphenoïdal angle of Virchow, arrived at a similar result. He demonstrated that the modifications of the base of the skull, that is, of a portion of the skeleton which stands in the most intimate relation to the brain, take place inversely in the man and ape. This angle diminishes from his birth in man, but, on the contrary, in the ape it becomes more and more obtuse, so as sometimes to become entirely extinct.

"But there is also another fact which is of a still more important character: it is that this inverse course of development has been ascertained to exist even in the brain itself. This fact, which was pointed out by Gratiolet, and dwelt upon by him on various occasions, has never been contested either at the *Société d'Anthropologie* or elsewhere, and possesses an importance and significance which may be readily comprehended.

"In man and the anthropomorphous ape, *when in an adult state*, there exists in the mode of arrangement of the cerebral folds a certain similarity on which much stress has been laid; but this resemblance has been, to some extent, a source of error, for the result is attained by an *inverse course of action*. In the ape, the temporo-sphenoïdal convolutions, which form the middle lobe, make their appearance, and are completed, before the anterior convolutions which form the frontal lobe. In man, on the contrary, the frontal convolutions are the first to appear, and those of the middle lobe are subsequently developed.

"It is evident that when two organised beings follow an inverse course in their growth, the more highly developed of the two cannot have descended from the other by means of evolution.

"Embryology next adds its evidence to that of anatomy and morphology, to show how much in error they are who have fancied that Darwin's ideas would afford them the means of maintaining the simial origin of man.

"In the face of all these facts, it may be easily understood that anthropologists, however little in harmony they may sometimes be on other points, are agreed on this, and have equally been led to the conclusion that there is nothing that permits us to look at the brain of the ape as the brain of man smitten with an arrest of development, or, on the other hand, the brain of man as a development of that of the ape (Gratiolet); that the study of animal organism in general, and that of the extremities in particular, reveals, in addition to a general plan, certain differences in shape and arrangement which specify two altogether special and distinct adaptations, and are incompatible with the idea of any filiation (Gratiolet and Alix); that in their course of improvement and development, apes do not tend to become allied to man, and conversely the human type, when in a course of degradation, does not tend to become allied to the ape (Bert); finally, that no possible point of transition can exist between man and the ape, unless under the condition of inverting the laws of development (Pruner-Bey), &c.

"What, we may ask, is brought forward by the partisans of the simial origin of man in opposition to these general facts, which here I must confine myself to merely pointing out, and to the multitude of details of which these are only the abstract?

"I have done my best to seek out the proofs alleged, but I everywhere meet with nothing but the same kind of argument—exaggerations of morphological similarities which no one denies; inferences drawn from a few exceptional facts which are then generalised upon, or from a few coincidences in which the relations of cause and effect are a matter of supposition; lastly, an appeal to *possibilities* from which conclusions of a more or less affirmative character are drawn.

"We will quote a few instances of this mode of reasoning.

"1st. The bony portion of the hand of man and of that of certain anthropomorphous apes present marked similarities. Would it not therefore have been possible for an almost imperceptible modification to have ultimately led to identity?

"MM. Gratiolet and Alix reply to this in the negative; for the muscular system of the thumb establishes a profound difference, and testifies to an *adaptation* to very different uses.

"2nd. It is only in man and the anthropomorphous apes that the articulation of the shoulder is so arranged as to allow of rotatory movements. Have we not here an unmistakable resemblance?

"The above-named anatomists again reply in the negative; for even if we only take the bones into account, we at once see that the movements could not be the same; but when we come to the muscular system, we find decisive differences again testifying to certain special *adaptations*."

"These rejoinders are correct, for when *locomotion* is the matter in question, it is evident that due consideration must be paid to the muscles, which are the active agents in that function at least as much as the bones, which only serve as points of attachment and are only passive.

"3rd. In some of the races of man, the arch of the skull, instead of presenting a uniform curve in the transverse direction, bends a little towards the top of the two sides, and rises towards the median line (New Caledonians, Australians, &c.). It is asked if this is not a preliminary step towards the bony crests which rise in this region in some of the anthropomorphous apes?

"Again we reply in the negative; for, in the latter, the bony crests arise from the walls of the skull, and do not form any part of the arch.

"4th. Is it not very remarkable that we find the orang to be brachycephalous, just like the Malay, whose country it inhabits, and that the gorilla and chimpanzee are dolichocephalous like the negro? Is not this fact a reason for our regarding the former animal as the ancestor of the Malays, and the latter of the African nations?

"Even if the facts brought forward were correct, the inference which is drawn from them would be far from satisfactory. But the coincidence which is appealed to does not exist. In point of fact, the orang, which is essentially a native of Borneo, lives among the Dyaks and not among the Malays; now the Dyaks are rather dolichocephalous than brachycephalous. With respect to gorillas being dolichocephalous, they cannot at least be so generally; as out of *three* female specimens of this ape which were examined, two were brachycephalous (Pruner-Bey).

"5th. The brains of microcephalous individuals present a mixture of human and simial characteristics, and point to some intermediate conformation, which was normal at some anterior epoch, but at the present time is only realised by an arrest of development and a fact of atavism.

"Gratiolet's investigations of the brain of the ape, normal man and small-brained individuals, have shown that the similarities pointed out are purely fallacious. People have thought that they could detect them, simply because they have not examined closely enough. In the last named, the human brain is simplified; but this causes no alteration in the *initial plan*, and this plan is not that which is ascertained to exist in the ape. Thus Gratiolet has expressed an opinion which no one has attempted to controvert: 'The human brain differs the more from that of the ape the less the former is developed, and an arrest of development could only exaggerate this natural difference.... The brains of microcephalous individuals, although often less voluminous and less convoluted than those of the anthropomorphous apes, do not on this account become like the latter.... The idiot, however low he may be reduced, is not a beast; he is nothing but a deteriorated man.'

"The laws of the development of the brain in the two types, laws which I mentioned before, explain and justify this language; and the laws of which it is the summary are a formal refutation of the comparison which some have attempted to make between the *contracted human brain*, and the *animal brain, however developed.*

"6th. The excavations which have been made in intact ancient beds have brought to light skulls of ancient races of man, and these skulls present characteristics which approximate them to the skull of the ape. Does not this pithecoïd stamp, which is very striking on the Neanderthal skull in particular, argue a transition from one type to another, and consequently *filiation*?

"This argument is perhaps the only one which has been brought forward with any degree of precision, and it is often recurred to. Is it, on this account, more demonstrative? Let the reader judge for himself.

"We may, in the first place, remark that Sir C. Lyell does not venture to pronounce affirmatively as to the high antiquity of the human remains discovered by Dr. Fuhlrott, and that he looked upon them, at the most, as contemporary with the Engis skull, in which the Caucasian type of head was reproduced.

"Let us, however, admit that the Neanderthal skull belongs to the remote antiquity to which it has been assigned; what, then, is in reality the significance of this skull? Is it actually a link between the head of the man and that of the ape? And does it not find some analogy in comparatively modern races?

"Many writings have been published on these questions, and, as it appears to me, some light has gradually been thrown upon the subject. There is no doubt that this skull is really remarkable for the enormous size of its superciliary ridges, the length and narrowness of the bony case, the slight elevation of the top of the skull. But these features are found to be much less exceptional than was at first supposed, in default of any means of instituting a just comparison; very far, indeed, from justifying the approximation which some have endeavoured to make, this skull is, in all its characteristics, essentially human. Mr. Busk, in England, has pointed out the great affinity which is established, by the prominence of the superciliary ridges and the depression of the upper region, between certain Danish skulls from Borreby and the Neanderthal skull. Dr. Barnard Davis has described the still greater similarities existing between this very *fossil* and a skull in his collection. Gratiolet forwarded to the Museum the skull of an idiot of the present time, which was almost identical with it in everything, although in slighter proportions, &c.

"The following appears to me to be decisive:

"In spite of its curious characteristics, the Neanderthal skull none the less belonged to an individual, who, to judge by other bones which have been found, diverged but little from the average type of the present Germanic races, and by no means approximated to that of the ape.

"Is it probable, proceeding even on the class of ideas which I am opposing, that in a being in a state of transition between man and the anthropomorphous apes, the body would have become entirely human in its character, whilst the head presented its simial peculiarities? If a fact like this is admitted, does it not render the hypothesis absolutely worthless?

"Notwithstanding all the discussion to which these curious remains have given rise, it appears to me impossible to look upon them in any other light than as the remains of an individuality, exceptional, no doubt, but clearly belonging to the human species, and, in addition to this, to the Celtic race, one of the branches of our Aryan stock. M. Pruner-Bey appears to me to have placed this fact beyond all question by the whole mass of investigations which he has published on this subject. The most convincing proofs are based on the very great similarity which may be noticed in a Celtic skull taken from a tumulus in Poitou to the skull which has become so well known and, indeed, so celebrated owing to the writings of Doctor Schaaffhausen. This similarity is not merely external. An internal cast taken from one skull fits perfectly into the interior of the other. It was, therefore, the *brains* and not merely the *skulls* which bore a resemblance to one another. The proof appears to me to be complete, and, with the learned author of this work, I feel no hesitation in concluding that the Neanderthal skull is one of Celtic origin.

"After all, neither experience nor observation have as yet furnished us with the slightest data with regard to man at his earliest origin. Science, therefore, which pretends to solidity of character, must put this problem on one side till fresh information is obtained. We really approach nearer to the truth when we confess our ignorance than when we attempt to disguise it either to ourselves or others.

"With regard to the simial origin of man, it is nothing but pure hypothesis, or rather nothing but a mere *jeu d'esprit* which everything proves utterly baseless, and in favour of which no solid fact has as yet been appealed to."

In dealing with this question in a more general point of view, we must add that the most enlightened science declares to us in unmistakable accents, that species is immutable, and that no animal species can be derived from another; they may change, but all bear witness to an independent creation. This truth, which has been developed at length by M. de Quatrefages in his numerous works, is a definitive and scientific judgment which must decide this question as far as regards any unprejudiced minds.

CHAPTER II.

Man in the condition of Savage Life during the Quaternary Epoch—The Glacial Period, and its Ravages on the Primitive Inhabitants of the Globe—Man in Conflict with the Animals of the Quaternary Epoch—The Discovery of Fire—The Weapons of Primitive Man—Varieties of Flint-hatchets—Manufacture of the earliest Pottery—Ornamental objects at the Epoch of the Great Bear and the Mammoth.

AFTER this dissertation, which was necessary to confute the theory which gives such a degrading explanation of our origin, we must contemplate man at the period when he was first placed upon the earth, weak and helpless, in the midst of the inclement and wild nature which surrounded him.

However much our pride may suffer by the idea, we must confess that, at the earliest period of his existence, man could have been but little distinguished from the brute. Care for his natural wants must have absorbed his whole being; all his efforts must have tended to one sole aim—that of insuring his daily subsistence.

At first, his only food must have been fruits and roots; for he had not as yet invented any weapon wherewith to destroy wild animals. If he succeeded in killing any creatures of small size he devoured them in a raw state, and made a covering of their skins to shelter himself against the inclemency of the weather. His pillow was a stone, his roof was the shadow of a wide-spreading tree, or some dark cavern which also served as a refuge against wild beasts.

For how many ages did this miserable state last? No one can tell. Man is an improvable being, and indefinite progress is the law of his existence. Improvement is his supreme attribute; and this it is which gives him the pre-eminence over all the creatures which surround him. But how wavering must have been his first steps in advance, and how many efforts must have been given to the earliest creation of his mind and to the first work of his hands—doubtless some shapeless attempt in which we nowadays, perhaps, should have some difficulty in recognising the work of any intelligent being!

Towards the commencement of the quaternary epoch, a great natural phenomenon took place in Europe. Under the influence of numerous and varied causes, which up to the present time have not been fully recognised, a great portion of Europe became covered with ice, on the one hand, making its way from the poles down to the most southern latitudes, and, on the other, descending into the plains from the summits of the highest mountain chains. Ice and ice-fields assumed a most considerable extension. As all the lower parts of the continent were covered by the sea, there were only a few plateaux which could afford a refuge to man and animals flying from this deadly cold. Such was the *Glacial Period*, which produced the annihilation of so many generations of animals, and must have equally affected man himself, so ill-defended against this universal and sudden winter.

Man, however, was enabled to resist the attacks of revolted nature. Without doubt, in this unhappy period, he must have made but little progress, even if his intellectual development were not completely stopped. At all events, the human species did not perish. The glacial period came to an end, the ice-fields shrank back to their original limits, and Nature reassumed its primitive aspect.

When the ice had gradually retired into the more northern latitudes, and had become confined to the higher summits, a new generation of animals—another *fauna*, as naturalists call it—made its appearance on the globe. This group of animals, which had newly come into being, differed much from those that had disappeared in the glacial cataclysm. Let us cast an inquiring glance on these strange and now extinct creatures.

First we have the mammoth (*Elephas primigenius*), or the woolly-haired and maned elephant, carcases of which were found, entire and in good preservation, in the ice on the coasts of Siberia. Next comes the rhinoceros with a complete nasal septum (*Rhinoceros tichorhinus*), likewise clad in a warm and soft fur, the nose of which is surmounted with a remarkable pair of horns. Then follow several species of the hippopotamus, which come as far north as the rivers of England and Russia; a bear of great size inhabiting caverns (*Ursus spelæus*), and presenting a projecting forehead and a large-sized skull; the cave lion or tiger (*Felis spelæa*), which much surpassed in strength the same animals of the existing species; various kinds of hyænas (*Hyæna spelæa*), much stronger than those of our epoch; the bison or aurochs (*Biso europæus*), which still exists in Poland; the great ox, the Urus of the ancients (*Bos primigenius*); the gigantic Irish elk (*Megaceros hibernicus*), the horns of which attained to surprising dimensions. Other animals made their appearance at the same epoch, but they are too numerous to mention; among them were some of the Rodent family. Almost all these species are now extinct, but man certainly existed in the midst of them.

The mammoth, elephant, rhinoceros, stag, and hippopotamus were then in the habit of roaming over Europe in immense herds, just as some of these animals still do in the interior of Africa. These animals must have had their favourite haunts—spots where they assembled together in thousands; or else it would be difficult to account for the countless numbers of bones which are found accumulated at the same spot.

Before these formidable bands, man could dream of nothing but flight. It was only with some isolated animal that he could dare to engage in a more or less unequal conflict. Farther on in our work, we shall see how he began to fabricate some rough weapons, with a view of attacking his mighty enemies.

The first important step which man made in the path of progress was the acquisition of fire. In all probability, man came to the knowledge of it by accident, either by meeting with some substance which had been set on fire by lightning or volcanic heat, or by the friction of pieces of wood setting a light to some very inflammable matter.

Fig. 7.—The Production of Fire.

In order to obtain fire, man of the quaternary epoch may have employed the same means as those made use of by the American aborigines, at the time when Christopher Columbus first fell in with them on the shores of the New World—means which savage nations existing at the present day still put in practice. He rubbed two pieces of dry wood one against the other, or turned round and round with great rapidity a stick sharpened to a point, having placed the end of it in a hole made in the trunk of a very dry tree (fig. 7).

As among the savages of the present day we find certain elementary mechanisms adapted to facilitate the production of fire, it is not impossible that these same means were practised at an early period of the human race.

It would take a considerable time to set light to two pieces of dry wood by merely rubbing them against one another; but if a bow be made use of, that is, the chord of an arc fixed firmly on a handle, so as to give a rapid revolution to a cylindrical rod of wood ending in a point which entered into a small hole made in a board, the board may be set on fire in a few minutes. Such a mode of obtaining fire may have been made use of by the men who lived in the same epoch with the mammoth and other animals, the species of which are now extinct.

The first rudiments of combustion having been obtained, so as to serve, during the daytime, for the purposes of warmth and cooking food, and during the night, for giving light, how was the fire to be kept up? Wood from the trees that grew in the district, or from those which were cast up by the currents of the rivers or sea; inflammable mineral oils; resin obtained from coniferous trees; the fat and grease of wild animals; oil extracted from the great cetaceans;—all these substances must have assisted in maintaining combustion, for the purposes both of warmth and light. The only fuel which the Esquimaux of the present day have either to warm their huts or light them during the long nights of their gloomy climate, is the oil of the whale and seal, which, burnt in a lamp with a short wick, serves both to cook their food and also to warm and illumine their huts.

Even, nowadays, in the Black Forest (Duchy of Baden), instead of candles, long splinters of very dry beech are sometimes made use of, which are fixed in a horizontal position at one end and lighted at the other. This forms an economical lamp, which is really not to be despised.

We have also heard of the very original method which is resorted to by the inhabitants of the Faroe Isles in the northern seas of Europe, in order to warm and light up their huts. This method consists in taking advantage of the fat and greasy condition of the young Stormy Petrel (Mother Carey's Chicken), so as to convert its body into a regular lamp. All that is necessary is to draw a wick through its body, projecting at the beak, which when lighted causes this really animal candle to throw out an excellent light until the last greasy morsel of the bird is consumed.

This bird is also used by the natives of the Isles as a natural fuel to keep up their fires and cook other birds.

Whatever may have been the means which were made use of by primitive man in order to procure fire, either the simple friction of two pieces of wood one against the other, continued for a long time, the *bow*, or merely a stick turning round rapidly by the action of the hand, without any kind of mechanism—it is certain that the acquisition of fire must be classed amongst the most beautiful and valuable discoveries which mankind has made. Fire must have put an end to the weariness of the long nights. In the presence of fire, the darkness of the holes and caverns in which man made his first retreat, must have vanished away. With the aid of fire, the most rigorous climates became habitable, and the damp which impregnated the body of man or his rough garments, made of the skin of the bear or some long-haired ruminant, could be evaporated. With fire near them, the danger arising from ferocious beasts must have much diminished; for a general instinct leads wild animals to dread the light and the heat of a fire. Buried, as they were, in the midst of forests infested with wild beasts, primitive men might, by means of a fire kept alight during the night, sleep in peace without being disturbed by the attacks of the huge wild beasts which prowled about all round them.

Fire, too, gave the first starting-point to man's industry. It afforded means to the earliest inhabitants of the earth for felling trees, for procuring charcoal, for hardening wood for the manufacture of their rudimentary implements, and for baking their primitive pottery.

Thus, as soon as man had at his disposal the means for producing artificial heat, his position began to improve, and the kindly flame of the hearth became the first centre round which the family circle was constituted.

Ere long man felt the need of strengthening his natural powers against the attacks of wild beasts. At the same time he desired to be able to make his prey some of the more peaceable animals, such as the stag, the smaller kinds of ruminants, and the horse. Then it was that he began to manufacture weapons.

He had remarked, spread about the surface of the ground, certain flints, with sharp corners and cutting edges. These he gathered up, and by the means of other stones of a rather tougher nature, he broke off from them pieces, which he fashioned roughly in the shape of a hatchet or hammer. He fixed these splinters into split sticks, by way of a handle, and firmly bound them in their places with the tendons of an animal or the strong stalks of some dried plant. With this weapon, he could, if he pleased, strike his prey at a distance.

When man had invented the bow and chipped out flint arrow-heads, he was enabled to arrest the progress of the swiftest animal in the midst of his flight.

Since the time when the investigations with regard to primitive man have been set on foot in all countries, and have been energetically prosecuted, enormous quantities have been found of these chipped flints, arrow-heads, and various stone implements, which archæologists designate by the common denomination of *hatchets*, in default of being able, in some cases, to distinguish the special use for which they had been employed. Before going any further, it will be necessary to enter into some details with regard to these flint implements—objects which are altogether characteristic of the earliest ages of civilisation.

For a long time past chipped stones of a somewhat similar character have been met with here and there in several countries, sometimes on the surface of, and sometimes buried deeply in, the ground; but no one understood what their significance was. If the common people ever distinguished them from ordinary stones, they attached to them some superstitious belief. Sometimes they called them "thunder-stones," because they attributed to them the power of preserving from lightning those who were in possession of them. It was not until the middle of the present century that naturalists and archæologists began to comprehend the full advantage which might be derived from the examination of these chipped stones, in reconstructing the lineaments of the earliest of the human race and in penetrating, up to a certain point, into their manners, customs, and industry. These stone-hatchets and arrow-heads are, therefore, very plentiful in the present day in collections of antiquities and cabinets of natural history.

Most of these objects which are found in Europe are made of flint, and this circumstance may be easily explained. Flint must have been preferred as a material, on account both of its hardness and its mode of cleavage, which may be so readily adapted to the will of the workman. One hard blow, skilfully applied, is sufficient to break off, by the mere shock, a sharp-edged flake of a blade-like shape. These sharp-edged blades of silex might serve as knives. Certainly they would not last long in use, for they are very easily notched; but primitive men must have been singularly skilful in making them.

Although the shapes of these stone implements are very varied, they may all be classed under a certain number of prevailing types; and these types are to be found in very different countries. The flint hatchets are at first very simple although irregular in their shape; but they gradually manifest a much larger amount of talent exhibited in their manufacture, and a better judgment is shown in adapting them to the special uses for which they were intended. The progress of the human intellect is written in ineffaceable characters on these tablets of stone, which, defended as they were, by a thick layer of earth, bid defiance to the injuries of time.

Let us not despise these first and feeble efforts of our primitive forefathers, for they mark the date of the starting-point of manufactures and the arts. If the men of the stone age had not persevered in their efforts, we, their descendants, should never have possessed either our palaces or our masterpieces of painting and sculpture. As Boucher de Perthes says, "The first man who struck one pebble against another to make some requisite alteration in its form, gave the first blow of the chisel which has resulted in producing the Minerva and all the sculpture of the Parthenon."

Archæologists who have devoted their energies to investigating the earliest monuments of human industry, have found it necessary to be on their guard against certain errors, or rather wilful deceptions, which might readily pervert their judgment and deprive their discoveries of all character of authenticity. There is, in fact, a certain class of persons engaged in a deceptive manufacture who have taken a delight in misleading archæologists by fabricating apocryphal flint and stone implements, in which they drive a rather lucrative trade. They assert, without the least scruple, the high antiquity of their productions, which they sell either to inexperienced amateurs, who are pleased to put them in their collections duly labelled and ticketed, or—which is a more serious matter—to workmen who are engaged in making excavations in fossiliferous beds. These workmen hide the fictitious specimens in the soil they are digging, using every requisite precaution so as to have the opportunity of subsequently extracting them and fingering a reward for them from some too trusting naturalist. These imitations are, moreover, so cleverly made, that it sometimes requires well-practised eyes to recognise them; but they may be recognised with some degree of facility by the following characteristics:—

Fig. 8.—*Dendrites* or Crystallisations found on the surface of wrought Flints.

The ancient flints present a glassy surface which singularly contrasts with the dull appearance of the fresh cleavages. They are also for the most part covered with a whitish coating or *patina*, which is nothing but a thin layer of carbonate of lime darkened in colour by the action of time. Lastly, many of these flints are ornamented with branching crystallisations, called *dendrites*, which form on their surface very delicate designs of a dark brown; these are owing to the combined action of the oxides of iron and manganese (fig. 8).

We must add that these flint implements often assume the colour of the soil in which they have been buried for so many centuries; and as Mr. Prestwich, a learned English geologist, well remarks, this agreement in colour indicates that they have remained a very considerable time in the stratum which contains them.

Among the stone implements of primitive ages, some are found in a state of perfect preservation, which clearly bears witness to their almost unused state; others, on the contrary, are worn, rounded, and blunted, sometimes because they have done good service in bygone days, and sometimes because they have been many times rolled over and rubbed by diluvial waters, the action of which has produced this result. Some, too, are met with which are broken, and nothing of them remains but mere vestiges. In a general way, they are completely covered with a very thick coating which it is necessary to break off before they can be laid open to view.

They are especially found under the soil in grottos and caves, on which we shall remark further in some detail, and they are almost always mixed up with the bones of extinct mammalian species.

Certain districts which are entirely devoid of caves contain, however, considerable deposits of these stone implements. We may mention in this category the alluvial quarternary beds of the valley of the Somme, known under the name of drift beds, which were worked by Boucher de Perthes with an equal amount of perseverance and success.

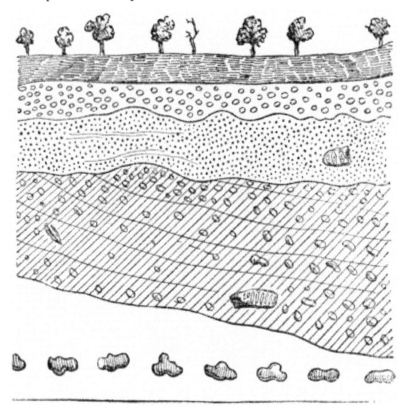

Fig. 9.—Section of a Gravel Quarry at Saint-Acheul, which contained the wrought Flints found by Boucher de Perthes.

This alluvium was composed of a gravelly deposit, which geologists refer to the great inundations which, during the epoch of the great bear and the mammoth, gave to Europe, by hollowing out its valleys, its present vertical outline. The excavations in the sand and gravel near Amiens and Abbeville, which were directed with so much intelligence by Boucher de Perthes, have been the means of exhuming thousands of worked flints, affording unquestionable testimony of the existence of man during the quaternary epoch.

All these worked flints may be classed under some of the principal types, from which their intended use may be approximately conjectured.

One of the types which is most extensively distributed, especially in the drift beds of the valley of the Somme, where scarcely any other kind is found, is the *almond-shaped* type (fig. 10).

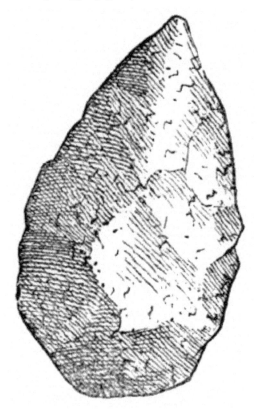

Fig. 10.—Hatchet of the *Almond-shaped* type, from the Valley of the Somme

The instruments of this kind are hatchets of an oval shape, more or less elongated, generally flattened on both sides, but sometimes only on one, carefully chipped all over their surface so as to present a cutting edge. The workmen of the Somme give them the graphic name of *cats' tongues*.

They vary much in size, but are generally about six inches long by three wide, although some are met with which are much larger. The Pre-historic Gallery in the Universal Exposition of 1867, contained one found at Saint-Acheul, and exhibited by M. Robert, which measured eleven inches in length by five in width. This remarkable specimen is represented in fig. 11.

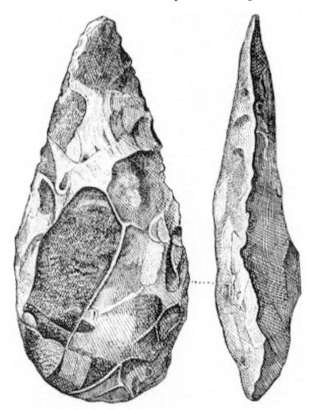

Fig. 11.—Flint Hatchet from Saint-Acheul of the so-called *Almond-shaped type*.

Another very characteristic form is that which is called the *Moustier type* (fig. 12), because they have been found in abundance in the beds in the locality of Moustier, which forms a portion of the department of Dordogne. This name is applied to the pointed flints which are only wrought on one side, the other face being completely plain.

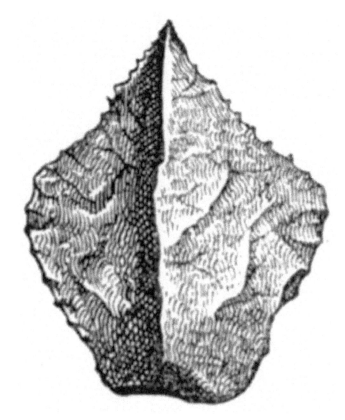

Fig. 12.—Wrought Flint (*Moustier type*).

To the same deposit also belongs the flint *scraper*, the sharp edge of which forms the arc of a circle, the opposite side being of some considerable thickness so as to afford a grasp to the hand of the operator.

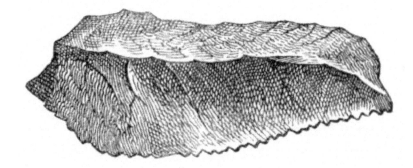

Fig. 13.—Flint Scraper.

Some of these instruments (fig. 13) are finely toothed all along their sharp edge; they were evidently used for the same purposes as our saws.

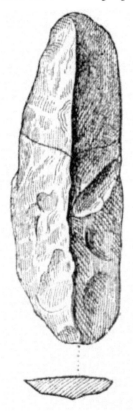

Fig. 14.—Flint Knife, found at Menchecourt, near Abbeville.

The third type (fig. 14) is that of *knives*. They are thin and narrow tongue-shaped flakes, cleft off from the lump of flint at one blow. When one of the ends is chipped to a point, these knives become scratchers. Sometimes these flints are found to be wrought so as to do service as augers.

The question is often asked, how these primitive men were able to manufacture their weapons, implements, and utensils, on uniform models, without the help of metallic hammers. This idea has, indeed, been brought forward as an argument against those who contend for the existence of quaternary man. Mr. Evans, an English geologist, replied most successfully to this objection by a very simple experiment. He took a pebble and fixed it in a wooden handle; having thus manufactured a stone hammer, he made use of it to chip a flint little by little, until he had succeeded in producing an oval hatchet similar to the ancient one which he had before him.

The flint-workers who, up to the middle of the present century, prepared gun-flints for the army, were in the habit of splitting the stone into splinters. But they made use of steel hammers to cleave the flint, whilst primitive man had nothing better at his disposal than another and rather harder stone.

Primitive man must have gone to work in somewhat the following way: They first selected flints, which they brought to the shape of those cores or *nuclei* which are found in many places in company with finished implements; then, by means of another and harder stone of elongated shape, they cleft flakes off the flint. These flakes were used for making knives, scratchers, spear or arrow-heads, hatchets, tomahawks, scrapers, &c. Some amount of skill must have been required to obtain the particular shape that was required; but constant practice in this work exclusively must have rendered this task comparatively easy.

Fig. 15.—Flint Core or Nucleus.

How, in the next place, were these clipped flints fitted with handles, so as to make hatchets, poniards and knives?

Some of them were fixed at right angles between the two split ends of a stick: this kind of weapon must have somewhat resembled our present hatchets. Others, of an oval shape and circular edge, might have been fastened transversely into a handle, so as to imitate a carpenter's adze. In case of need, merely a forked branch or a piece of split wood might serve as sheath or handle to the flint blade. Flints might also have been fixed as double-edged blades by means of holes cut in pieces of wood, to which a handle was afterwards added.

These flint flakes might, lastly, be fitted into a handle at one end. The wide-backed knives, which were only sharp on one side, afforded a grasp for the hand without further trouble, and might dispense with a handle. The small flints might also be darted as projectiles by the help of a branch of a tree forming a kind of spring, such as we may see used as a toy by children.

The mere description of these stone hatchets, fitted on to pieces of wood, recall to our mind the natural weapons used by some of the American savages, and the tribes which still exist in a state of freedom in the Isles of Oceania. We allude to the tomahawk, a name which we so often meet with in the accounts of voyages round the world. Among those savage nations who have not as yet bent their necks beneath the yoke of civilisation, we might expect to find—and, in fact, we do find—the weapons and utensils which were peculiar to man in primitive ages. A knowledge of the manners and customs of the present Australian aborigines has much conduced to the success of the endeavours to reconstruct a similar system of manners and customs in respect to man of the quaternary age.

It was with the weapons and implements that we have just described that man, at the epoch of the great bear and mammoth, was able to repulse the attacks of the ferocious animals which prowled round his retreat and often assailed him (fig. 16).

Fig. 16.—Man in the Great Bear and Mammoth Epoch.

But the whole life of primitive man was not summed up in defending himself against ferocious beasts, and in attacking them in the chase. Beyond the needs which were imposed upon him by conflict and hunting, he felt, besides, the constant necessity of quenching his thirst. Water is a thing in constant use by man, whether he be civilised or savage. The fluid nature of water renders it difficult to convey it except by enclosing it in bladders, leathern bottles, hollowed-out stumps of trees, plaited bowls, &c. Receptacles of this kind were certain ultimately to become dirty and unfit for the preservation of water; added to this they could not endure the action of fire. It was certainly possible to hollow out stone, so as to serve as a receptacle for water; but any kind of stone which was soft enough to be scooped out, and would retain its tenacity after this operation, is very rarely met with. Shells, too, might be used to hold a liquid; but then shells are not to be found in every place. It was, therefore, necessary to resolve the problem—how far it might be possible to make vessels which would be strong, capable of holding water, and able to stand the heat of the fire without breaking or warping. What was required was, in fact, the manufacture of pottery.

The potter's art may, perhaps, be traced back to the most remote epochs of man. We have already seen, in the introduction to this work, that, in 1835, M. Joly found in the cave of Nabrigas (Lozère), a skull of the great bear pierced with a stone arrow-head, and that by the side of this skull were also discovered fragments of pottery, on which might still be seen the imprint of the fingers which moulded it. Thus, the potter's art may have already been exercised in the earliest period which we can assign to the development of mankind.

Other causes also might lead us to believe that man, at a very early period of his existence, succeeded in the manufacture of rough pottery.

The clay which is used in making all kinds of pottery, from the very lowest kitchen utensil up to the most precious specimens of porcelain, may be said to exist almost everywhere. By softening it and kneading it with water, it may be moulded into vessels of all shapes. By mere exposure to the heat of the sun, these vessels will assume a certain amount of cohesion; for, as tradition tells us, the towers and palaces of ancient Nineveh were built entirely with bricks which had been baked in the sun.

Yet the idea of hardening any clayey paste by means of the action of fire is so very simple, that we are not of opinion that pottery which had merely been baked in the sun was ever made use of to any great extent, even among primitive man. Mere chance, or the most casual observation, might have taught our earliest forefathers that a morsel of clay placed near a fire-hearth became hardened and altogether impenetrable to water, that is, that it formed a perfect specimen of pottery. Yet the art, though ancient, has not been universally found among mankind.

Ere long, experience must have taught men certain improvements in the manufacture of pottery. Sand was added to the clay, so as to render it less subject to "flying" on its first meeting the heat of the fire; next, dried straw was mixed with the clay in order to give it more coherence.

In this way those rough vessels were produced, which were, of course, moulded with the hand, and still bear the imprints of the workman's fingers. They were only half-baked, on account of the slight intensity of heat in the furnace which they were then obliged to make use of, which was nothing more than a wood fire, burning in the open air, on a stone hearth.

From these data we give a representation (fig. 17) of the *workshop of the earliest potter*.

Fig. 17.—The First Potter.

In the gravel pits in the neighbourhood of Amiens we meet with small globular bodies with a hole through the middle, which are, indeed, nothing but fossil shells found in the white chalk (fig. 18). It is probable that these stony beads were used to adorn the men contemporary with the diluvial period. The natural holes which existed in them enabled them to be threaded as bracelets or necklaces. This, at least, was the opinion of Dr. Rigollot; and it was founded on the fact that he had often found small heaps of these delicate little balls collected together in the same spot, as if an inundation had drifted them into the bed of the river without breaking the bond which held them together.

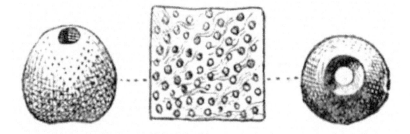

Fig. 18.—Fossil Shells used as Ornaments, and found in the Gravel at Amiens.

The necklaces, which men and women had already begun to wear during the epoch of the great bear and the mammoth, were the first outbreak of the sentiment of adornment, a feeling so natural to the human species. The way in which these necklaces were put together is, however, exactly similar to that which we meet with during the present day among savage tribes—a thread on which a few shells were strung, which was passed round the neck.

It has been supposed, from another series of wrought flints, found at Saint-Acheul by Boucher de Perthes, that the men of the epoch of the great bear and mammoth may have executed certain rough sketches of art-workmanship, representing either figures or symbols. Boucher de Perthes has, in fact, found flints which he considered to show representations, with varying degrees of resemblance, of the human head, in profile, three-quarter view, and full face; also of animals, such as the rhinoceros and the mammoth.

There are many other flints, evidently wrought by the hand of man, which were found by Boucher de Perthes in the same quaternary deposits; but it would be a difficult matter to decide their intention or significance. Some, perhaps, were religious symbols, emblems of authority, &c. The features which enable us to recognise the work of man in these works of antediluvian art, are the symmetry of shape and the repetition of successive strokes by which the projecting portions are removed, the cutting edges sharpened, or the holes bored out.

The natural colour of all the wrought flints we have just been considering, which bring under our notice the weapons and utensils of man in the earliest epoch of his existence, is a grey which assumes every tint, from the brightest to the darkest; but, generally speaking, they are stained and coloured according to the nature of the soil from which they are dug out. Argillaceous soils colour them white; ochreous gravels give them a yellowish brown hue. Some are white on one side and brown on the other, probably from having lain between two different beds.

This *patina* (to use the established term) is the proof of their long-continued repose in the beds, and is, so to speak, the stamp of their antiquity.

CHAPTER III.

The Man of the Great Bear and Mammoth Epoch lived in Caverns—Bone Caverns in the Quaternary Rock during the Great Bear and Mammoth Epoch—Mode of Formation of these Caverns—Their Division into several Classes—Implements of Flint, Bone, and Reindeer-horn found in these Caverns—The Burial-place at Aurignac—Its probable Age—Customs which it reveals—Funeral Banquets during the Great Bear and Mammoth Epoch.

HAVING given a description of the weapons and working implements of the men belonging to the great bear and mammoth epoch, we must now proceed to speak of the habitations.

Caverns hollowed out in the depth of the rocks formed the first dwellings of man. We must, therefore, devote some degree of attention to the simple and wild retreats of our forefathers. As the objects which have been found in these caverns are both numerous and varied in their character, they not only throw a vivid light on the manners and customs of primitive man, but also decisively prove the fact of his being contemporary with mammals of species now extinct, such as the mammoth, the great bear, and the *Rhinoceros tichorhinus*.

But before proceeding any further, it is necessary to inquire in what way these caverns could have been formed, in which we find accumulated so many relics of the existence of primitive man.

M. Desnoyers, Librarian of the Museum of Natural History at Paris, is of opinion that these caverns are crevices of the same class as metalliferous *lodes*, only instead of containing metallic ores they must have been originally filled by the deposits of certain thermal springs.

Fig. 19.—Theoretical Section of a Vein of Clay in the Carboniferous Limestone, *before* the hollowing out of Valleys by diluvial Waters.

Fig. 19 represents, according to M. Desnoyers' treatise on *caverns*, one of these primordial veins in the carboniferous limestone. At the time of the diluvial inundation, these veins were opened by the impetuous action of the water. When thus cleared out and brought to the light of day, they assumed the aspect of caves, as represented in fig. 20.

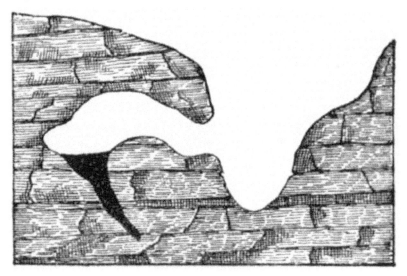

Fig. 20.—Theoretical section of the same Vein of Clay converted into a Cavern, *after* the hollowing out of Valleys by diluvial Waters.

The European diluvial inundation was, as we know, posterior to the glacial epoch.

It is also likely that caverns were sometimes produced by the falling in of portions of some of the interior strata, or that they were formerly the natural and subterranean channels of certain watercourses; many instances of this kind being now known in different countries.

We must also add that it is not probable that all caverns originated in the same way; but that one or other of the several causes just enumerated must have contributed to their formation.

Under the general denomination of *caverns*, all kinds of subterranean cavities are comprehended; but it will be as well to introduce several distinctions in this respect. There are, in the first place, simple clefts or crevices, which are only narrow pits deviating but slightly from the vertical. Next we have grottos (or *baumes* as they are called in the south of France), which generally have a widely opening inlet, and are but of small extent. Lastly, we must draw a distinction between these and the real bone caverns, which consist of a series of chambers, separated by extremely narrow passages, and are often of very considerable dimensions. Some of these caverns occupy an extent of several leagues underground, with variations of level which render their exploration very difficult. They are generally very inaccessible, and it is almost always necessary to ply the pick-axe in order to clear a way from one chamber to another.

In most of these grottos and caverns the ground and sides are covered with calcareous deposits, known by the name of *stalactite* and *stalagmite*, which sometimes meet one another, forming columns and pillars which confer on some of these subterranean halls an elegance replete with a kind of mysterious charm.

These deposits are caused by the infiltrated water charged with carbonate of lime, which, oozing drop by drop through the interstices of the rock, slowly discharge the carbonic acid which held the carbonate of lime in solution, and the salts gradually precipitating form the crystalline or amorphous deposits which constitute these natural columns.

The calcareous deposits which spread over the ground of the caverns are called *stalagmite*, and the name of *stalactite* is given to those which hang down from the roof, forming pendants, natural decorations, and ornaments as of alabaster or marble, producing sometimes the most magnificent effects.

Under the stalagmite the largest number of animal bones have been found. This crust, which has been to them a preservatory grave, is so thick and hard that a pick-axe is required in order to break it. Thanks to the protecting cover, the bones have been sheltered from all the various causes of decomposition and destruction. The limestone formed a kind of cement which, uniting clay, mud, sand, flints, bones of men and animals, weapons and utensils into a compact mass, has preserved them for the study and consideration of scientific men in our own days.

The soil called *bone-earth* is, in fact, found under the crystalline bed which covers the ground of the caverns.

Fig. 21, which represents a section of the cave of Galeinreuth, in Bavaria, will enable us clearly to understand the position occupied by the bones in most of these caverns.

Fig. 21.—The Cave of Galeinreuth, in Bavaria.

Bone-earth consists of a reddish or yellowish clay, often mixed with pebbles, which seem to have come from some distant beds, for they cannot be attributed to the adjacent rocks. This stratum varies considerably in depth; in some spots it is very thin, in others it rises almost to the top of the cavern, to a height of forty or fifty feet. But in this case it is, in reality, composed of several strata belonging to different ages, and explorers ought to note with much attention the exact depth of any of the organic remains found in their mass.

There are, however, in several bone-caverns certain peculiarities which demand a special explanation. Caves often contain large heaps of bones, situated at heights which it would have been absolutely inaccessible to the animals which lived in these places. How, then, was it possible that these bones could have found their way to such an elevated position? It is also a very strange fact, that no cavern has ever produced an entire skeleton or even a whole limb of the skeleton of a man, and scarcely of any animal whatever. The bones, in fact, not only lie in confusion and utter disorder, but, up to the present time, it has been impossible to find all the bones which in times past formed an individual. It must, therefore, be admitted, that the accumulation of bones and human remains in most of the caves are owing to other causes than the residence of man and wild animals in these dark retreats.

It is supposed, therefore, that the bones in question were deposited in these hollows by the rushing in of the currents of diluvial water, which had drifted them along in their course. A fact which renders this hypothesis likely is that drift-pebbles are constantly found in close proximity to these bones. Now these pebbles come from localities at considerable distances from the cavern; often, indeed, terrestrial and fluviatile shells accompany these bones. It may sometimes be remarked that the femurs and tibias of large mammals have their points rubbed off, and the smallest bones are reduced to rounded fragments. These are all evident indications that these bones had been carried along by rapid currents of water, which swept away everything in their course; or, in other words, by the current of the waters of the deluge which signalised the quaternary epoch.

During this period of the existence of primitive man, all these caverns were not applied to the same purpose. Some were the dens of wild beasts, others formed the habitations of man, and others again were used as burial-places.

There is no difficulty in the idea that dens of wild beasts might very readily be occupied by man, after he had killed or driven out the fierce inhabitants; no discovery, however, has as yet confirmed this supposition. It can hardly be doubted that primitive man seldom dared to take up his abode in dens which had been, for some time, the refuge of any of the formidable carnivora; if he did, it was only after having assured himself that these retreats had been altogether abandoned by their terrible inhabitants.

We shall now proceed to consider these three classes of caverns.

Caves which, during the quaternary epoch, have served as dens for wild animals, are very numerous. Experienced *savants* are enabled to recognise them by various indications. The bones they contain are never fractured; but it may be seen that they have been gnawed by carnivorous animals, as they still bear the marks of their teeth. Into these retreats the cave-lion (*Felis spelæa*) and the hyæna (*Hyæna spelæa*) were accustomed to drag their prey, in order there to tear it to pieces and devour it, or divide it into portions for their young ones. In fact, in these caverns, excrements of the hyæna mixed with small and undigested bones are often found. The cave bear retired into the same retreats, but he probably only came there to pass the period of his hibernal sleep. Lastly, the same dens no doubt offered a refuge to sick or dying animals, who resorted thither in order to expire in peace. We have a proof of this in the traces of wounds and caries on some of the bones of animals found by Schmerling in the caverns of the Meuse; also in the skull of a hyæna, the median ridge of which had been bitten and appeared to be half healed.

Those caverns which formed a shelter for primitive man are, like the preceding ones, to be recognised by a mere inspection of the bones contained in them. The long bones of the ox, horse, stag, rhinoceros, and other quadrupeds which formed the food of man during the quaternary epoch, are always split; and they are all broken in the same way, that is, lengthwise. The only cause for their having been split in this manner must have been the desire of extracting the marrow for the purpose of eating. Such a mode of breaking them would never have been practised by any animal.

This apparently trivial circumstance is, however, of the highest importance. In fact, it leads to the following conclusion: "That man, having eaten large mammals of species now extinct, must have been contemporary with these species."

We shall now proceed to examine the caverns which were used as burial-places for man.

To M. Édouard Lartet, the celebrated palæontologist, the honour must be ascribed of having been the first to collect any important data bearing on the fact that caverns were used for burial-places by the primitive man of the great bear and mammoth epoch. We have thus been led to discover the traces of a funeral custom belonging to the man of these remote ages; we allude to the *funeral banquet*. The source of this information was the discovery of a pre-historic burial-place at Aurignac (Haute-Garonne), of which we have given an account in the Introduction to this work, which, however, we must again here refer to.

Near the town of Aurignac rises the hill of Fajoles, which the inhabitants of the country, in their *patois*, call "*mountagno de las Hajoles*" (beech-tree mountain), a circumstance showing that it was formerly covered with beech-trees. As we have already stated, in the Introduction to this work, it was on one of the slopes of this hill that, in the year 1842, an excavator, named Bonnemaison, discovered a great slab of limestone placed in a vertical position and closing up an arched opening. In the cave closed up by this slab the excavator discovered the remains of seventeen human skeletons!

We have already told how these skeletons were removed to the village cemetery, and thus, unfortunately, for ever lost to the researches of science.

Eighteen years after, in 1860, M. Lartet, having heard of the event, repaired to the spot, accompanied by Bonnemaison; he quite understood how it had happened that, during a long course of centuries, the cave had escaped the notice of the inhabitants of the country. The entrance to it was concealed by masses of earth which, having been brought down from the top of the hill by the action of the water, had accumulated in front of the entrance, hiding a flat terrace, on which many vestiges of pre-historic times were found. As no disturbance of the ground had taken place in this spot subsequent to the date of the burial, this *talus* had been sufficient to protect the traces of the men who were contemporary with the mammoth, and to shield their relics from all exterior injury.

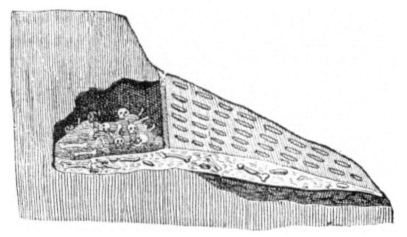

Fig. 22.—Section of the Sepulchral Cave at Aurignac.

Fig. 22, taken from M. Lartet's article, represents a vertical section of the sepulchral cave at Aurignac.

After a rapid inspection of the cave and its surroundings, M. Lartet resolved to make complete and methodical excavations, aided by intelligent workmen labouring under his superintendence; the following are the results he obtained.

A bed of "made ground" two feet thick covered the ground of the cave. In this were found some human remains which had escaped the first investigations; also bones of mammals in good preservation, and exhibiting no fractures or teeth-marks, wrought flints, mostly of the *knife* type (fig. 23), and carved reindeer horns, among which there was an instrument carefully tapered off and rounded, but deprived of its point (fig. 24), the other end being bevelled off, probably to receive a handle.

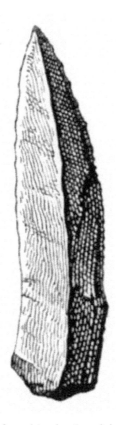

Fig. 23.—Flint Knife found in the Sepulchral Cave at Aurignac.

Fig. 24.—Implement made of Reindeer's or Stag's Horn, found in the Sepulchral Cave at Aurignac.

We must here add, that at the time of his discovery Bonnemaison collected, from the midst of the bones, eighteen small discs which were pierced in the centre, and doubtless intended to be strung together in a necklace or bracelet. These discs, which were formed of a white compact substance were recognised as sea-shells of a *Cardium* species.

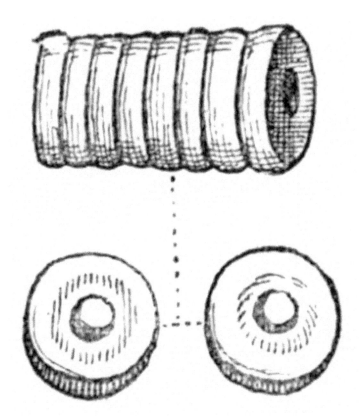

Fig. 25.—Series of perforated Discs of the *Cardium* Shell found in the Sepulchral Cave at Aurignac.

The cavern of Aurignac was a burial-place of the quaternary epoch, for M. Lartet found in it a quantity of the bones of the cave-bear, the bison, the reindeer, the horse, &c.

In fig. 26, we give a representation of a fragment of the lower jaw of a great bear as an example of the state of the bones found in this cavern.

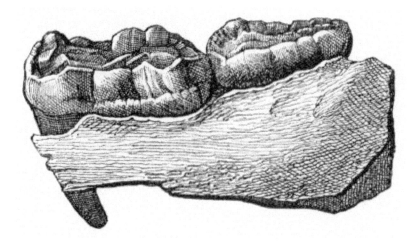

Fig. 26.—Fragment of the Lower Jaw of a Cave-Bear, found in the Sepulchral Cave at Aurignac.

The perfect state of preservation of these bones shows that they were neither broken to furnish food for man nor torn by carnivorous animals, particularly by hyænas, as is seen in a great many caverns. We must therefore conclude from this peculiarity, that the stone which closed the entrance to the cave was moved away for every interment and carefully put back into its place immediately afterwards.

In order to explain the presence of so many foreign objects by the side of the human skeletons—such as animals' bones—implements of flint and reindeers' horn—necklaces or bracelets—we must admit as probable that a funeral custom existed among the men of the great bear and mammoth epoch, which has been preserved in subsequent ages. They used to place in the tomb, close to the body, the weapons, hunting trophies, and ornaments of all sorts, belonging to the defunct. This custom still exists among many tribes in a more or less savage state.

In front of the cave, there was, as we have already said, a kind of flat spot which had afterwards become covered with earth which had fallen down from the top of the hill. When the earth which covered this flat spot was cleared away, they met with another deposit containing bones. This deposit was situated on a prolongation of the ground on which the skeletons were placed in the interior of the cavern. Under this deposit, was a bed of ashes and charcoal, 5 to 7 inches thick. This was, therefore, the site of an ancient fire-hearth.

In other words, in front of the sepulchral cave there was a kind of terrace upon which, after the interment of the body in the cavern, a feast called the *funeral banquet* was held.

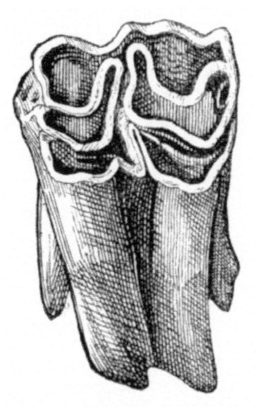

Fig. 27.—Upper Molar of a Bison, found in the Ashes of the Fire-hearth of the Sepulchral Cave at Aurignac.

In this bed, situated in front of the cavern an immense number of the most interesting relics were discovered—a large number of the teeth and broken bones of herbivorous animals (fig. 27); a hundred flint knives; two chipped flints, which archæologists believe to be sling projectiles; a rounded pebble with a depression in the middle, which, according to Mr. Steinhauer, keeper of the Ethnographical Museum at Copenhagen, was used to flake off flint-knives; lastly, a large quantity of implements made of reindeers' horn, which exhibit the most varied shapes. We may mention, for instance, the arrow-heads fashioned very simply, without wings or barbs (fig. 28); some of these heads appear to have been subjected to the action of fire, as if they had been left in the body of the animal during the process of cooking; a bodkin made of roebuck's horn (fig. 29) very carefully pointed, and in such a good state of preservation that it might still be used, says M. Lartet, to perforate the skins of animals before sewing them; and this must, in fact, have been its use; a second instrument, similar to the preceding, but less finely pointed, which M. Lartet is inclined to consider as an instrument for tatooing; some thin blades of various sizes, which, according to Steinhauer, much resemble the reindeer-horn polishers still used by the Laplanders to flatten down the seams of their coarse skin-garments; another blade, accidentally broken at both ends, one of the sides of which is perfectly polished and shows two series of transversal lines at equal distances apart; the lateral edges of this blade are marked with deeper notches at almost regular intervals (fig. 30). M. Lartet considers that these lines and notches are signs of numeration, and Mr. Steinhauer has propounded the idea that they are hunting-marks. Both hypotheses are possible, and the more so as they do not contradict each other.

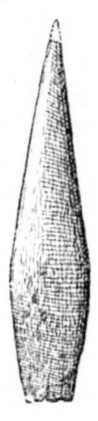

Fig. 28.—Arrow-head made of Reindeer's Horn, found in the Sepulchral Cave of Aurignac.

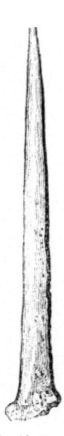

Fig. 29.—Bodkin made of Roebuck's Horn, found in the Sepulchral Cave of Aurignac.

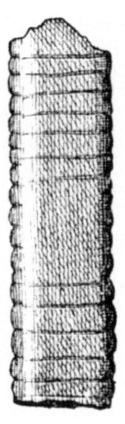

Fig. 30.—Truncated Blade in Reindeer's Horn, bearing two Series of transversal Lines and Notches, probably used for numeration.

Among the bones, some were partly carbonised, others, only scorched, but the greater number had not been subjected at all to the action of fire. All the bones having medullary hollows, and commonly called marrow-bones, were broken lengthwise, a certain indication that this operation had been effected to extract the marrow, and that these bones had been used at a feast carried on according to the manners and customs of that epoch, when the marrow out of animal bones was regarded as the most delicious viand—many men of our own days being also of this opinion.

A certain number of these bones exhibited shallow cuts, showing that a sharp instrument had been used to detach the flesh from them. Nearly all those which had not been subjected to the action of fire bore the mark of the teeth of some carnivorous animal. This animal, doubtless, came to gnaw them after man had taken his departure from the spot. This carnivorous animal could have been none other than the hyæna, as is shown by the excrements left in the place.

The ossiferous mound situated immediately above the fire-hearth contained, like the subjacent ashes, a large number of the bones of certain herbivorous animals.

The discovery of the fire-hearth situated in front of the cave of Aurignac, and the various remains which were found intermingled underneath it, enable us to form some idea of the way in which funeral ceremonies took place among the men of the great bear epoch. The parents and friends of the defunct accompanied him to his last resting-place; after which, they assembled together to partake of a feast in front of the tomb soon to be closed on his remains. Then everyone took his departure, leaving the scene of their banquet free to the hyænas, which came to devour the remains of the meal.

This custom of funeral-feasts is, doubtless, very natural, as it has been handed down to our days; though it now chiefly exists among the poorer classes.

In accordance with the preceding data we here represent (fig. 31) a *funeral feast during the great bear and mammoth epoch.*

Fig. 31.—Funeral Feast during the Great Bear and Mammoth Epoch.

On a flat space situated in front of the cave destined to receive the body of the defunct, some men covered merely with bears' skins with the hair on them are seated round a fire, taking their part in the funeral-feast. The flesh of the great bear and mammoth forms the *menu* of these primitive love-feasts. In the distance may be seen the colossal form of the mammoth, which forms the chief dish of the banquet. The manner of eating is that which distinguishes the men of that epoch; they suck the marrow from the long bones which have previously been split lengthwise, and eat the flesh of the animals cooked on the hearth. The dead body is left at the entrance of the cavern; the primitive grave-stone will soon close on it for ever.

The relics found in the interior of the sepulchral cave of Aurignac have led to a very remarkable inference, which shows how interesting and fertile are the studies which have been made by naturalists on the subject of the antiquity of man. The weapons, the trophies, the ornaments, and the joints of meat, placed by the side of the defunct—does not all this seem to establish the fact that a belief in a future life existed at an extraordinarily remote epoch? What could have been the use of these provisions for travelling, and these instruments of war, if the man who had disappeared from this world was not to live again in another? The great and supreme truth—that the whole being of man does not die with his material body is, therefore, innate in the human heart; since it is met with in the most remote ages, and even existed in the mental consciousness of the man of the stone age.

An instinct of art also appears to have manifested itself in the human race at this extremely ancient date. Thus, one of the articles picked up in the sepulchral cave of Aurignac consisted of a canine tooth of a young cave-bear, perforated so as to allow of its being suspended in some way or other. Now this tooth is so carved that no one can help recognising in it a rough outline of some animal shape, the precise nature of which is difficult to determine, although it may, perhaps, be the head of a bird. It was, doubtless, an amulet or jewel belonging to one of the men interred in the cave, and was buried with him because he probably attached a great value to it. This object, therefore, shows us that some instincts of art existed in the men who hunted the great bear and mammoth.

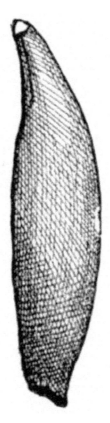

Fig. 32.—Carved and perforated Canine Tooth of a young Cave-Bear.

We shall close this account of the valuable discoveries which were made in the sepulchral cave of Aurignac, by giving a list of the species of mammals the bones of which were found either in the interior or at the exterior of this cavern. The first six species are extinct; the others are still living:—

The great cave-bear (*Ursus spelæus*); the mammoth (*Elephas primigenius*); the rhinoceros (*Rhinoceros tichorhinus*); the great cave-lion (*Felis spelæa*); the cave-hyæna (*Hyæna spelæa*); the gigantic stag (*Megaceros hibernicus*); the bison, the reindeer, the stag, the horse, the ass, the roe, the wild boar, the fox, the wolf, the wild-cat, the badger, and the polecat.

We think it as well to place before the eyes of our readers the exact forms of the heads of the three great fossil animals found in the cave of Aurignac, which geologically characterise the great bear and mammoth epoch, and evidently prove that man was contemporary with these extinct species. Figs. 33, 34, and 35 represent the heads of the cave-bear, the *Rhinoceros tichorhinus*, and the *megaceros* or gigantic stag; they are taken from the casts which adorn the great hall of the Archæological and Pre-historic Museum at Saint-

Germain, and are among the most curious ornaments of this remarkable museum.

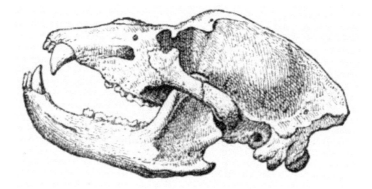

Fig. 33.—Head of a Cave-Bear found in the Cave of Aurignac.

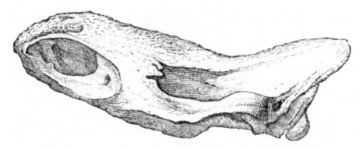

Fig. 34.—Head of the *Rhinoceros Tichorhinus* found in the Cave of Aurignac.

Fig. 35.—Head of a great Stag (*Megaceros hibernicus*) found in the Cave of Aurignac.

Of all these species, the fox has left behind him the largest number of remains. This carnivorous animal was represented by about eighteen to twenty individual specimens. Neither the mammoth, great cave-lion, nor wild boar appear to have been conveyed into the cave in an entire state; for two or three molar or incisive teeth are the only remains of their carcases which have been found.

But still it is a certain fact that the men who fed on the *Rhinoceros tichorinus* buried their dead in this cavern. In fact, M. Lartet asserts that the bones of the rhinoceros had been split by man in order to extract the marrow. They had also been gnawed by hyænas, which would not have been the case if these bones had not been thrown away, and left on the ground in a fresh state.

The burial-place of Aurignac dates back to the earliest antiquity, that is to say, it was anterior to the European diluvial period. Thus, according to M. Lartet, the great cave-bear was the first of the extinct species to disappear; then the mammoth and *Rhinoceros tichorhinus* were lost sight of; still later, the reindeer first, and then the bison, migrated to the northern and eastern regions of Europe. Now, the *diluvium*, that is to say, the beds formed by drifted pebbles and originating in the great derangement caused by the inundation of the quaternary epoch, does not contain any traces of the bones of the cave-bear. It, therefore, belongs to an epoch of the stone age more recent than the cave of Aurignac. [6] All this goes to prove that this sepulchral cave, which has furnished the science of the antiquity of man with so much valuable information, belonged to the great bear and mammoth epoch, which preceded the diluvial cataclysm.

FOOTNOTE:

[6] 'Nouvelles Recherches sur la Coexistence de l'Homme et des grands Mammifères fossiles.' ('Annales de Sciences naturelles, Zoologie,' vol. xv.)

CHAPTER IV.

Other Caves of the Epoch of the Great Bear and Mammoth—Type of the Human Race during the Epochs of the Great Bear and the Reindeer—The Skulls from the Caves of Engis and Neanderthal.

WITH regard to the bone-caves, which have furnished us with such valuable information as to the men who lived in the epoch of the great bear and the mammoth, we have laid down a necessary distinction, dividing them into caves which served as dens for wild beasts, those which have afforded a refuge for man, and those which were used as his burial-places. In order to complete this subject and set forth the whole of the discoveries which have been made by science on this interesting point, we will say a few words as to the principal bone-caves belonging to the same epoch which have been studied in France, England and Belgium.

We will, in the first place, call attention to the fact that these caverns, taken together, embrace a very long period of time, perhaps an enormous number of centuries, and that hence a considerable difference must result in the nature of the remains of human industry which they contain. Some certainly manifest a perceptible superiority over others in an industrial point of view; but the reason is that they belong to a period somewhat nearer our own, although still forming a part of the epoch of the great bear and mammoth.

We shall divide the caves in France into three groups—those of the east, those of the west and centre, and those of the south.

In the first group, we shall mention the *Trou de la Fontaine* and the *Cave of Sainte-Reine*, both situated in the environs of Toul (Meurthe). These two caves have furnished bones of bears, hyænas, and the rhinoceros, along with the products of human industry. That of Sainte-Reine has been explored by M. Guérin, and especially by M. Husson, who has searched it with much care.

The second group includes the grottos *des Fées*, of Vergisson, Vallières, and La Chaise.

The Grotte des Fées, at Arcy (Yonne), has been searched and described by M. de Vibraye, who ascertained the existence of two distinct beds, the upper one belonging to the reindeer epoch, the lower one to the great bear epoch. These two beds were divided from each other by matter which had formed a part of the roof of the cave, and had fallen down on the earlier deposit. In the more ancient bed of the two, M. de Vibraye collected fractured bones of the bear and cave-hyæna, the mammoth, and the *Rhinoceros tichorhinus*, all intermingled with flints wrought by the hand of man, amongst which were chips of hyaline quartz (rock-crystal.) His fellow-labourer, M. Franchet, extracted from it a human *atlas* (the upper part of the vertebral column).

The cave of Vergisson (Saône-et-Loire), explored by M. de Ferry, furnished the same kind of bones as the preceding cave, and also bones of the bison, the reindeer, the horse, the wolf, and the fox, all intermixed with wrought flints and fragments of rough pottery. The presence of this pottery indicated that the cave of Vergisson belonged to the latter period of the great bear epoch.

The cave of Vallières (Loir-et-Cher), was worked, first by M. de Vibraye, and subsequently by the Abbé Bourgeois. There was nothing particular to be remarked.

The cave of La Chaise, near Vouthon (Charente), explored by MM. Bourgeois and Delaunay, furnished bones of the cave-bear, the rhinoceros, and the reindeer, flint blades and scrapers, a bodkin and a kind of hook made of bone, an arrow-head in the shape of a willow-leaf likewise of bone, a bone perforated so as to hang on a string, and, what is more remarkable, two long rods of reindeer's horn, tapering at one end and bevelled off at the other, on which figures of animals were graven. These relics betray an artistic feeling of a decided character as existing in the men, the traces of whom are found in this cave.

Among the caves in the south of France, we must specify those of Périgord, those of Bas-Languedoc, and of the district of Foix (department of Ariége).

The caves of Périgord have all been explored by MM. Lartet and Christy, who have also given learned descriptions of them. We will mention the caves of the *Gorge d'Enfer* and *Moustier*, in the valley of the Vézère, and that of *Pey de l'Azé*, all three situate in the department of Dordogne (arrondissement of Sarlat).

The two caves of the *Gorge d'Enfer* were, unfortunately, cleared out in 1793, in order to utilise the deposits of saltpetre which they contained in the manufacture of gunpowder. They have, however, furnished flints chipped into the shapes of scrapers, daggers, &c., a small pebble of white quartz, hollowed out on one side, which had probably been used as a mortar, and instruments of bone or reindeer's horn, three of which showed numerous notches. Bones of the great bear clearly indicated the age of these settlements.

The cave of Moustier, situated about 80 feet above the Vézère, is celebrated for the great number and characteristic shapes of its stone implements, which we have before spoken of. Hatchets of the almond-shaped type, like those of the *diluvium* of Abbeville and Saint-Acheul, were very plentiful. Biconvex spear-heads were also found, of very careful workmanship, and instruments which might be held in the hand, some of them of considerable dimensions; but no pieces of bone or of reindeer's horn were discovered which had been adapted to any purpose whatever. The bones were those of the great bear and cave-hyæna, accompanied by separate *laminæ* of molars of the mammoth, the use of which it is impossible to explain. Similar fragments were met with in some of the other Périgord settlements, and M. Lartet also found some at Aurignac.

Next to the cave of Pey de l'Azé, on which we shall not dwell, come the caverns of Bas-Languedoc, which we shall only enumerate. They consist of the caves of Pondres and Souvignargues (Hérault), which were studied in 1829 by M. de Christol, who recognised, from the data he derived from them, the co-existence of man and the great extinct mammals; also those of Pontil and La Roque, the first explored by M. Paul Gervais, the second by M. Boutin.

We shall now consider the caves of the department of Ariége, some of which furnish objects of very considerable interest. They consist of the caves of *Massat, Lherm,* and *Bouicheta.*

Two caves, very remarkable on account of their extent, have been explored by M. Fontan; they are situate in the valley of Massat, which contains others of less importance. One is placed at the foot of a limestone mountain, about 60 feet above the bottom of the valley; the opening of the other is much higher up; only the latter belongs to the great bear epoch.

From the results of his explorations, M. Fontan is of opinion that the ground in them has been greatly altered by some violent inundation which has intermingled the remains of various geological epochs. This *savant* found in the cave of Massat the bones of the bear, the hyæna and the great cave-lion, the fox, the badger, the wild boar, the roe, &c., two human teeth, and a bone arrow-head. Two beds of ashes and charcoal were also remarked at different depths.

In the upper cave of Massat was found the curious stone on which is designed with tolerable correctness a sketch of the great cave-bear (fig. 36). This singular record marks out for us the earliest trace of the art of design, which we shall find developing itself in a more decisive way during the prehistoric period which follows the one we are now considering.

Fig. 36.—Sketch of the Great Bear on a Stone found in the Cave of Massat.

The caves of Lherm and Bouicheta were inspected by MM. Garrigou and Filhol, who found in them bones of most of the great mammals belonging to extinct species, and particularly those of the great bear, many of which are broken, and still show the marks of the instruments which were used for cutting the flesh off them. Some have been gnawed by hyænas, as proved by the deep grooves with which they are marked. Lower jaw-bones of the great bear, and of the great cave-lion, have been found fashioned, according to a uniform plan, in the shape of hoes. MM. Garrigou and Filhol were of opinion that these jaw-bones, when thus modified, might have been used as offensive weapons.

The cave of Lherm contained also human bones; namely, three teeth, a fragment of a *scapula*, a broken *ulna* and *radius*, and the last joint of the great toe; all these remains presented exactly the same appearance and condition as those of the *Ursus spelæus*, and must, therefore, have belonged to the same epoch.

We have stated that numerous caves have been explored in England, Belgium, and several other countries. We shall not undertake to give with regard to each details which would only be a reproduction of those which precede. We therefore confine ourselves to mentioning the most celebrated of the caverns belonging to the epoch of the great bear and the mammoth.

In England we have the Kent's Hole and Brixham caverns, near Torquay in Devonshire, the latter of which is many hundred yards in extent; the caves of the Gower peninsula, in Glamorganshire (South Wales), which have been carefully studied within the last few years by Messrs. Falconer and Wood; in these were found flint instruments along with bones of the *Elephas antiquus* and the *Rhinoceros hemitæchus*, species which were still more ancient than the mammoth and the *Rhinoceros tichorhinus*; those of Kirkdale, in Yorkshire, explored by Dr. Buckland, the geologist; those near Wells in Somersetshire, Wokey Hole, Minchin Hole, &c.

We must mention, in the north of Italy, the caves of Chiampo and Laglio, on the edge of the Lake of Como, in which, just as at Vergisson, fragments of rough pottery have been discovered, indicating some degree of progress in the manufacture; also the caves in the neighbourhood of Palermo, and especially those of San Ciro and Macagnone.

In the last-mentioned cave, in the midst of an osseous *breccia* which rose to the roof, Dr. Falconer collected flint instruments, splinters of bone, pieces of baked clay and wood charcoal mixed up with large land-shells (*Helix vermiculata*), in a perfect state of preservation, horses' teeth, and the excrements of the hyæna, all cemented together in a deposit of carbonate of lime. In a lower bed were found the bones of various species of the hippopotamus, the *Elephas antiquus*, and other great mammals.

Lastly, Spain, Algeria, Egypt, and Syria also present to our notice caves belonging to the Stone Age.

In the New World various bone-caverns have been explored. We must especially mention Brazil, in which country Lund searched no less than eight hundred caves of different epochs, exhuming in them a great number of unknown animal species. In one of these caves, situated near the Lake of Sumidouro, Lund found some human bones which had formed a part of thirty individuals of different ages, and were "in a similar state of decomposition, and in similar circumstances to the bones of various extinct species of animals."

Thus far we have designedly omitted to mention the Belgian caves. They have, in fact, furnished us with such remarkable relics of former ages that, in dealing with them, we could not confine ourselves to a mere notice. The caves in the neighbourhood of Liége, which were explored in 1833 by Schmerling, deserve to be described in some detail.

Schmerling examined more than forty caves in the Valley of the Meuse and its tributaries. The access to some of these caves was so difficult that in order to reach them it was necessary for the explorer to let himself down by a cord, and then to crawl flat on his face through narrow galleries, so as to make his way into the great chambers; there he was obliged to remain for hours, and sometimes whole days, standing up to his knees in mud, with water dripping from the walls upon his head, while overlooking the workmen breaking up with their pick-axes the layer of stalagmite, so as to bring to light the bone earth—the records on which are inscribed the palpable evidences of the high antiquity of man. Schmerling was compelled to accomplish a perilous expedition of this kind in his visit to the cave of Engis, which has become celebrated by the two human skulls found there by him.

Nearly all the caves in the province of Liége contain scattered bones of the great bear, the cave-hyæna, the mammoth, and the rhinoceros, intermixed with those of species which are still living, such as the wolf, the wild boar, the roe, the beaver, the porcupine, &c. Several of them contained human bones, likewise much scattered and rubbed; they were found in all positions, and at every elevation, sometimes above and sometimes below the above-mentioned animal remains; from this it may be concluded that these caves had been filled with running water, which drifted in all kinds of *débris*. None of them, however, contained any gnawed bones, or the fossil excrement of any animal species, which puts an end to the hypothesis that these caves had been used as dens by wild beasts. Here and there bones were found belonging to the same skeleton, which were in perfect preservation, and lying in their natural juxtaposition; they were probably drifted into the cave by gently flowing water, while still covered with their flesh, and no movement of the ground had since separated them. But no complete skeleton has as yet been discovered, even among the smaller species of mammiferous animals, the disjunction of which is generally less complete.

In almost all the caves Schmerling met with flint implements chipped into the form of hatchets and knives, and he calls attention to the fact "that none of them could have been introduced into the caves at a posterior epoch, as they were found in the same position as the animal remains which accompanied them." In the cave of Clokier, about two and a half miles from Liége, he picked up a polished bone in the shape of a needle, having an eye pierced at the base; in the cave of Engis he likewise found a carved bone, and also some worked flints.

We here close our enumeration of the various sources of the archæological records which have served to reconstruct the history of primitive man during that period of the stone age which we have designated under the name of the epoch of the great bear and the mammoth. Before concluding our remarks as to this period, there is one question which we must enter upon, although there is a great deficiency in any positive records by which it might be solved. What was the organic type of man during this epoch? Could we, for instance, determine what amount of intellect man possessed in this earliest and ancient date of his history?

The answer to this question—although a very uncertain answer—has been supposed to have been found in the caves of Engis and Engihoul, of which we have just spoken as having been explored by Schmerling with such valuable results.

The cave of Engis contained the remains of three human beings, among which were two skulls, one that of a youth, the other that of an adult. The latter only was preserved, the former having fallen into dust while it was being extracted from the ground. Two small fragments of a human skull were likewise found at Engihoul; also a great many of the bones of the hands and feet of three individuals.

The Engis skull has been a subject of protracted argument to the palæontologists and anatomists of the present day. Floods of ink have been spilt upon the question; discussions without end have taken place with respect to this piece of bone, in order to fix accurately the amount of intellect possessed by the inhabitants of Belgium during the epoch of the great bear and the mammoth. Up to a certain point the development of the brain may, in fact, be ascertained from the shape of the cranial envelope, and it is well known that a remarkable similarity exists between the cerebral capacity and the intellectual development of all mammiferous animals. But in a question of this kind we must carefully avoid a quicksand on which anthropologists too often make shipwreck; this danger consists in basing a theory on a too limited number of elements, and of generalising conclusions which are perhaps drawn from one special case. Because we find a portion of a skull—not even a whole skull—belonging to a human being contemporary with the great bear, we assume that we can determine the amount of intellect possessed by man during this epoch. But what proof have we that this skull is not that of an idiot, or, on the contrary, the skull of an individual possessing a superior degree of intelligence? What deduction can be logically drawn from the examination of one single skull? None whatever! "*Testis unus testis nullus*;" and what is said by jurisprudence, which is nothing but good sense in legal matters—science, which is nothing but good sense in learned questions, ought likewise to repeat. If we found ten or twelve skulls, each presenting the same characteristics, we should be justified in thinking that we had before our eyes the human type corresponding to the epoch we are considering; but, we again ask, what arguments could be based on a few fragments of one single skull?

These reservations having been laid down, let us see what some of our great anatomical reasoners have thought about the Engis skull.

The representation which we here give (fig. 37) of the Engis skull was taken from the cast in the Museum of Saint-Germain, and we may perceive from it that the skull is not complete; the entire base of the skull is wanting, and all the bones of the face have disappeared. Consequently it is impossible either to measure the facial angle or to take account of the development of the lower jaw.

Fig. 37.—Portion of a Skull of an Individual belonging to the Epoch of the Great Bear and the Mammoth, found in the Cave of Engis.

We shall not, therefore, surprise any of our readers when we state that the opinions on this subject differ in the most extraordinary degree. In the eyes of Professor Huxley, the English anatomist, this skull offers no indication of degradation; it presents "a good average," and it might just as well be the head of a philosopher as the head of an uncivilised savage. To others—for instance, to Carl Vogt—it indicates an altogether rudimentary degree of intellect.

Thus Hippocrates-Huxley says *yes*, Galen-Vogt says *no*, and Celsus-Lyell says neither *yes* nor *no*. This causes us but little surprise, but it induces us not to waste more time in discussing a question altogether in the dark, that is, upon altogether incomplete data.

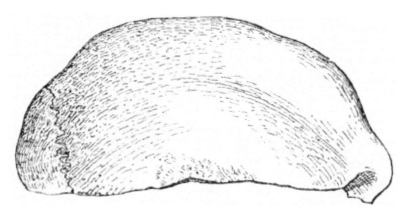

Fig. 38.—Portion of the so-called Neanderthal Skull.

We will now turn our attention to another skull, equally celebrated, which was found in 1857 by Dr. Fuhlrott, near Dusseldorf, in a deep ravine known by the name of Neanderthal. This skull (fig. 38) was discovered in the midst of a small cave under a layer of mud about 5 feet in thickness. The entire skeleton was doubtless buried on the same spot, but the workmen engaged in clearing out the cave must have inadvertently scattered a great portion of the bones, for the largest only could be collected.

It is well to call attention to the fact that no animal remains were found near these bones; there is, therefore, no certain proof that the latter can be assigned to the epoch of the great bear: they might, in fact, be either more recent or more modern. Most geologists are, however, of opinion that they ought to be referred to the above-named early date.

The Neanderthal skull, of which we possess even a smaller portion than of the preceding, differs from the Engis skull. It is characterised by an extraordinary development of the frontal sinuses; that is, by an enormous projection of the superciliary ridges, behind which the frontal bone presents a considerable depression. The cranium is very thick, and of an elongated elliptical shape; the forehead is narrow and low.

These remarks were made by Professor Schaaffhausen, who also established the fact of the identity in length of the femur, the humerus, the radius, and the ulna, with the same bones of a modern European of equal size. But the Prussian *savant* was surprised at the really remarkable thickness of these bones, and also at the large development of the projections and depressions which served for the insertion of the muscles.

Fig. 38 represents this skull, which is drawn from the cast in the Museum of St. Germain.

Professor Schaaffhausen's opinion with regard to this skull is, that it manifests a degree of intelligence more limited than that of the races of negroes who are least favoured by nature, in other words, it approaches the nature of the beast more nearly than any other known human skull. But, on the other hand, Mr. Busk and Dr. Barnard Davis look upon this skull as very closely allied to the present race of men; and Professor Gratiolet produced before the Anthropological Society of Paris an idiot's head of the present day, which showed all the osteological characteristics peculiar to the Neanderthal skull. Lastly, an anthropologist of great authority, Dr. Pruner-Bey, has brought forward all requisite evidence to prove that the Neanderthal skull is identical, in all its parts, with the cranium of the Celt.

We see, therefore, that the opinion propounded by Dr. Schaaffhausen at the commencement of his studies was not able to stand its ground before the opposition resulting from subsequent labours on the point; and that this head of a man belonging to the epoch of the great bear and mammoth, which he regarded as manifesting the most limited amount of intelligence, differed in no way from the heads belonging to Celts of historic times, whose moral qualities and manly courage make Frenchmen proud to call themselves their descendants.

We need scarcely add that the examination of this latter skull, which dated back to the first origin of mankind, is sufficient to set at naught all that has been written as to the pretended analogy of structure existing between primitive man and the ape, and to wipe out for ever from scientific phraseology the improper and unhappy term *fossil man*, which has not only been the cause of so many lamentable misunderstandings, but has also too long arrested the formation and the progress of the science of the first starting-point of man.

Other remains of human skulls, appearing to date back to a very ancient epoch, have been found in various countries, since the discovery of those above-named. We will mention, a jaw-bone found by M. Édouard Dupont in the cave of Naulette, near Dinant, in Belgium—a frontal and parietal bone, extracted from the *Lehm* in the valley of the Rhine, at Eggisheim near Colmar, by Dr. Faudel—a skull found by Professor Bocchi, of Florence, in the Olmo pass, near Arezzo—lastly, the celebrated jaw-bone from Moulin-Quignon, near Abbeville, found in 1863 by Boucher de Perthes, in the *diluvium*, of which bone we have given an illustration in the introduction to this volume. It is acknowledged by all anthropologists that this portion of the skull of the man of Moulin-Quignon bears a perfect resemblance to that of a man of small size of the present age.

From the small number of skulls which we possess, it is impossible for us to estimate what was the precise degree of intelligence to be ascribed to man at the epoch of the great bear and mammoth. No one, assuredly, will be surprised at the fact, that the human skull in these prodigiously remote ages did not present any external signs of great intellectual development. The nature of man is eminently improvable; it is, therefore, easily to be understood, that in the earliest ages of his appearance on the earth his intelligence should have been of a limited character. Time and progress were destined both to improve and extend it; the flame of the first-lighted torch was to be expanded with the lapse of centuries!

II.

Epoch of the Reindeer, or of Migrated Animals.

CHAPTER I.

Mankind during the Epoch of the Reindeer—Their Manners and Customs—Food—Garments—Weapons, Utensils, and Implements—Pottery—Ornaments—Primitive Arts—The principal Caverns—Type of the Human Race during the Epoch of the Reindeer.

WE have now arrived at that subdivision of the stone age which we designate by the name of the *Reindeer Epoch*, or the *Epoch of migrated animals*. Many ages have elapsed since the commencement of the quaternary geological epoch. The mighty animals which characterised the commencement of this period have disappeared, or are on the point of becoming extinct. The great bear (*Ursus spelæus*) and the cave-hyæna (*Hyæna spelæa*) will soon cease to tread the soil of our earth. It will not be long before the final term will be completed of the existence of the cave-lion (*Felis spelæa*), the mammoth, and the *Rhinoceros tichorhinus*. Created beings diminish in size as they improve in type.

To make up for these losses, numerous herds of reindeer now inhabit the forests of western Europe. In that part of the continent which was one day to be called France, these animals make their way as far as the Pyrenees. The horse (*Equus caballus*), in no way different from the present species, is the companion of the above-named valuable ruminant; also the bison (*Biso europæus*), the urus (*Bos primigenius*), the musk-ox (*Ovibos moschatus*), the elk, the deer, the chamois, the ibex, and various species of rodents, amongst others, the beaver, the hamster-rat, the lemming, the spermophilus, &c.

After the intense cold of the glacial period the temperature has become sensibly milder, but it is still much lower than at the present day in the same countries; as the reindeer, an animal belonging to a hyperborean climate, can both enjoy life and multiply in the comparatively southern part of Europe.

The general composition of the *fauna* which we have just described is a striking proof of the rigorous cold which still characterised the climate of central Europe. Animals which then inhabited those countries are now only met with in the high northern latitudes of the old and new worlds, in close proximity to the ice and snow, or on the lofty summits of great mountain-chains. To localities of this kind have now retired the reindeer, the musk-ox, the elk, the chamois, the wild-goat, the hamster-rat, the lemming and the spermophilus. The beaver, too, is at the present day confined almost entirely to Canada.

Mr. Christy, an English naturalist, has remarked with much acuteness that the accumulations of bones and other organic remains in caves actually imply the existence of a rigorous climate. Under the influence of even a merely moderate temperature, these accumulations of bones and animal remains would, in fact, have given forth putrid exhalations which would have prevented any human being from living in close contiguity to these infectious heaps. The Esquimaux of the present day live, in this respect, very much like the people of primitive ages, that is, close by the side of the most fetid *débris*; but, except in the cold regions of the north, they would be quite unable to do this.

Fig. 39.—Man of the Reindeer Epoch.

What progress was made by the man of the reindeer epoch (fig. 39) beyond that attained by his ancestors? This is the question we are about to consider. But we must confine the sphere of our study to the only two countries in which a sufficient number of investigations have been made in respect to the epoch of the reindeer. We allude to that part of Europe which nowadays forms France and Belgium.

During the reindeer epoch, man wrought the flint to better effect than in the preceding period. He also manufactured somewhat remarkable implements in bone, ivory, and reindeers' horn. In the preceding period, human bones were found in caves, mixed up indiscriminately with those of animals; in the epoch we are now considering, this promiscuous intermingling is no longer met with.

We shall first pass in review man as existing in this epoch, in respect to his habitation and food. We shall then proceed to speak of the productions of his industry, and also of the earliest essays of his artistic genius. Lastly, we shall briefly consider his physical organisation.

With respect to his habitation, man, during the reindeer epoch, still took up his abode in caves. According to their depth and the light penetrating them, he either occupied the whole extent of them or established himself in the outlet only. About the centre of the cavern some slabs of stone, selected from the hardest rocks, such as sandstone or slate, were bedded down in the ground, and formed the hearth for cooking his food. During the long nights of winter the whole family must have assembled round this hearth.

Sometimes, in order the better to defend himself against the various surprises to which he was exposed, the man of the reindeer epoch selected a cavern with a very narrow inlet which could only be entered by climbing.

A cave formed naturally in the deepest clefts and hollows of some rock constituted, in every climate, the earliest habitation of man. In cold climates it was necessary for him to find some retreat in which to pass the night, and in warmer latitudes he had to ward off the heat of the day. But these natural dwellings could only be met with in districts where rocks existed which offered facilities for cover in the way of clefts and holes. When man took up his abode in a level country, he was compelled to construct for himself some place of shelter. By collecting together stones, brought from various directions, he then managed to build an artificial cavern. Choosing a spot where some natural projection overhung the ground, he enlarged, as far as he was able, this natural roof, and, bringing art to the assistance of nature, he ultimately found himself in possession of a convenient retreat.

We must not omit to add that the spot in which he established his dwelling was always in the vicinity of some running stream.

In this way, therefore, the inhabitants of the plains formed their habitations during the epoch which we are considering.

We have, also, certain proofs that primitive tribes, during this period, did not take up their abode in natural caverns exclusively, but that they were able to make for themselves more convenient sheltering-places under the cover of some great overhanging rock. In various regions of France, especially in Périgord, numerous ancient open-air human settlements have been discovered. They must have been mere sheds or places of shelter, leaning against the base of some high cliff, and protected against the inclemency of the weather by projections of the rock which, more or less, hung over them, forming a kind of roof. The name of *rock-shelters* has been given to these dwellings of primitive man.

These wild retreats are generally met with in the lower part of some valley in close proximity to a running stream. They, like the caverns, contain very rich deposits of the bones of mammals, birds and fishes, and also specimens of hatchets and utensils made of flint, bone, and horn. Traces of hearths are also discovered.

One of the most remarkable of these natural shelters belonging to the reindeer epoch has been discovered at Bruniquel, in the department of Tarn-et-Garonne, not far from Montauban.

Fig. 40.—Rock-shelter at Bruniquel, a supposed Habitation of Man during the Reindeer Epoch.

On the left bank of the river Aveyron, under the overhanging shelter of one of the highest rocks of Bruniquel and in close proximity to a *château*, the picturesque ruins of which still stand on the brow of the cliff above, there was discovered, in 1866, a fire-hearth of the pre-historic period; this hearth and its surroundings have afforded us the most complete idea of one of the rock-shelters of man during the reindeer epoch.

This rock, known by the name of Montastruc, is about 98 feet high, and it overhangs the ground below for an extent of 46 to 49 feet. It covers an area of 298 square yards. In this spot, M. V. Brun, the Director of the Museum of Natural History at Montauban, found a host of objects of various descriptions, the study of which has furnished many useful ideas for the history of this epoch of primitive humanity.

By taking advantage of the photographic views of the pre-historic settlement of Bruniquel, which M. V. Brun has been kind enough to forward to us, we have been enabled to compose the sketch which is presented in fig. 40 of a rock-shelter, or an open-air settlement of man in the reindeer epoch.

Men during the reindeer epoch did not possess any notion of agriculture. They had not as yet subdued and domesticated any animal so as to profit by its strength, or to ensure by its means a constant supply of food. They were, therefore, like their forefathers, essentially hunters; and pursued wild animals, killing them with their spears or arrows. The reindeer was the animal which they chiefly attacked. This mammal, which then existed all over Europe, in the centre as well as in the south (although it has now retired or migrated into the regions of the extreme north), was for the man of this period all that it nowadays is to the Laplander—the most precious gift of nature. They fed upon its flesh and made their garments of its skin, utilising its tendons as thread in the preparation of their dress; its bones and its antlers they converted into all kinds of weapons and implements. Reindeer's horn was the earliest raw material in the manufactures of these remote ages, and to the man of this epoch was all that iron is to us.

The horse, the ox, the urus, the elk, the ibex, and the chamois, all formed a considerable part of the food of men during this epoch. They were in the habit of breaking the long bones and the skulls of the recently-killed animals, in order to extract the marrow and the brain, which they ate all steaming with the natural animal heat, as is done in the present day by certain tribes in the Arctic regions. The meat of this animal was cooked on their rough hearths; for they did not eat it raw as some naturalists have asserted. The animal bones which have been found, intermingled with human remains, in the caverns of this epoch bear evident traces of the action of fire.

To this animal prey they occasionally added certain birds, such as the great heath-cock, willow-grouse, owl, &c. When this kind of game fell short, they fell back upon the rat. Round the hearthstone, in the cave of Chaleux, M. Dupont found more than twenty pounds weight of the bones of water-rats, half roasted.

Fish is an article of food which has always been much sought after by man. By mere inference we might, therefore, readily imagine that man during the reindeer epoch fed on fish as well as the flesh of animals, even if the fact were not attested by positive evidence. This evidence is afforded by the remains of fish-bones which are met with in the caves of this epoch, intermingled with the bones of mammals, and also by sketches representing parts of fishes, which are found roughly traced on a great number of fragments of bone and horn implements.

The art of fishing, therefore, must certainly have been in existence during the reindeer epoch. We cannot assert that it was practised during that of the great bear and the mammoth; but, as regards the period we are now considering, no doubt can be entertained on the point. In an article on the 'Origine de la Navigation et de la Pêche,' M. G. de Mortillet expresses himself as follows:

"The epoch of the reindeer presents to our notice several specimens of fishing-tackle. The most simple is a little splinter of bone, generally about one to two inches long, straight, slender, and pointed at both ends. This is the primitive and elementary fish-hook. This small fragment of bone or reindeer horn was fastened by the middle and covered with a bait; when swallowed by a fish, or even by an aquatic bird, it became fixed in the interior of the body by one of the pointed ends, and the voracious creature found itself caught by the cord attached to the primitive hook. At the museum of Saint-Germain, there are several of these hooks which came from the rich deposits of Bruniquel, near Montauban (Tarn-et-Garonne).

"Hooks belonging to the reindeer epoch have also been found in the caves and retreats of Dordogne, so well explored by MM. Lartet and Christy. Along with those of the simple form which we have just described, others were met with of a much more perfect shape. These are likewise small fragments of bone or reindeer's horn, with deep and wide notches on one side, forming a more or less developed series of projecting and sharp teeth, or barbs. Two of them are depicted in PLATE B, VI. of the 'Reliquiæ Aquitanicæ.' M. Lartet is in possession of several of them; but the most remarkable specimen forms a part of the beautiful collection of M. Peccadeau de l'Isle, of Paris."[7]

There are strong reasons for believing that man during this epoch did not confine himself to a diet of an exclusively carnivorous character, for vegetable food is in perfect harmony with the organisation of our species. By means of wild fruits, acorns, and chestnuts, he must have introduced some little variety into his ordinary system of sustenance.

From the data which we have been considering, we furnish, in fig. 41, a representation of *a feast during the reindeer epoch*. Men are engaged in cleaving the head of a urus, in order to extract and devour the smoking brains. Others, sitting round the fire in which the flesh of the same animal is being cooked, are sucking out the marrow from the long bones of the reindeer, which they have broken by blows with a hatchet.

Fig. 41.—A Feast during the Reindeer Epoch.

It becomes a very interesting question to know whether the men of these remote periods practised cannibalism or not. On this point we have as yet no certain information. We will, however, state some facts which seem to make in favour of this idea.

Human skulls have been found in Scotland mixed up promiscuously with sculptured flints, remains of pottery, and children's bones; on the latter, Professor Owen thinks that he can recognise the trace of human teeth.

At Solutré, in Mâconnais, M. de Ferry has discovered human finger-joints among the remains of cooking of the epoch of the great bear and mammoth, and of that of the reindeer.

The appearance of certain bones from the caves of Ariége, dug up by MM. Garrigou and Filhol, has led both these *savants* to the opinion "that pre-historic man may have been anthropophagous."

The same conclusion would be arrived at from the explorations which have been undertaken in the grottos and caves of Northern Italy by M. Costa de Beauregard. This latter *savant* found in the caves the small shin-bone of a child which had been carefully emptied and cleansed, leading to the idea that the marrow had been eaten.

At a point near Finale, on the road from Genoa to Nice, in a vast cave which was for a long period employed as a habitation for our race, M. Issel discovered some human bones which had evidently been calcined. Their whitish colour, their lightness, and their friability left no room for doubt on the point. Added to this, the incrustations on their surface still contained small fragments of carbon. Moreover, many of the bones showed notches which could not have been made without the help of some sharp instrument.

It is, therefore, probable that men in the stone age practised anthropophagy; we have, really, no cause to be surprised at this; since, in our own days, various savage tribes are addicted to cannibalism, under a considerable diversity of circumstances.

Not the least trace has been discovered of animals' bones being gnawed by dogs in any of the human settlements during the reindeer epoch. Man, therefore, had not as yet reduced the dog to a state of domesticity.

How did primitive man dress himself during this epoch? He must have made garments out of the skins of the quadrupeds which he killed in hunting, and especially of the reindeer's hide. There can be no doubt on this point. A large number of reindeers' antlers found in Périgord have at their base certain cuts which evidently could only have been produced in flaying the animal.

It is no less certainly proved that these men knew how to prepare animals' skins by clearing them of their hair, and that they were no longer compelled, like their ancestors, to cover themselves with rough bear-skins still covered with their fur. To what purpose could they have applied the flint scrapers which are met with everywhere in such abundance, except for scraping the hair off the skins of wild beasts? Having thus taken off the hair, they rendered them supple by rubbing them in with brains and the marrow extracted from the long bones of the reindeer. Then they cut them out into some very simple patterns, which are, of course, absolutely unknown to us; and, finally, they joined together the different pieces by rough sewing.

The fact that man at this epoch knew how to sew together reindeer skins so as to convert them into garments, is proved by the discovery of numerous specimens of instruments which must have been used for this work; these are—and this is most remarkable—exactly the same as those employed nowadays by the Laplanders, for the same purpose. They consist of bodkins or stilettoes made of flint and bone (fig. 42), by means of which the holes were pierced in the skin; also very carefully fashioned needles, mostly of bone or horn (fig. 43).

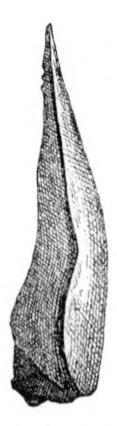

Fig. 42.—Flint Bodkin or Stiletto for sewing Reindeer Skins, found in the Cave of Les Eyzies (Périgord).

Fig. 43.—Bone Needle for sewing.

The inspection of certain reindeer bones has likewise enabled us to recognise the fact that the men of this age used for thread the sinewy fibres of this animal. On these bones transverse cuts may be noticed, just in those very spots where the section of the tendon must have taken place.

No metal was as yet known; consequently, man continued to make use of stone instruments, both for the implements of labour, and also for offensive and defensive weapons. The hatchet was but little employed as a weapon of war, and the flint-knife was the arm most extensively used. We must add to this, another potent although natural weapon; this was the lower jaw-bone of the great bear, still retaining its sharp and pointed canine tooth. The elongated and solid bone furnished the handle, and the sharp tooth the formidable point; and with this instrument man could in the chase attack and pierce any animal with which he entered into a hand-to-hand conflict.

It may be noticed that this weapon is placed in the hand of the man in fig. 39, which represents him during the reindeer epoch.

It must certainly be the case that the human race possesses to a very high degree the taste for personal ornament, since objects used for adornment are found in the most remote ages of mankind and in every country. There can be no doubt that the men and women who lived in the reindeer epoch sacrificed to the graces. In the midst of their precarious mode of life, the idea entered into their minds of manufacturing necklaces, bracelets, and pendants, either with shells which they bored through the middle so as to be able to string them as beads, or with the teeth of various animals which they pierced with holes with the same intention, as represented in fig. 44.

Fig. 44.—The Canine Tooth of a Wolf, bored so as to be used as an ornament.

The horny portion of the ear of the horse or ox (fig. 45), was likewise used for the same purpose, that is, as an object of adornment.

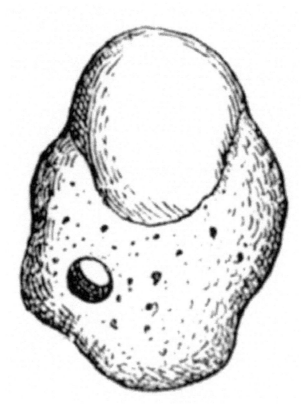

Fig. 45.—Ornament made of the bony part of a Horse's Ear.

It becomes a question whether man at this epoch had any belief in a future life, and practised anything which bore a resemblance to religious worship. The existence, round the fire-hearths of the burial-caverns in Belgium, of large fossil elephant (mammoth's) bones—a fact which has been pointed out by M. Édouard Dupont—gives us some reason for answering this question in the affirmative. According to M. Morlot, the practice of placing bones round caverns still survives, as a religious idea, among the Indians. We may, therefore, appeal to this discovery as a hint in favour of the existence of some religious feeling among the men who lived during the reindeer epoch.

In the tombs of this epoch are found the weapons and knives which men carried during their lifetime, and sometimes even a supply of the flesh of animals used for food. This custom of placing near the body of the dead provisions for the journey to be taken *post mortem* is, as remarked in reference to the preceding period, the proof of a belief in another life.

Certain religious, or rather superstitious, ideas may have been attached to some glittering stones and bright fragments of ore which have been picked up in several settlements of these primitive tribes. M. de Vibraye found at Bourdeilles (Charente), two nodules of hydrated oxide of iron mixed with *débris* of all kinds; and at the settlement of Laugerie-Basse (Dordogne), in the middle of the hearth, a small mass of copper covered with a layer of green carbonate. In other spots there have been met with pieces of jet, violet fluor, &c., pierced through the middle, doubtless to enable them to be suspended to the neck and ears. The greater part of these objects may possibly be looked upon as amulets, that is, symbols of some religious beliefs entertained by man during the reindeer epoch.

The social instinct of man, the feeling which compels him to form an alliance with his fellow-man, had already manifested itself at this early period. Communication was established between localities at some considerable distance from one another. Thus it was that the inhabitants of the banks of the Lesse in Belgium travelled as far as that part of France which is now called Champagne, in order to seek the flints which they could not find in their own districts, although they were indispensable to them in order to manufacture their weapons and implements. They likewise brought back fossil shells, of which they made fantastical necklaces. This distant intercourse cannot be called in question, for certain evidences of it can be adduced. M. Édouard Dupont found in the cave of Chaleux, near Dinant (Belgium), fifty-four of these shells, which are not found naturally anywhere else than in Champagne. Here, therefore, we have the rudiments of commerce, that is, of the importation and exchange of commodities which form its earliest manifestations in all nations of the world.

Again, it may be stated that there existed at this epoch real manufactories of weapons and utensils, the productions of which were distributed around the neighbouring country according to the particular requirements of each family. The cave of Chaleux, which was mentioned above, seems to have been one of these places of manufacture; for from the 8th to the 30th of May, during twenty-two days only, there were collected at this spot nearly 20,000 flints chipped into hatchets, daggers, knives, scrapers, scratchers, &c.

Workshops of this kind were established in the settlements of Laugerie-Basse and Laugerie-Haute in Périgord. The first was to all appearance a special manufactory for spear-heads, some specimens of which have been found by MM. Lartet and Christy of an extremely remarkable nature; exact representations of them are delineated in fig. 46. In the second were fabricated weapons and implements of reindeers' horn, if we may judge by the large quantity of remains of the antlers of those animals, which were met with by these *savants*, almost all of which bear the marks of sawing.

Fig. 46.—Spear-head found in the Cave of Laugerie-Basse (Périgord).

It is not, however, probable that the objects thus manufactured were exported to any great distance, as was subsequently the case, that is, in the polished stone epoch. How would it be possible to cross great rivers, and to pass through wide tracts overgrown with thick forests, in order to convey far and wide these industrial products; at a time, too, when no means of communication existed between one country and another? But it is none the less curious to be able to verify the existence of a rudimentary commerce exercised at so remote an epoch.

The weapons, utensils and implements which were used by man during the reindeer epoch testify to a decided progress having been made beyond those of the preceding period. The implements are made of flint, bone, or horn; but the latter kind are much the most numerous, chiefly in the primitive settlements in the centre and south of France. Those of Périgord are especially remarkable for the abundance of instruments made of reindeers' bones.

The great diversity of type in the wrought flints furnishes a very evident proof of the long duration of the historical epoch we are considering. In the series of these instruments we can trace all the phases of improvement in workmanship, beginning with the rough shape of the hatchets found in the *diluvium* at Abbeville, and culminating in those elegant spear-heads which are but little inferior to any production of later times.

We here give representations (fig. 47, 48, 49, 50), of the most curious specimens of the stone and flint weapons of the reindeer epoch. Knives and other small instruments, such as scrapers, piercers, borers, &c., form the great majority; hatchets are comparatively rare. Instruments are also met with which might be used for a double purpose, for instance, borers and also piercers. There are also round stones which must have been used as hammers; it may, at least, be noticed that they have received repeated blows.

Fig. 47.—Worked Flint from Périgord (Knife).

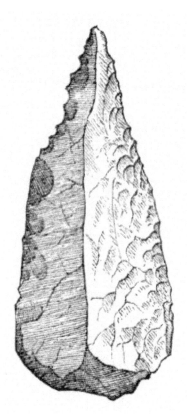

Fig. 48.—Worked Flint from Périgord (Hatchet).

Fig. 49.—Chipped Flint from Périgord (Knife).

Fig. 50.—Chipped Flint from Périgord (Scraper).

Sir J. Lubbock is of opinion that some of these stones were employed in heating water, after they had been made red-hot in the fire. According to the above-named author, this plan of procuring hot water is still adopted among certain savage tribes who are still ignorant of the art of pottery, and possess nothing but wooden vessels, which cannot be placed over a fire. [8]

We must also mention the polishers formed of sandstone or some other material with a rough surface. They could only be used for polishing bone and horn, as the reindeer epoch does not admit of instruments of polished stone.

There have also been collected here and there pebbles of granite or quartzite hollowed out at the centre, and more or less perfectly rounded on the edges. It has been conjectured that these were mortars, although their small dimensions scarcely countenance this hypothesis. Neither is it probable that they were used for pounding seed, as fancied by M. de Vibraye. Nor does the idea which has been entertained of their being used for producing fire seem to have any sufficient ground.

Among the most interesting specimens in the vast collection of flints belonging to the reindeer epoch which have been found in the countries of France and Belgium, we must mention the delicate and very finely-toothed double-edged saws. The one we here represent (fig. 51) is in the Archæological Museum of Saint-Germain. It does not measure more than three-quarters of an inch in length, and about one-tenth of an inch in width. It was found by M. V. Brun in one of the *rock-shelters* at Bruniquel.

Fig. 51.—Small Flint Saw, found in the Rock-shelter at Bruniquel.

Saws of this kind were, no doubt, employed for fashioning the antlers of the reindeer, and other ruminants that shed their horns. The antler was cut into on each side, and the fracture was finished by hand.

The objects of bone and reindeer-horn found in the caves of Périgord show a still greater variety, and a no less remarkable skilfulness in workmanship.

We may mention, for instance, the arrow and javelin-heads. Some are slender and tapering off at both ends; in others, the base terminates in a single or double bevel. Among the latter, the greater part seem made to fix in a cleft stick; some are ornamented with lines and hatching over their surface. Others have notches in them, somewhat similar to an attempt at barbing.

Fig. 52.—The Chase during the Reindeer Epoch.

We now come to the barbed dart-heads, designated by the name of *harpoons*. They taper-off considerably towards the top, and are characterised by very decided barbs, shaped like hooks, and distributed sometimes on one side only, and sometimes on both (figs. 53, 54). In the latter case the barbs are arranged in pairs, and are provided with a small furrow or middle groove, which, according to some naturalists, was intended to hold some subtle poison. Like the present race of Indians of the American forests, primitive man may possibly have poisoned his arrows; and the longitudinal groove, which is noticed in so many reindeer arrow-heads, may have served to contain the poison.

Fig. 53.—Barbed Arrow of Reindeer Horn.

Fig. 54—Arrow of Reindeer Horn with double Barbs.

We must not, however, fail to state that this opinion has been abandoned since it has been ascertained that the North American Indians used in former times to hunt the bison with wooden arrows furnished with grooves or channels of a similar character. These channels are said to have been intended to give a freer vent to the flow of the animal's blood, which was thus, so to speak, sucked out of the wound. This may, therefore, have been the intention of the grooves which are noticed on the dart-heads of the reindeer epoch, and the idea of their having been poisoned must be dismissed.

These barbed darts or harpoons are still used by the Esquimaux of the present day, in pursuing the seal. Such arrows, like those of the primitive hordes of the reindeer epoch which are represented above (figs. 53, 54), are sharply pointed and provided with barbs; they are fastened to a string and shot from a bow. The Esquimaux sometimes attach an inflated bladder to the extremity of the arrow, so that the hunter may be apprized whether he has hit his mark, or in order to show in what direction he should aim again.

We give here (fig. 55) a drawing of a fragment of bone found in the cave of Les Eyzies (Périgord); a portion of one of these harpoons remains fixed in the bone.

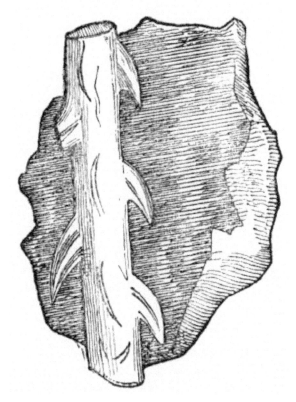

Fig. 55.—Animal Bone, pierced by an Arrow of Reindeer Horn.

We must assign to the class of implements the bone bodkins or stilettoes of different sizes, either with or without a handle (figs. 56, 57), and also a numerous series of needles found in the caves of Périgord, some of which are very slender and elegant, and made of bone, horn, and even ivory. In some of the human settlements of the reindeer epoch, bones have been found, from which long splinters had been detached, fitted for the fabrication of needles. The delicate points of flint have also been found which were used to bore the eyes of the needles, and, lastly, the lumps of sandstone on which the latter were polished.

Fig. 56.—Tool made of Reindeer Horn, found in the Cave of Laugerie-Basse (Stiletto?).

Fig. 57.—Tool made of Reindeer Horn, found in the Cave of Laugerie-Basse (Needle?).

We must, likewise, point out the *smoothers*, intended to flatten down the seams in the skins used for garments.

One of the most important instruments of this epoch is a perfect drill with a sharpened point and cutting edge. With this flint point rapidly twirled round, holes could be bored in any kind of material—bone, teeth, horn, or shells. This stone drill worked as well as our tool made of steel, according to the statement of certain naturalists who have tried the effect of them.

The primitive human settlement at Laugerie-Basse has furnished several specimens of an instrument, the exact use of which has not been ascertained. They are rods, tapering off at one end, and hollowed out at the other in the shape of a spoon. M. Édouard Lartet has propounded the opinion that they were used by the tribes of this epoch as spoons, in order to extract the marrow from the long bones of the animals which were used for their food. M. Lartet would not, however, venture to assert this, and adds: "It is, perhaps, probable that our primitive forefathers would not have taken so much trouble." Be this as it may, one of these instruments is very remarkable for the lines and ornaments in relief with which it is decorated, testifying to the existence in the workman of some feeling of symmetry (fig. 58).

Fig. 58.—Spoon of Reindeer Horn.

In various caves—at Les Eyzies, Laugerie-Basse, and Chaffant, *commune* of Savigné (Vienne)—whistles of a peculiar kind have been found (fig. 59). They are made from the first joint of the foot of the reindeer or some other ruminant of the stag genus. A hole has been bored in the base of the bone, a little in front of the metatarsal joint. If one blows into this hole, placing the lower lip in the hollow answering to the above-named joint, a shrill sound is produced, similar to that made by blowing into a piped key. We ourselves have had the pleasure of verifying the fact, at the Museum of Saint-Germain, that these primitive whistles act very well.

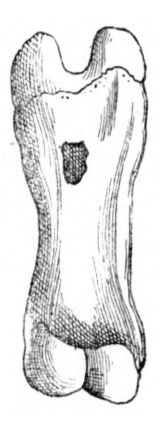

Fig. 59.—Knuckle-Bone of Reindeer's Foot, bored with a hole and used as a Whistle.

The settlements at Périgord have also furnished a certain number of staves made of reindeer horn (figs. 60, 61), the proper functions of which no one has succeeded in properly explaining. They are invariably bored with one or more holes at the base, and are covered with designs to which we shall hereafter refer. M. Lartet has thought that they were perhaps symbols or staves of authority.

Fig. 60.—Staff of authority in Reindeer's Horn, found in the Cave of Périgord.

Fig. 61.—Another Staff of authority in Reindeer's Horn.

This explanation appears the correct one when we consider the care with which these bâtons were fashioned. If the hypothesis of their being symbols of authority be adopted, the varying number of the holes would not be without intention; it might point to some kind of hierarchy, the highest grade of which corresponded to the bâton with the most holes. Thus, in the Chinese empire, the degree of a mandarin's authority is estimated by the number of buttons on his silk cap. And just as in the Mussulman hierarchy there were pachas of from one to three tails, so it may be fancied that among primitive man of the reindeer epoch there were chiefs of from one to three holes!

We have already stated that in the epoch of the great bear and the mammoth the art of manufacturing a rough description of pottery was, perhaps, known in Europe. The men of the reindeer epoch made, however, but little progress in this respect. Nevertheless, if certain relics really belong to this period, they may have known how to make rough vessels, formed of clay, mixed with sand, and hardened by the action of fire. This primitive art was, as yet, anything but generally adopted: for we very rarely find *débris* of pottery in close contiguity with other remains of the reindeer epoch.

The Archæological Museum of Saint Germain is in possession of a hollow vessel, a natural geode, very large and very thick (fig. 62). It was found in the cave of La Madelaine (department of Dordogne); on one side it has evidently been subjected to the action of fire, and may therefore be presumed to have been used as a large vessel for culinary purposes.

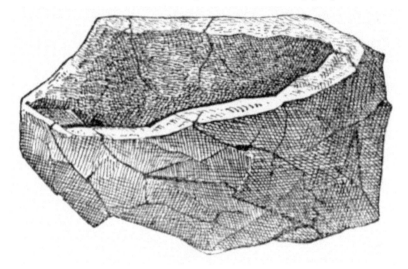

Fig. 62.—A Geode, used as a cooking Vessel (?), found in the Cave of La Madelaine (Périgord).

In a cave at Furfooz, near Dinant in Belgium, to which we shall subsequently refer, M. Édouard Dupont found, intermingled with human bones, an urn, or specimen of rough pottery, which is perhaps one of the most ancient monuments of the ceramic art as practised by our primitive ancestors. This urn (fig. 63) was partly broken; by the care of M. Hauzeur it has been put together again, as we represent it from the work of M. Le Hon.[9]

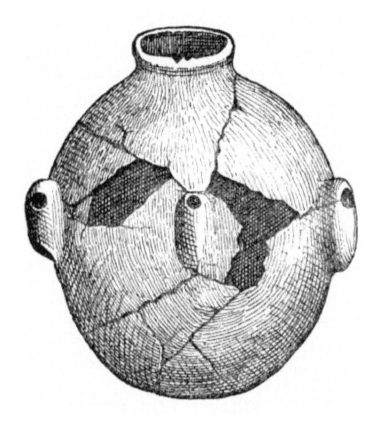

Fig. 63.—Earthen Vase found in the Cave of Furfooz (Belgium).

It is in the reindeer epoch that we find the earliest traces of any artistic feeling manifested in man.

It is a circumstance well worthy of remark, that this feeling appears to have been the peculiar attribute of the tribes which inhabited the south-west of the present France; the departments of Dordogne, Vienne, Charente, Tarn-et-Garonne, and Ariége, are, in fact, the only localities where designs and carvings representing organised beings have been discovered. The departments in the east have not furnished anything of a similar character, any more than Belgium, which has been so thoroughly explored by M. Édouard Dupont, or Wurtemburg, where M. Fraas has lately described various settlements of this primitive epoch.

It is not sufficient to allege, in order to explain this singular circumstance, that the caves in the south of France belong to a later period of the reindeer epoch, and that the others go back to the earliest commencement of the same age. Apart from the fact that this assertion is in no way proved, a complete and ready answer is involved in the well verified circumstance, that even in later ages—in the polished stone, and even in the bronze epoch—no representation of an animal or plant is found to have been executed in these localities. No specimen of the kind has, in fact, been found in the *kitchen-middens* of Denmark, or in the lacustrine settlements of the stone age, or even of the bronze age.

It must, then, be admitted that the tribes which were scattered over those portions of the European continent which now correspond to the south-west of France, possessed a special talent in the art of design. There is, moreover, nothing unreasonable in such a supposition. An artistic feeling is not always the offspring of civilisation, it is rather a gift of nature. It may manifest its existence in the most barbarous ages, and may make its influence more deeply felt in nations which are behindhand in respect to general progress than in others which are much further advanced in civilisation.

There can be no doubt that the rudiments of engraving and sculpture of which we are about to take a view, testify to faculties of an essentially artistic character. Shapes are so well imitated, movements are so thoroughly caught, as it were, in the sudden fact of action, that it is almost always possible to recognise the object which the ancient workman desired to represent, although he had at his disposal nothing but the rudest instruments for executing his work. A splinter of flint was his sole graving-tool, a piece of reindeer horn, or a flake of slate or ivory, was the only plate on which primitive man could stamp his reproductions of animated nature.

Perhaps they drew on stone or horn with lumps of red-chalk or ochre, for both these substances have been found in the caves of primitive man. Perhaps, too, as is the case with modern savages, the ochre and red-chalk were used besides for painting or tatooing his body. When the design was thus executed on stone or horn, it was afterwards engraved with the point of some flint instrument.

Those persons who have attentively examined the interesting gallery of the *Histoire du Travail* in the International Exposition of 1867, must have remarked a magnificent collection of these artistic productions of primeval ages. There were no less than fifty-one specimens, which were exhibited by several collectors, and were for the most part extremely curious. In his interesting work, 'Promenades Préhistoriques à l'Exposition Universelle,' M. Gabriel de Mortillet has carefully described these objects. In endeavouring to obtain some knowledge of them, we shall take as our guide the learned curator of the Archæological Museum of Saint-Germain.

We have, in the first place, various representations of the mammoth, which was still in existence at the commencement of the reindeer epoch.

The first (fig. 64) is an outline sketch, drawn on a slab of ivory, from the cave of La Madelaine. When MM. Lartet and Christy found it, it was broken into five pieces, which they managed to put together very accurately. The small eye and the curved tusks of the animal may be perfectly distinguished, as well as its huge trunk, and even its abundant mane, the latter proving that it is really the mammoth—that is the fossil—and not the present species of elephant.

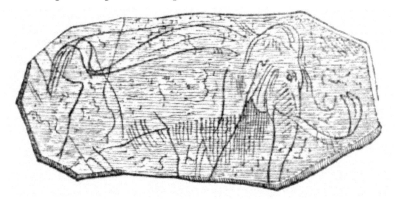

Fig. 64.—Sketch of a Mammoth, graven on a Slab of Ivory.

The second figure is an entire mammoth, graven on a fragment of reindeer horn, from the rock-shelters of Bruniquel, and belongs to M. Peccadeau de l'Isle. This figure forms the hilt of a poniard, the blade of which springs from the front part of the animal. It may be recognised to be the mammoth by its trunk, its wide flat feet, and especially by its erect tail, ending in a bunch of hair. In point of fact, the present species of elephant never sets up the tail, and has no bunch of hair at the end of it.

A third object brought from the pre-historic station of Laugerie-Basse (M. de Vibraye's collection) is the lower end of a staff of authority carved in the form of a mammoth's head. The prominent forehead, and the body of the animal stretching along the base of the staff, may both be very distinctly seen.

On another fragment of a staff of authority, found at Bruniquel by M. V. Brun, the cave-lion (*Felis spelæa*) is carved with great clearness. The head, in particular, is perfectly represented.

Representations of reindeer, either carved or scratched on stone or horn, are very common; we mention the following:—

In the first place the hilt of a dagger in reindeer's horn (fig. 65) of the same type as that shaped in the form of a mammoth. This specimen is remarkable, because the artist has most skilfully adapted the shape of the animal to the purpose for which the instrument was intended. The hilt represents a reindeer, which is carved out as if lying in a very peculiar position; the hind legs are stretched along the blade, and the front legs are doubled back under the belly, so as not to hurt the hand of anyone holding the dagger; lastly, the head is thrown back, the muzzle turned upwards, and the horns flattened down so as not to interfere with the grasp.

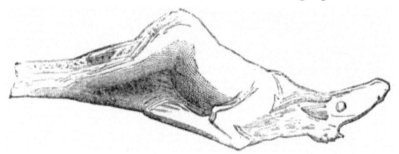

Fig. 65.—Hilt of a Dagger, carved in the shape of a Reindeer.

This is, at all events, nothing but a rough sketch. The same remark, however, does not apply to two ivory daggers found at Bruniquel by M. Peccadeau de l'Isle. These objects are very artistically executed, and are the most finished specimens that have been found up to the present time. Both of them represent a reindeer with the head thrown back as in the preceding plate; but whilst in one dagger the blade springs from the hinder part of the body, in the same way as in the rough-hewn horn, in the other it proceeds from the front of the body, between the head and the forelegs. The hind legs are stretched out and meet again at the feet, thus forming a hole between them, which was probably used as a ring on which to suspend the dagger.

We must not omit to mention a slab of slate, on which is drawn in outline a reindeer fight. It was found at Laugerie-Basse by M. de Vibraye. The artist has endeavoured to portray one of those furious contests in which the male reindeer engages during the rutting season, in order to obtain possession of the females; he has executed his design in a spirited manner, marked by a certain *naïveté*.

There are a good many other fragments on which reindeer are either drawn or carved; we shall not dwell upon them, but add a few remarks as to several specimens on which are representations of the stag, the horse, the bison, the ibex, &c.

A representation of a stag (fig. 66) is drawn on a fragment of stag's horn found in the cave of La Madelaine by MM. Lartet and Christy. The shape of the antlers, which are very different to those of the reindeer, leave no doubt as to the identity of the animal.

Fig. 66.—Representation of a Stag, drawn on a Stag's Horn.

The ox and the bison are represented in various fashions. We will mention here a carved head which was found in the cave of Laugerie-Basse by M. de Vibraye. It forms the base of a staff of authority.

Fig. 67.—Representation of some large herbivorous Animal on a Fragment of Reindeer's Horn.

We must, doubtless, class under the same category a fragment of reindeer's horn, found at Laugerie-Basse, on which the hind-quarters of some large herbivorous animal are sketched out with a bold and practised touch (fig. 67). Various indications have led M. Lartet to think that the artist has not endeavoured to represent a horse, as was at first imagined, but a bison of rather a slender shape. Unfortunately the fragment is broken at the exact spot where the bushy mane should begin, which characterises the species of the bison sub-genus.

Fig. 68.—Arts of Drawing and Sculpture during the Reindeer Epoch.

In the same locality another fragment of reindeer's horn was found, on which some horned animal is depicted (fig. 69), which appears to be an ibex, if we may judge by the lines under the chin which seem to indicate a beard.

Fig. 69.—Representation of an Animal, sketched on a Fragment of Reindeer's Horn.

In the cave of Les Eyzies, in the department of Dordogne, MM. Lartet and Christy came upon two slabs of quartziferous schist, on both of which are scratched animal forms which are deficient in any special characteristics. In one (fig. 70), some have fancied they could recognise the elk; but, as the front part only of the other has been preserved, it is almost impossible to determine what mammiferous animal it is intended to represent. An indistinct trace of horns seems to indicate a herbivorous animal.

Fig. 70.—Fragment of a Slab of Schist, bearing the representation of some Animal, and found in the Cave of Les Eyzies.

On each side of a staff of authority made of reindeer's horn, found by MM. Lartet and Christy in the cave of the Madelaine, may be noticed three horses in demi-relief, which are very easily recognisable.

On a carved bone, found at Bruniquel by M. de Lastic, the head of a reindeer and that of a horse are drawn in outline side by side; the characteristics of both animals are well maintained.

Lastly, we may name a round shaft formed of reindeer's horn (fig. 71), found at Laugerie-Basse by MM. Lartet and Christy, on which is carved an animal's head, with ears of a considerable length laid back upon the head. It is not easy to determine for what purpose this shaft was intended; one end being pointed and provided with a lateral hook. It was perhaps used as a harpoon.

Fig. 71.—A kind of Harpoon of Reindeer's Horn, carved in the shape of an Animal's Head.

Representations of birds are more uncommon than those of mammals.

There are, on the other hand, a good many rough delineations of fish, principally on the so-called wands of authority, on which numbers may often be noticed following one another in a series. We have one delineation of a fish, skilfully drawn on a fragment of the lower jaw-bone of a reindeer, which was found at Laugerie-Basse.

Also in the cave of La Vache (Ariége), M. Garrigou found a fragment of bone, on which there is a clever design of a fish.

Very few representations of reptiles have come to light, and those found are in general badly executed. We must, however, make an exception in favour of the figure of a tadpole, scratched out on an arrow-head, found in the cave of the Madelaine.

Designs representing flowers are very rare; in the *Galerie du Travail*, at the Exposition, only three specimens are exhibited; they came from La Madelaine and Laugerie-Basse, and were all three graven on spear-heads.

But did the men of the reindeer epoch make no attempts to portray their own personal appearance? Have not the excavations dug in the settlements of primitive man, found in Périgord, ever brought to light any imitation of the human form? Nothing could exceed the interest of such a discovery. Research has not been entirely fruitless in this respect, and it is hoped that the first attempt in the art of statuary of this primitive people may yet be discovered. In the cave of Laugerie-Basse, M. de Vibraye found a little ivory statuette, which he takes to be a kind of idol of an indecent character. The head and legs, as well as the arms, are broken off.

Another human figure (fig. 72), which, like the preceding one, is long and lean, is graven on a staff of authority, a fragment of which was found in the cave of La Madelaine by MM. Lartet and Christy. The man is represented standing between two horses' heads, and by the side of a long serpent or fish, having the appearance of an eel. On the reverse side of the same bâton, which is not given in the figure, the heads of two bisons are represented.

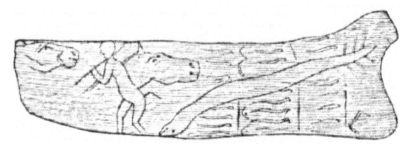

Fig. 72.—Staff of Authority, on which are graven representations of a Man, two Horses, and a Fish.

On a fragment of a spear-head, found in the same settlement of Laugerie-Basse, there is a series of human hands, provided with four fingers only, represented in demi-relief. M. Lartet has called attention to the fact, that certain savage tribes still depict the hand without noticing the thumb.

In fig. 39, which represents man during the reindeer epoch, such as we must suppose him to have been from the sum total of our present stock of information on the point, we see a man clothed in garments sewn with a needle, carrying as his chief weapon the jaw-bone of a bear armed with its sharp fang, and also provided with his flint hatchet or knife. Close to him a woman is seated, arrayed in all the personal ornaments which are known to have been peculiar to this epoch.

The question now arises, what were the characteristics of man during the reindeer epoch, with regard to his physical organisation?

We know a little of some of the broader features of his physiognomy from studying the objects found in the Belgian bone-caves, of which we have spoken in the introduction to this work. These caves were explored by M. Édouard Dupont, assisted by M. Van Beneden, a Belgian palæontologist and anatomist. The excavations in question were ordered by King Leopold's Government, which supplied the funds necessary for extending them as far as possible. The three caves, all situated in the valley of the Lesse, are the *Trou des Nutons*, the *Trou du Frontal*, at Furfooz, near Dinant, and the *Caverne de Chaleux*, in the neighbourhood of the town from which its name is derived.

The *Trou des Nutons* and the *Trou du Frontal* have been completely thrown into confusion by a violent inroad of water; for the *débris* that they contained were intermingled in an almost incredible confusion with a quantity of earthy matter and calcareous rocks, which had been drifted in by the inundation.

In the *Trou des Nutons*, which is situated about 164 feet above the level of the Lesse, M. Van Beneden recognised a great many bones of the reindeer, the urus, and many other species which are not yet extinct. These bones were indiscriminately mixed up with bones and horns of the reindeer carved into different shapes, knuckle-bones of the goat polished on both sides, a whistle made from the tibia of a goat, from which sounds could still be produced, fragments of very coarse pottery, some remains of fire-hearths, &c.

The *Trou du Frontal* was thus named by M. Édouard Dupont, from the fact of a human frontal-bone having been found there on the day that the excavations commenced. This was not the only discovery of the kind that was to be made. Ere long they fell in with a great quantity of human bones, intermixed with a considerable number of the bones of reindeer and other animals, as well as implements of all kinds. M. Van Beneden ascertained that the bones must have belonged to thirteen persons of various ages; some of them are the bones of infants scarcely a year old. Among them were found two perfect skulls which are in good preservation; these remains are also very valuable, because they afford data from which deductions may be drawn as to the cranial conformation of the primitive inhabitants of the banks of the Lesse.

M. Édouard Dupont is of opinion that this cave was used as a burial-place. It is, in fact, very probable that such was the purpose for which it was intended; for a large flag-stone was found in it, which was probably used to close up the mouth of the cave, and to shield the dead bodies from profanation. If this be the case, the animal bones which were scattered around are the remains of the funeral banquets which it was the custom to provide during the epoch of the great bear and the mammoth.

It is interesting to establish the existence of such a similarity between the customs of men who were separated by vast tracts of land and an interval of many thousands of years.

Immediately above the *Trou du Frontal* there is a cave called *Trou Rosette*, in which the bones of three persons of various ages were found intermingled with the bones of reindeer and beavers; fragments of a blackish kind of pottery were also found there, which were hollowed out in rough grooves by way of ornamentation, and merely hardened in the fire. M. Dupont is of opinion that the three men whose remains were discovered were crushed to death by masses of rock at the time of the great inundation, traces of which may still be seen in the valley of the Lesse.

By the falling in of its roof, which buried under a mass of rubbish all the objects which were contained in it at the time of the catastrophe and thus kept them in their places, the cave of Chaleux escaped the complete disturbance with which the above-mentioned caverns were visited. The bones of mammals, of birds, and of fish were found there; also some carved bones and horns of the reindeer, some fossil shells, which, as we have before observed, came from Champagne, and were used as ornaments; lastly, and chiefly, wrought flints numbering at least 30,000. In the hearth, which was placed in the middle of the cave, a stone was discovered with certain signs on it, which, up to the present time, have remained unexplained. M. Dupont, as we have previously stated, collected in the immediate vicinity about twenty-two pounds' weight of the bones of the water-rat either scorched or roasted; this proves that when a more noble and substantial food failed them, the primitive inhabitants of this country were able to content themselves with these small and unsavoury rodents.

The two skulls which were found at Furfooz have been carefully examined by MM. Van Beneden and Pruner-Bey, who are both great authorities on the subject of anthropology. These skulls present considerable discrepancies, but Pruner-Bey is of opinion that they are heads of a male and female of the same race. In order to justify his hypothesis the learned anthropologist says, that there is often more difference between the skulls of the two sexes of the same race, than between the skulls of the same sex belonging to two distinct races.

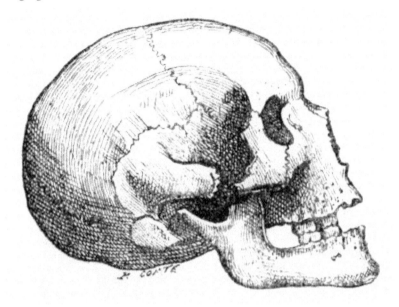

Fig. 73.—Skull found at Furfooz, by M. Édouard Dupont.

One of these skulls is distinguished by a projecting jaw; the other, which is represented in fig. 73, has jaws even with the facial outline. The prominent jaw of the first, which is the indication of a degraded race (like that of the negro), does not prevent its having a higher forehead and a more capacious cranium than the other skull. We find here an actual intermingling of the characteristics which belong to the inferior races with those peculiar to the Caucasian race, which is considered to be the most exalted type of the human species.

According to Pruner-Bey, the Belgian people during the reindeer epoch were a race of small stature but very sturdy; the face was lozenge-shaped, and the whole skull had the appearance of a pyramid. This race of a Turanian or Mongolian origin was the same as the Ligurian or Iberian race, which still exists in the north of Italy (Gulf of Genoa), and in the Pyrenees (Basque districts).

These conclusions must be accepted with the highest degree of caution, for they do not agree with the opinions of all anthropologists. M. Broca is of opinion that the Basques have sprung from a North African race, which spread over Europe at a time when an isthmus existed where the Straits of Gibraltar are now situated. This idea is only reasonable; for certain facts prove that Europe and Africa were formerly connected by a neck of land;

this was afterwards submerged, at the spot where the Straits of Gibraltar now exist, bringing about the disjunction of Europe and Africa. It will be sufficient proof, if we point to the analogy subsisting between the *fauna* of the two countries, which is established by the existence of a number of wild monkeys which, even in the present day, inhabit this arid rock, and are also to be met with on the opposite African shore.

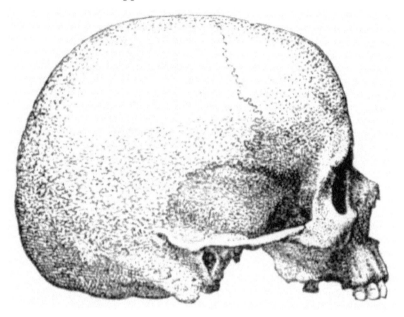

Fig. 74.—Skull of an old Man, found in a *Rock-shelter* at Bruniquel.

In the interesting excavations which were made in the *rock-shelters* at Bruniquel, M. V. Brun found a quantity of human bones, and particularly two skulls—one that of an old man, the other that of an adult. We here (fig. 74) give a representation of the old man's skull taken from a photograph which M. V. Brun has been kind enough to send us.

If we measure the facial angle of this skull, we shall find that it does not differ from the skulls of the men who at the present time inhabit the same climates. From this fact, it may be gathered how mistaken the idea may be which looks upon primitive man, or the man of the stone epoch as a being essentially different from the men of the present day. The phrase *fossil man*, we must again repeat, should be expunged from the vocabulary of science; we should thus harmonise better with established facts, and should also do away with a misunderstanding which is highly detrimental to the investigations into the origin of man.

In concluding this account of the manners and customs of man during the reindeer epoch, we must say a few words as to the funeral rites of this time, or rather, the mode of burial peculiar to this period of primitive man's history.

Those who lived in caves buried their dead in caves. It is, also, a fact to be remarked, that man often uses the same type for both his burial-places and dwelling-places.

The burial-places of the Tartars of Kasan, says M. Nilsson, are exact likenesses, on a small scale, of their dwelling-places, and like them, are constructed of beams placed close to one another. A Circassian burial-place is perfectly similar to a Circassian dwelling. The tombs of the Karaite Jews, in the valley of Jehoshaphat, resemble their houses and places of worship, and the Neo-Grecian tombs, in the Crimea, are likewise imitations of their churches.[10]

We shall not, therefore, be surprised to learn that man during the reindeer epoch buried his dead in caves, just in the same way as was done by his ancestors during the epoch of the great bear and the mammoth, that is to say, the dead were interred in the same kind of caves as those which were then generally used as places of abode.

Fig. 75 represents a funeral ceremonial during the reindeer epoch.

Fig. 75.—A Funeral Ceremony during the Reindeer Epoch.

The corpse is borne on a litter of boughs, a practice which is still in use among some modern savages. Men provided with torches, that is branches of resinous trees, preceded the funeral procession, in order to light the interior of the cavern. The cave is open, ready to receive the corpse, and it will be closed again after it is deposited there. The weapons, ornaments, and utensils which he had prized during his lifetime, are brought in to be laid by the side of the dead.

We will sum up the principal facts which we have laid before our readers in this account of the condition of mankind during the reindeer epoch, by quoting an eloquent passage from a report addressed by M. Édouard Dupont to the Belgian Minister of the Interior, on the excavations carried on by this eminent Belgian geologist in the caves in the neighbourhood of Furfooz.

"The data obtained from the fossils of Chaleux, together with those which have been met with in the caves of Furfooz, present us," says M. Dupont, "with a striking picture of the primitive ages of mankind in Belgium.

"These ancient tribes and all their customs, after having been buried in oblivion for thousands and thousands of years, are again vividly brought before our eyes; and, like the wondrous bird, which, in its ashes, found a new source of life, antiquity lives again in the relics of its former existence.

"We may almost fancy that we can see them in their dark and subterranean retreats, crouching round their hearths, and skilfully and patiently chipping out their flint instruments and shaping their reindeer-horn tools, in the midst of all the pestilential emanations arising from the various animal remains which their carelessness has allowed to remain in their dwellings. Skins of wild beasts are stripped of their hair, and, by the aid of flint needles, are converted into garments. In our mind's eye, we may see them engaged in the chase, and hunting wild animals—their only weapons being darts and spears, the fatal points of which are formed of nothing but a splinter of flint.

"Again, we are present at their feasts, in which, during the period when their hunting has been fortunate, a horse, a bear, or a reindeer becomes the more noble substitute for the tainted flesh of the rat, their sole resource in the time of famine.

"Now, we see them trafficking with the tribes inhabiting the region now called France, and procuring the jet and fossil shells with which they love to adorn themselves, and the flint which is to them so precious a material. On one side they are picking up the fluor spar, the colour of which is pleasing to their eyes; on the other, they are digging out the great slabs of sandstone which are to be placed as hearthstones round their fire.

"But, alas! inauspicious days arrive, and certainly misfortune does not seem to spare them. A falling in of the roof of their cave drives them out of their chief dwelling-place. The objects of their worship, their weapons, and their utensils—all are buried there, and they are forced to fly and take up their abode in another spot.

"The ravages of death break in upon them; how great are the cares which are now lavished upon those whom they have lost! They bear the corpse into its cavernous sepulchre; some weapons, an amulet, and perhaps an urn, form the whole of the funeral furniture. A slab of stone prevents the inroad of wild beasts. Then begins the funeral banquet, celebrated close by the abode of the dead; a fire is lighted, great animals are cut up, and portions of their smoking flesh are distributed to each. How strange the ceremonies that must then have taken place! ceremonies like those told us of the savages of the Indian and African solitudes. Imagination may easily depict the songs, the dances and the invocations, but science is powerless to call them into life.

"The sepulchre is often reopened; little children and adults came in turn to take their places in the gloomy cave. Thirteen times the same ceremonial occurs, and thirteen times the slab is moved to admit the corpses.

"But the end of this primitive age is at last come. Torrents of water break in upon the country. Its inhabitants, driven from their abodes, in vain take refuge on the lofty mountain summits. Death at last overtakes them, and a dark cavern is the tomb of the wretched beings, who, at Furfooz, were witnesses of this immense catastrophe.

"Nothing is respected by the terrible element. The sepulchre, the object of such care on the part of the artless tribe, is burst open before the torrent, and the bones of the dead bodies, disjointed by the water, are dispersed into the midst of the crumbling earth and stones. Their former habitation alone is exempt from this common destruction, for it has been protected by a previous catastrophe—the sinking in of its roof on to the ground of the cave."

Having now given a sketch of the chief features presented by man and his surroundings during the reindeer epoch; having described the most important objects of his skill, and dwelt upon the products of his artistic faculties; it now remains for us to complete, in a scientific point of view, the study of this question, by notifying the sources from which we have been able to gather our data, and to bring home to our minds these interesting ideas. Under this head, we may state that almost all the information which has been obtained has been derived from caves; and it will, therefore, be best to make a few brief remarks on the caverns which have been the scene of these various discoveries.

Honour to whom honour is due. In mentioning these localities, we must place in the first class the settlements of Périgord, which have contributed to so great an extent towards the knowledge which we possess of primitive man. The four principal ones are, the cave of Les Eyzies and the rock-shelters or caverns of La Madelaine, Laugerie-Haute, and Laugerie-Basse.

All of them have been explored by MM. Lartet and Christy, who, after having directed the excavations with the greatest ability, have set forth the results of their researches in a manner no less remarkable.[11]

The settlement of Laugerie-Basse has also been explored by M. de Vibraye, who collected there some very interesting specimens.

We have no intention of reverting to what we have before stated when describing the objects found in these various localities. We will content ourselves with mentioning the lumbar vertebral bone of a reindeer found in the cave of Eyzies, of which we have given a representation in fig. 55; it was pierced through by an arrow-head, which may still be seen fixed in it. If any doubts could still exist of the co-existence, in France, of man and the reindeer, this object should suffice to put an end to them for ever.

We will mention, as next in importance, the cave and rock-shelters at Bruniquel (Tarn-et-Garonne). They have been carefully examined by a great many explorers, among whom we must specify M. Garrigou, M. de Lastic (the proprietor of the cavern), M. V. Brun, the learned Director of the Museum of Natural History at Montauban, and M. Peccadeau de l'Isle.

It is to be regretted that M. de Lastic sold about fifteen hundred specimens of every description of the relics which had been found on his property, to Professor Owen, for the British Museum. In this large quantity of relics, there were, of course, specimens which will never be met with elsewhere; which, therefore, it would have been better in every respect to have retained in France.

The cave of Bruniquel has also furnished us with human bones, amongst which are two almost perfect skulls, one of which we have previously represented; also two half jaw-bones which resemble those found at Moulin-Quignon. M. V. Brun has given, in his interesting work, a representation of these human remains.[12]

We will now mention the *Cave of Bize* near Narbonne (Aude); the *Cave of La Vache* in the valley of Tarascon (Ariége), in which M. Garrigou collected an immense quantity of bones, on one of which some peculiar characters are graven, constituting, perhaps, a first attempt in the art of writing; the *Cavern of Massat* in the same department, which has been described by M. Fontan, and is thought by M. Lartet to have been a summer dwelling-place, the occupiers of which lived on raw flesh and snails, for no traces of a hearth are to be seen, although it must have been used for a considerable time as a shelter by primitive man; the *Cave of Lourdes*, near Tarbes (Hautes-Pyrénées), in which M. Milne-Edwards met with a fragment of a human skull, belonging to an adult individual; the *Cave of Espalungue*, also called the *Grotto of Izeste* (Basses-Pyrénées), where MM. Garrigou and Martin found a human bone, the fifth left metatarsal; the *Cave of Savigné* (Vienne), situated on the banks of the Charente, and discovered by M. Joly-Leterme, an architect of Saumur, who there found a fragment of a stag's bone, on which the bodies of two animals are graven with hatchings to indicate shadows; the *Grottos of La Balme and Bethenas*, in Dauphiné, explored by M. Chantre; lastly, the settlement of Solutré, in the neighbourhood of Mâcon, from which MM. Ferry and Arcelin have exhumed two human skulls, together with some very fine flint instruments of the Laugerie-Haute type.

These settlements do not all belong to the same epoch, although most of them correspond to the long period known as the reindeer epoch. It is not always possible to determine their comparative chronology. From the state of their *débris* it can, however, be ascertained, that the caves of Lourdes and Espalungue date back to the most ancient period of the reindeer epoch; whilst the settlements of Périgord, of Tarn-et-Garonne, and of Mâconnais are of a later date. The cave of Massat seems as if it ought to be dated at the beginning of the wrought stone epoch, for no bones have been found there, either of the reindeer or the horse; the remains of the bison are the sole representatives of the extinct animal species.

In concluding this list of the French bone-caves which have served to throw a light upon the peculiar features of man's existence during the reindeer epoch, we must not omit to mention the Belgian caves, which have been so zealously explored by M. Édouard Dupont. From the preceding pages, we may perceive how especially important the latter have been in the elucidation of the characteristics of man's physical organisation during this epoch.

France and Belgium are not the only countries which have furnished monuments relating to man's history during the reindeer epoch. We must not omit to mention that settlements of this epoch have been discovered both in Germany and also in Switzerland.

In 1866 a great quantity of bones and broken instruments were found at the bottom of an ancient glacier-moraine in the neighbourhood of Rabensburg, not far from the lake of Constance. The bones of the reindeer formed about ninety-eight hundredths of these remains. The other *débris* were the bones of the horse, the wolf, the brown bear, the white fox, the glutton and the ox.

In 1858, on a mountain near Geneva, a cave was discovered about 12 feet deep and 6 feet wide, which contained, under a layer of carbonate of lime, a great quantity of flints and bones. The bones of the reindeer formed the great majority of them, for eighteen skeletons of this animal were found. The residue of the remains were composed of four horses, six ibex, intermingled with the bones of the marmot, the chamois, and the hazelhen; in short, the bones of the whole animal population which, at the present time, has abandoned the valleys of Switzerland, and is now only to be met with on the high mountains of the Alps.

FOOTNOTES:

[7] 'Origine de la Navigation et de la Pêche.' Paris, 1867, p. 25.

[8] 'Pre-Historic Times,' 2d ed. p. 319.

[9] 'L'Homme Fossile.' Brussels, 1868 (page 71).

[10] 'The Primitive Inhabitants of Scandinavia,' by Sven Nilsson, p. 155. London, 1868.

[11] 'Reliquiæ Aquitanicæ,' by Éd. Lartet and H. Christy. London, 1865, &c.

[12] 'Notice sur les Fouilles Paléontologiques de l'Age de la Pierre exécutées à Bruniquel et Saint-Antonin,' by V. Brun. Montauban, 1867.

III.

The Polished-stone Epoch; or, the Epoch of Tamed Animals.

CHAPTER I.

The European Deluge—The Dwelling-place of Man during the Polished-stone Epoch—The Caves and Rock-shelters still used as Dwelling-places—Principal Caves belonging to the Polished-stone Epoch which have been explored up to the present Time—The Food of Man during this period.

AIDED by records drawn from the bowels of the earth, we have now traversed the series of antediluvian ages since the era when man first made his appearance on the earth, and have been enabled, though but very imperfectly, to reconstruct the history of our primitive forefathers. We will now leave this epoch, through the dark night of which science seeks almost in vain to penetrate, and turn our attention to a period the traces of which are more numerous and more easily grasped by our intelligence—a period, therefore, which we are able to characterise with a much greater degree of precision.

A great catastrophe, the tradition of which is preserved in the memory of all nations, marked in Europe the end of the quaternary epoch. It is not easy to assign the exact causes for this great event in the earth's history; but whatever may be the explanation given, it is certain that a cataclysm, caused by the violent flowing of rushing water, took place during the quaternary geological epoch; for the traces of it are everywhere visible. These traces consist of a reddish clayey deposit, mixed with sand and pebbles. This deposit is called in some countries *red diluvium*, and in others *grey diluvium*. In the valley of the Rhone and the Rhine it is covered with a layer of loamy deposit, which is known to geologists by the name of *loess* or *lehm*, and as to the origin of which they are not all agreed. Sir Charles Lyell is of opinion that this mud was produced by the crushing of the rocks by early Alpine glaciers, and that it was afterwards carried down by the streams of water which descended from these mountains. This mud covers a great portion of Belgium, where it is from 10 to 30 feet in thickness, and supplies with material a large number of brickfields.

This deposit, that is the *diluvial beds*, constitutes nearly the most recent of all those which form the earth's crust; in many European countries, it is, in fact the ground trodden under the feet of the present population.

The inundation to which the *diluvium* is referred closes the series of the quaternary ages. After this era, the present geological period commences, which is characterised by the almost entire permanency of the vertical outline of the earth, and by the formation of peat-bogs.

The earliest documents afforded us by history are very far from going back to the starting-point of this period. The history of the ages which we call historical is very far from having attained to the beginning of the present geological epoch.

In order to continue our account of the progressive development of primitive man, we must now turn our attention to the *Polished-stone Epoch*, or the *Epoch of Tamed Animals*, which precedes the Metal Age.

As the facts which we shall have to review are very numerous, we will, in the first place, consider this epoch as it affects those parts of our continent which form the present France and Belgium; next, with reference to Denmark and Switzerland, in which countries we shall have to point out certain manners and customs of man of an altogether special character.

We shall consider in turn:—

1st. The habitation of man during the polished-stone epoch.

2nd. His system of food.

3rd. His arts and manufactures.

4th. The weapons manufactured by him, and their use in war.

5th. His attainments in agriculture, fishing, and navigation.

6th. His funeral ceremonies.

7th. Lastly, the characteristics of mankind during this epoch.

Habitation.—In that part of the European continent which now forms the country called France, man, during that period we designate under the name of the polished-stone epoch, continued for a considerable time to inhabit rock-shelters and caves which afforded him the best retreat from the attacks of wild beasts.

This fact has been specially proved to have been the case in the extreme south of the above-mentioned country. Among the investigations which have contributed towards its verification, we must give particular notice to those made by MM. Garrigou and Filhol in the caves of the Pyrenees (Ariége). These two *savants* have also explored the caves of Pradières, Bedeilhac, Labart, Niaux, Ussat, and Fontanel.[13]]

In one of these caves, which we have already mentioned in the preceding chapter, but to which we must again call attention—for they belong both to the polished stone, and also to the reindeer epoch—MM. Garrigou and Filhol found the bones of a huge ox, the urus or *Bos primigenius*, a smaller kind of ox, the stag, the sheep, the goat, the antelope, the chamois, the wild boar, the wolf, the dog, the fox, the badger, the hare, and possibly those of the horse. Neither the bones of the reindeer nor the bison are included in this list of names; on account of the mildness of the climate, these two species had already migrated towards the north and east in search of a colder atmosphere.

The remains of hearths, bones split lengthwise, and broken skulls, indicate that the inhabitants of these caves lived on much the same food as their ancestors. It is probable that they also ate raw snails, for a large quantity of their shells were found in this cave, and also in the cavern of Massat,[14] the presence of which can only be accounted for in this way.

These remains were found intermingled with piercers, spear-heads, and arrow-heads, all made of bone; also hatchets, knives, and scratchers, made of flint, and also of various other substances, which were more plentiful than flint in that country, such as siliceous schist, quartzite, leptinite and serpentine stones. These instruments were carefully wrought, and a few had been polished at one end on a slab of flag-stone.

In the cave of Lourdes (Hautes-Pyrénées), which has been explored by M. Alphonse Milne-Edwards, two layers were observed; one belonging to the reindeer epoch, and the other to the polished-stone epoch.[15] The cave of Pontil (Hérault), which has been carefully examined by Professor Gervais,[16] has furnished remains of every epoch including the bronze age; we must, however, except the reindeer epoch, which is not represented in this cave.

Lastly, we will mention the cave of Saint-Jean-d'Alcas (Aveyron), which has been explored, at different times, by M. Cazalis de Fondouce. This is a sepulchral cave, like that of Aurignac. When it was first explored, about twenty years ago, five human skulls, in good preservation, were found in it—a discovery, the importance of which was then unheeded, and the skulls were, in consequence, totally lost to science. Flint, jade, and serpentine instruments, carved bones, remains of rough pottery, stone amulets, and the shells of shell-fish, which had formed necklaces and bracelets, were intermingled with human bones.

At Saint-Jean-d'Alcas, M. Cazalis de Fondouce did not meet with any remains of funeral banquets such as were found at Aurignac and Furfooz; he only noticed two large flag-stones lying across one another at the mouth of the cave, so as to make the inlet considerably narrower.

This cave, according to a recent publication of M. Cazalis, must be referred to a more recent epoch than was at first supposed, for some fragments of metallic substances were found in it. It must, therefore, have belonged to a late period of the polished-stone epoch. [17]

Man's System of Feeding during the Polished-stone Epoch.—In order to obtain full information on the subject of man's food in the north and centre of Europe during the polished-stone epoch, we must appeal to the interesting researches of which Denmark has been the scene during the last few years; but these researches, on account of their importance, require a detailed account.

FOOTNOTES:

[13] 'L'Homme Fossile des Cavernes de Lombrive et de Lherm.' Toulouse, 1862. Illustrated. 'L'Age de Pierre dans les Vallées de Tarascon' (Ariége). Tarascon, 1863.

[14] 'Sur deux Cavernes découvertes dans la Montagne de Kaer à Massat' (Ariége). Quoted by Lyell, Appendix to 'The Antiquity of Man,' p. 247.

[15] 'De l'Existence de l'Homme pendant la Période quaternaire dans la grotte de Lourdes' (Hautes-Pyrénées). ('Annales des Sciences Naturelles,' 4th series, vol. xvii.)

[16] 'Mémoires de l'Académie de Montpellier' ('Section des Sciences'), 1857, vol. iii, p. 509.

[17] 'Sur une Caverne de l'Age de la Pierre, située près de Saint-Jean-d'Alcas' (Aveyron), 1864. 'Derniers Temps de l'Age de la Pierre Polie dans l'Aveyron', Montpellier, 1867. Illustrated.

Fig. 76.—Man of the Polished-stone Epoch.

CHAPTER II.

The *Kjoekken-Moeddings* or "Kitchen-middens" of Denmark—Mode of Life of the Men living in Denmark during the Polished-stone Epoch—The Domestication of the Dog—The Art of Fishing during the Polished-stone Epoch—Fishing-nets—Weapons and Instruments of War—Type of the Human Race; the Borreby Skull.

ALTHOUGH classed in the lowest rank on account of the small extent of its territory and the number of its inhabitants, the Danish nation is, nevertheless, one of the most important in Europe, in virtue of the eminence to which it has attained in science and arts. This valiant, although numerically speaking, inconsiderable people, can boast of a great number of distinguished men who are an honour to science. The unwearied researches of their archæologists and antiquarians have ransacked the dust of bygone ages, in order to call into new life the features of a vanished world. Their labours, guided by the observations of naturalists, have brought out into the clear light of day some of the earliest stages in man's existence and progress.

There is no part of the world more adapted than Denmark to this kind of investigation. Antiquities may be met with at every step; the real point in question is to know how to examine them properly, so as to obtain from them important revelations concerning the manners, customs, and manufactures of the pre-historic inhabitants. The Museum of Copenhagen, which contains antiquities from various Scandinavian states, is, in this respect, without a rival in the world.

Among the objects arranged in this well-stocked Museum a great many specimens may be observed which have come from the so-called *kitchen-middens*.

In the first place, what are these *kjoekken-moeddings*, or kitchen-middens, with their uncouth Scandinavian name?

Immense accumulations of shells have been observed on different points of the Danish coast, chiefly in the north, where the sea enters those narrow deep creeks, known by the name of *fiords*. These deposits are not generally raised more than about 3 feet above the level of the sea; but in some steep places their altitude is greater. They are about 3 to 10 feet in thickness, and from 100 to 200 feet in width; their length is sometimes as much as 1000 feet, with a width of from 150 to 250 feet. On some of the more level shores they form perfect hills, on which, as at Havelse, windmills are sometimes built.

What do we meet with in these heaps? An immense quantity of sea-shells, especially those of the oyster, broken bones of mammiferous animals, remains of birds and fish; and, lastly, some roughly-wrought flints.

The first idea formed with regard to these kitchen-middens was that they were nothing but banks of fossil shells, beds which had formerly been submerged, and subsequently brought to light by an upheaval of the earth caused by some volcanic cause. But M. Steenstrup, a Danish *savant*, opposed this opinion, basing his contradiction on the fact that these shells belong to four different species which are never found together, and consequently they must have been brought together by man. M. Steenstrup also called attention to the fact that almost all these shells must have belonged to full-grown animals, and that there were hardly any young ones to be found amongst them. A peculiarity of this kind is an evident indication of the exercise of some rational purpose, in fact, of an act of the human will.

When all the *débris* and relics which we have enumerated were discovered in these kitchen-middens, when the remains of hearths—small spots which still retained traces of fire—were found in them, the origin of these heaps were readily conjectured. Tribes once existed there who subsisted on the products of fishing and hunting, and threw out round their cabins the remains of their meals, consisting especially of the *débris* of shell-fish. These remains gradually accumulated, and constituted the considerable heaps which we are discussing; hence the name of *kjoekken-moedding*, composed of two words—*kjoekken*, kitchen; and *moedding*, heap of refuse. These "kitchen-middens," as they are called, are, therefore, the refuse from the meals of the primitive population of Denmark.

If we consider the heaps of oyster-shells and other *débris* which accumulate in the neighbourhood of eating-houses in certain districts, we may readily understand, comparing great things with small, how these Danish kitchen-middens were produced. I myself well recollect having noticed in the environs of Montpellier small hillocks of a similar character, formed by the accumulation of oyster-shells, mussels, and clams.

When the conviction was once arrived at that these kitchen-middens were the refuse of the meals of the primitive inhabitants, the careful excavation of all these heaps scattered along the Danish coast became an extremely interesting operation. It might be justly expected that some data would be collected as to the customs and manufactures of the ancient dwellers in these countries. A commission was, in consequence, appointed by the

Danish Government to examine these deposits, and to publish the results of its labours.

This commission was composed of three *savants*, each of whom were eminent in their respective line—Steenstrup, the naturalist, Forchhammer, a geologist, and the archæologist, Worsaae—and performed its task with as much talent as zeal. The observations which were made are recorded in three reports presented to the Academy of Sciences at Copenhagen. From these documents are borrowed most of the details which follow.

Before proceeding to acquaint our readers with the facts brought to light by the Danish commission, it will be well to remark that Denmark does not stand alone in possessing these kitchen-middens. They have been discovered in England—in Cornwall and Devonshire—in Scotland, and even in France, near Hyères (Bouches-du-Rhône).[18]

MM. Sauvage and Hamy have pointed out to M. de Mortillet the existence of deposits of this kind in the Pas-de-Calais. They may be noticed, say these naturalists, at La Salle (Commune of Outreau) at certain parts of the coast of Portel, and especially a very large heap at Cronquelets (Commune of Etaples.) They chiefly consist of the *cardium edule*, which appear to abound in the kitchen-middens of the Pas-de-Calais.

Messrs. Evans, Prestwich, and Lubbock observed one of these deposits at Saint-Valery, near the mouth of the Somme. Added to this, they have been described by various travellers as existing in different parts of the world. Dampier studied them in Australia, and Darwin in Tierra del Fuego, where deposits of the same character are now in the course of formation. M. Pereira da Costa found one on the coast of Portugal; Sir C. Lyell has testified to the existence of others on the coasts of Massachusetts and Georgia, in the United States; M. Strobel, on the coasts of Brazil. But those in Denmark are the only deposits of this kind which have been the subject of investigations of a deliberate and serious character.

Almost all these kitchen-middens are found on the coast, along the *fiords*, where the action of the waves is not much felt. Some have, however, been found several miles inland; but this must be owing to the fact that the sea once occupied these localities, from which it has subsequently retired. They are not to be met with on some of the Danish coasts, as those of the western side; this, on the one hand, may be caused by their having been washed away by the sea, which has there encroached on the land, or, on the other hand, by the fact that the western coast was much less sheltered than the other parts of the Danish peninsula. They are not unfrequently to be found in the adjacent islands.

These kitchen-middens form, in a general way, undulating mounds, which sink in a gentle incline from the centre to the circumference. The spot where they are thickest indicates the site of the habitations of man. Sometimes, we may notice one principal hillock, surrounded by smaller mounds; or else, in the middle of the heaps, there is a spot which must have been the site of the encampment.

These refuse deposits are almost entirely made up of shells of various kinds of molluscs; the principal species are the oyster, the cockle, the mussel, and the periwinkle. Others, such as whelks, *helices* (edible snails), *nassa*, and *trigonella*, are also found; but they are comparatively few in number.

Fishes' bones are discovered in great abundance in the kitchen-middens. They belong to the cod, herring, dab, and eel. From this we may infer that the primitive inhabitants of Denmark were not afraid of venturing out to brave the waves of the sea in their frail skiffs; for the herring and the cod cannot, in fact, be caught except at some little distance from the shore.

Mammalian bones are also plentifully distributed in the Danish kitchen-middens. Those most commonly met with are the remains of the stag, the roe, and the boar, which, according to M. Steenstrup's statement, make up ninety-seven hundredths of the whole mass. Others are the relics of the urus, the wolf, the dog, the fox, the wild-cat, the lynx, the marten, the otter, the porpoise, the seal, the water-rat, the beaver and the hedgehog.

The bison, the reindeer, the elk, the horse, and the domestic ox have not left behind them any trace which will permit us to assume that they existed in Denmark at the period when these deposits were formed.

Amongst other animals, we have mentioned the dog. By various indications, we are led to the belief that this intelligent creature had been at this time reduced to a state of domesticity. It has been remarked that a large number of the bones dispersed in these kitchen-middens are incomplete; exactly the same parts are almost always missing, and certain bones are entirely wanting. M. Steenstrup is of opinion that these deficiencies may be owing to the agency of dogs, which have made it their business to ransack the heaps of bones and other matters which were thrown aside by their masters. This hypothesis was confirmed, in his idea, when he became convinced, by experience, that the bones which were deficient in these deposits were precisely those which dogs are in the habit of devouring, and that the remaining portions of those which were found were not likely to have been subject to their attacks on account of their hardness and the small quantity of assimilable matter which was on or in them.

Although primitive man may have elevated the dog to the dignity of being his companion and friend, he was, nevertheless, sometimes in the habit of eating him. No doubt he did not fall back upon this last resort except in cases when all other means of subsistence failed him. Bones of the dog, broken by the hand of man, and still bearing the marks of having been cut with a knife, are amongst the remains found, and place the fact beyond any question.

We find, besides, the same taste existing here which we have seen manifested in other ages and different countries. All the long bones have been split in order to extract their marrow—the dainty so highly appreciated by man during the epochs of the reindeer and the mammoth.

Some remains of birds have been found in the kitchen-middens; but most of the species are aquatic—a fact which may be readily explained by the seaboard position of the men who formed these deposits.

As the result of this review of the various substances which were made use of for food by the men of the polished-stone epoch, we may infer that they were both hunters and fishermen.

Animals of rapid pace were hunted down by means of the dart or arrow, and any more formidable prey was struck down at close quarters by some sharp stone weapon.

Fishing was practised, as at the present day, by means of the line and net.

We have already seen that men, during the reindeer epoch, probably used hooks fastened at the end of lines. These hooks, as we have before remarked, were made with splinters of bone or reindeer horn. During the polished-stone epoch this fishing instrument was much improved, and they now possessed the real hook with a recurvate and pointed end. This kind of hook was found by Dr. Uhlmann in one of the most ancient lacustrine stations of Switzerland. But a curved hook was both difficult to make and also not very durable; instead of it was used another and more simple sort—the straight skewer fixed to serve as a hook. This is a simple fragment of bone, about an inch long, very slender and pointed at the two ends (fig. 77). Sometimes it is a little flattened in the middle, or bored with a hole, into which the line was fastened.

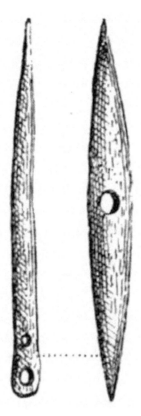

Fig. 77.—Bone Skewers used as Fish-hooks.

This little splinter of bone, when hidden by the bait and fastened to a line, was swallowed by the fish and could not be disgorged, one of the pointed ends being certain to bury itself in the entrails of the creature.

Some of our readers will perhaps be surprised to learn that men of the polished-stone epoch were in the habit of fishing with nets; but it is a fact that cannot be called into question, for the very conclusive reason, that the remains of these nets have been found.

How could it possibly come to pass that fishing-nets of the polished-stone epoch should have been preserved to so late a period as our times? This is exactly the question we are about to answer.

On the lakes of Switzerland and of other countries, there used to exist certain habitations of man. These are the so-called *lacustrine dwellings* which we shall have hereafter to consider in some considerable detail, when we come to the Bronze Age. The men who lived on these lakes were necessarily fishers; and some traces of their fishing-nets have been discovered by a circumstance which chemistry finds no difficulty in explaining. Some of these lake-dwellings were destroyed by fire; as, for instance, the lacustrine settlements of Robenhausen and Wangen in Switzerland. The outsides of these cabins, which were almost entirely constructed of wood, burnt, of course, very readily; but the objects inside, chiefly consisting of nets—the sole wealth of these tribes—could not burn freely for want of oxygen, but were only charred with the heat. They became covered with a slight coating of some empyreumatic or tarry matter—an excellent medium for insuring the preservation of any organic substance. These nets having been scorched by the fire, fell into the water with the *débris* of the hut, and, in consequence of their precipitate fall, never having come in actual contact with the flame, have been preserved almost intact at the bottom of the lakes. When, after a long lapse of centuries, they have been again recovered, these *débris* have been the means of affording information as to the manufacture both of the fishing-nets, and also as to the basket-work, vegetable provisions, &c., of these remote ages.

In one of Dr. Keller's papers on these *lacustrine dwellings*, of which we shall have more to say further on, we find a description and delineation of certain fishing-nets which were recovered from the lake of Robenhausen. In the Museum of Saint-Germain we inspected with curiosity several specimens of these very nets, and we here give a representation of one of them. There were nets with wide meshes like that shown in fig. 78, and also some more closely netted. The mesh is a square one, and appears to have been made on a frame by knotting the string at each point of intersection. All these nets are made of flax, for hemp had not yet been cultivated.

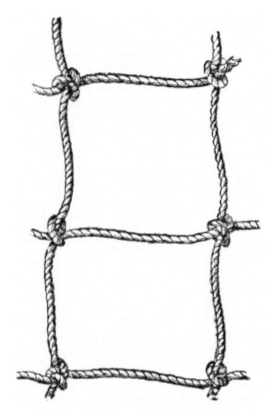

Fig. 78.—Fishing-net with wide Meshes.

These nets were held suspended in the water by means of floats, made, not of cork, but of the thick bark of the pine-tree, and were held down to the bottom of the water by stone weights. We give a representation here (fig. 79), of one of these stone weights taken from a specimen exhibited in the Museum of Saint-Germain.

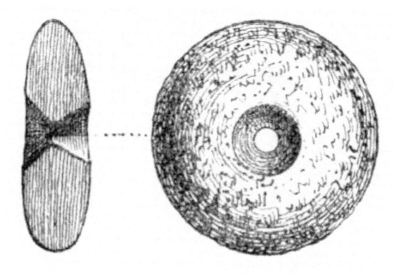

Fig. 79.—Stone Weight used for sinking the Fishing-nets.

These stone weights, large quantities of which are to be seen in museums, and especially in that of Saint-Germain, are, in almost every case, nothing but pebbles bored through the centre. Sometimes, however, they were round pieces of soft stone, having a hole made in the middle. Through this hole the cord was passed and fastened by a knot on the other side. By means of the floats and weights the nets were made to assume any position in the water which was wished.

The large size of the meshes in the nets belonging to the polished-stone epoch proves, that in the lakes and rivers of this period the fish that were used for food were of considerable dimensions. Added to this, however, the monstrous hooks belonging to this epoch which have been found in the Seine tend to corroborate this hypothesis.

Thus, then, the art of fishing had arrived in the polished-stone epoch to a very advanced stage of improvement.

In plate 80 we give a representation of fishing as carried on during the polished-stone epoch.

Fig. 80.—Fishing during the Polished-stone Epoch.

Returning to the subject of the ancient Danes, we must add, that these men, who lived on the sea-coasts, clad themselves in skins of beasts, rendered supple by the fat of the seal and marrow extracted from the bones of some of the large mammals. For dwelling-places they used tents likewise made of skins prepared in the same way.

Arts and Manufactures.—What degree of skill in this respect was attained by the men who lived during the polished-stone epoch? To give an answer to this question, we must again ransack those same kitchen-middens which have been the means of furnishing us with such accurate information as to the system of food of the man of that period. We shall also have to turn our attention to the remains found in the principal caves of this epoch.

An examination of the instruments found in the kitchen-middens shows us that the flints are in general of a very imperfect type, with the exception, however, of the long splinters or knives, the workmanship of which indicates a considerable amount of skill.

Fig. 81 represents a flint knife from one of the Danish deposits, delineated in the Museum of Saint-Germain; and fig. 82 a *nucleus*, that is, a piece of flint from which splinters have been taken off, which were intended to be used as knives.

Fig. 81.—Flint Knife, from one of the Danish Beds.

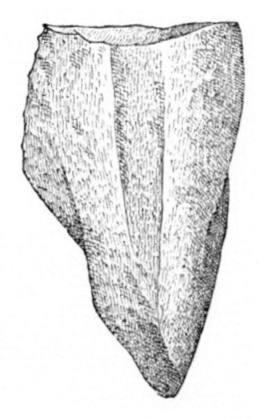

Fig. 82.—Nucleus off which Knives are flaked.

We also give a representation of a hatchet (fig. 83) and a scraper (fig. 84), which came from the same source.

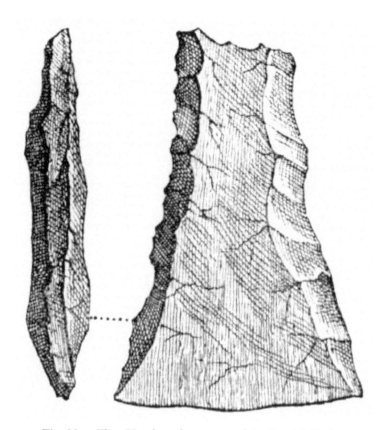

Fig. 83.—Flint Hatchet, from one of the Danish Beds.

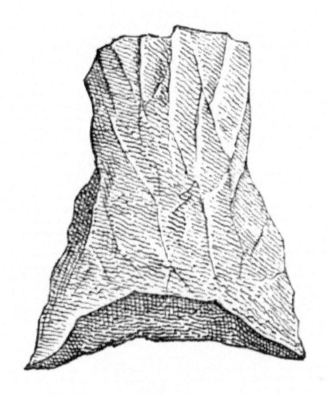

Fig. 84.—Flint Scraper, from one of the Danish Beds.

Besides these instruments, bodkins, spear-heads, and stones for slings have also been found in the kitchen-middens, without taking into account a quantity of fragments of flint which do not appear to have been wrought with any special purpose in view, and were probably nothing but rough attempts, or the mere refuse of the manufacture.

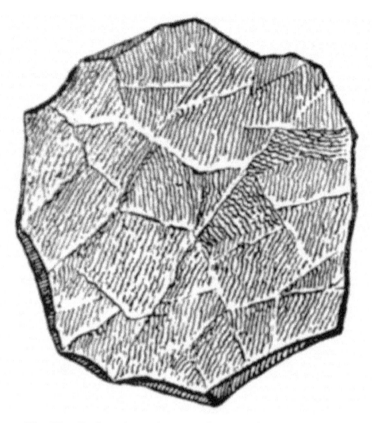

Fig. 85.—Refuse from the Manufacture of wrought Flints.

In the same deposits there are also found a good many pebbles, which, according to the general opinion, must have been used as weights to sink the fishing-nets to the bottom of the water. Some are hollowed out with a groove all round them, like that depicted in fig. 86, which is designed from a specimen in the Museum of Saint-Germain. Others have a hole bored through the middle. This groove or hole was, doubtless, intended to hold the cord which fastened the stone weight to the net.

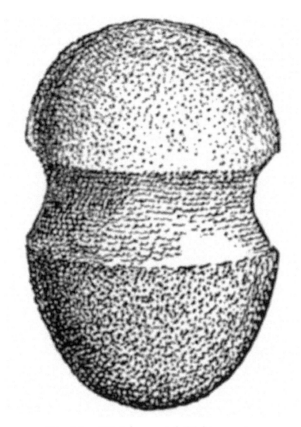

Fig. 86.—Weight to sink Fishing-nets.

Weapons and Tools.—We shall now pass on to the weapons and tools which were in use among the people in the north of Europe during the period we are considering.

During the latter period of the polished-stone epoch working in stone attained to a really surprising degree of perfection among the people of the North. It is, in fact, difficult to understand how, without making use of any metallic tools, men could possibly impart to flint, when fashioned into weapons and implements of all kinds, those regular and elegant shapes which the numerous excavations that have been set on foot are constantly bringing to light. The Danish flint may, it is true, be wrought with great facility; but nevertheless, an extraordinary amount of skill would be none the less necessary in order to produce that rectitude of outline and richness of contour which are presented by the Danish specimens of this epoch—specimens which will not be surpassed even in the Bronze Age.

The hatchets found in the north of Europe, belonging to the polished-stone epoch, differ very considerably from the hatchets of France and

Belgium. The latter are rounded and bulging at the edges; but the hatchets made use of by the people of the North (fig. 87) were flatter and cut squarely at the edge. They were nearly in the shape of a rectangle or elongated trapezium, with the four angles cut off. Their dimensions are sometimes considerable; some have been found which measured nearly 16 inches in length.

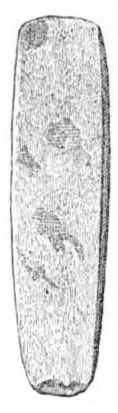

Fig. 87.—Danish Axe of the Polished-stone Epoch.

Independently of this type, which is the most plentiful, the northern tribes used also to manufacture the drilled hatchet, which is combined in various ways with the hammer. In these instruments, the best workmanship and the most pleasing shapes are to be noticed. The figs. 88, 89 and 90, designed in the Museum of Saint-Germain, from authentic specimens sent by the Museum of Copenhagen, represent double-edged axes and axe-hammers. They are all pierced with a round hole in which the handle was fixed. The cutting edge describes an arc of a circle, and the other end is wrought into sharp angular edges.

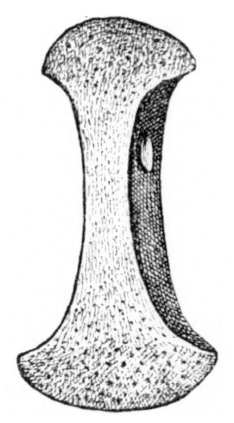

Fig. 88.—Double-edged Axe.

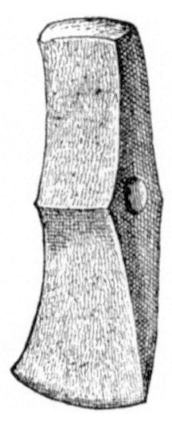

Fig. 89.—Danish Axe-hammer, drilled for handle.

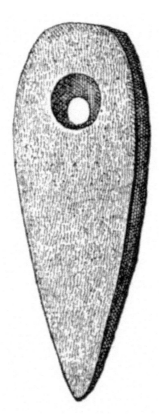

Fig. 90.—Danish Axe-hammer, drilled for handle.

These hatchets are distinguished from those of the reindeer epoch by a characteristic which enables us to refer them without hesitation to their real date, even in cases in which they have not yet been subject to the operation of polishing. The hatchets of the reindeer epoch have their cutting edge at the narrowest end, whilst those of the polished-stone epoch are sharp at their widest end. This observation does not apply specially to the Danish hatchets; it refers equally to those of other European countries.

The spear-heads are masterpieces of good taste, patience, and skill. There are two sorts of them. The most beautiful (figs. 91, 92) assume the shape of a laurel-leaf; they are quite flat, and chipped all over with an infinite amount of art. Their length is as much as 15 inches. Others are shorter and thicker in shape, and terminate at the base in an almost cylindrical handle. Sometimes they are toothed at the edge (fig. 93). These spear-heads were evidently fixed at the end of a staff, like the halberds of the middle ages and the modern lance.

Fig. 91.—Spear-head from Denmark.

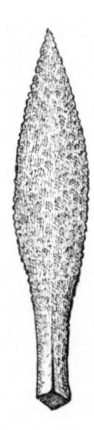

Fig. 92.—Spear-head from Denmark.

The poniards (fig. 94) are no less admirable in their workmanship than the spear-heads, from which they do not perceptibly differ, except in having a handle, which is flat, wide, solid, and made a little thicker at the end. This handle is always more or less ornamented, and is sometimes covered with delicate carving. To chip a flint in this way must have required a skilful and well-practised hand.

Fig. 93.—Toothed Spear-head of Flint.

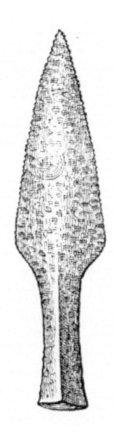

Fig. 94.—Flint Poniard, from Denmark.

After these somewhat extraordinary instruments, we must mention the arrow-heads, the shapes of which are rather varied in their character.

The arrow-heads most frequently found are formed in the shape of a triangular prism, terminating at the lower end in a stem intended to be inserted into a stick (fig. 95); others are deeply indented at the base and quite flat. Many are finely serrated on the edges, and occasionally even on the inside edge of the indentation.

Figs. 95, 96, 97, and 98 represent the various types of Danish arrow-heads, all of which are in the Museum of Saint-Germain, and from which these designs were made.

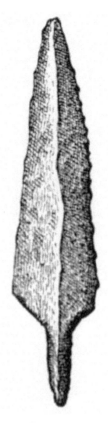

Fig. 95.—Type of the Danish Arrow-head.

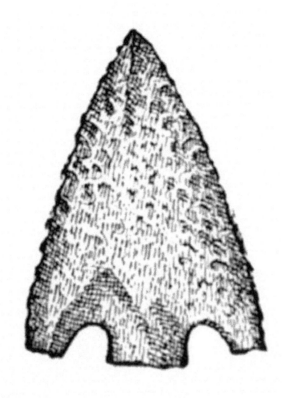

Fig. 96.—Another Type of Arrow-head.

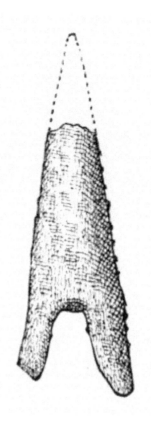

Fig. 97.—Arrow-head.

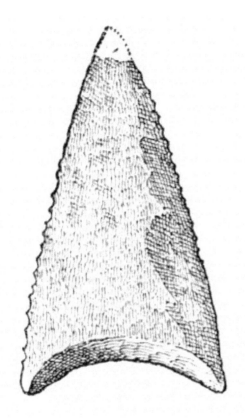

Fig. 98.—Arrow-head from Denmark.

The chisels and gouges equally merit a special mention.

The chisel (fig. 99) is a kind of quadrangular prism, chipped in a bevel down to the base.

Fig. 99.—Flint Chisel from Denmark.

The gouges are hollowed out on one of their faces, so as to act as the tool the name of which has been applied to them.

We next come to some curious instruments, of which we have given designs taken from the specimens in the Museum of Saint-Germain; the purpose they were applied to is still problematical. They are small flakes, or blades, in the shape of a crescent (figs. 100, 101). The inner edge, which was either straight or concave, is usually serrated like a saw; the convex side must have been fixed into a handle; for the traces of the handle may still be detected upon many of them. These instruments were probably made use of as scrapers in the preparation of skins for garments; perhaps, also, they were used as knives or as saws.

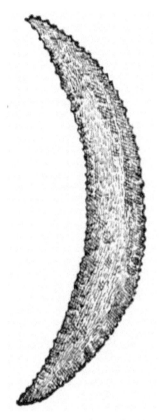

Fig. 100.—Small Stone Saw from the Danish Deposits.

Fig. 101.—Another Stone Saw from Denmark.

We must now turn our attention to instruments made of bone or stag's horn. They are much less numerous than those of stone, and have nothing about them of a very remarkable character. The only implement that is worthy of notice is the harpoon (fig. 102). It is a carved bone, and furnished with teeth all along one side, the other edge being completely smooth. The harpoon of the reindeer epoch was decidedly superior to it.

Fig. 102.—Bone Harpoon of the Stone Age from Denmark.

On account of its singularity, we must not omit to mention an object made of bone, composed of a wide flat plate, from which spring seven or eight teeth of considerable length, and placed very close together; there is a kind of handle, much narrower, and terminating in a knob, like the top of a walking-stick. This is probably one of the first combs which ever unravelled the thickly-grown heads of hair of primitive man.

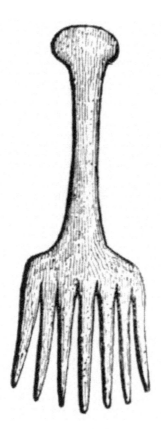

Fig. 103.—Bone Comb from Denmark.

It is a well-known fact that amber is very plentiful on the coasts of the Baltic. Even in the Stone Age, it was already much appreciated by the northern tribes, who used to make necklaces of it, either by merely perforating the rough morsels of amber and stringing them in a row, or by cutting them into spherical or elliptical beads, as is the case nowadays.

Fig. 104 represents a necklace and also various other ornaments made of yellow amber, which have been drawn from specimens in the Museum of Saint-Germain.

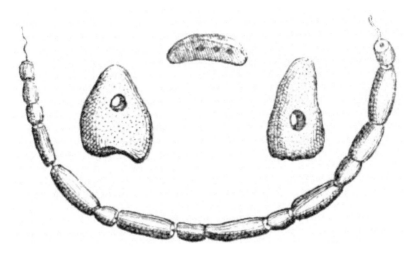

Fig. 104.—Necklace and various Ornaments of Amber.

Although these northern tribes of the polished-stone epoch were such skilful workmen in flint, they were, nevertheless, but poor hands at pottery. The *débris* of vessels collected from the Danish *kitchen-middens*, and also from the peat-bogs and tombs, are in every way rough, and testify to a very imperfect knowledge of the art of moulding clay. They may be said to mark the first efforts of a manufacturing art which is just springing into existence, which is seeking for the right path, although not, as yet, able to find it. The art of pottery (if certain relics be relied on) was more advanced at a more ancient period, that is, during the reindeer epoch.

We have already stated that during the reindeer epoch there existed certain manufactories of weapons and tools, the productions of which were distributed all round the adjacent districts, although over a somewhat restricted circle. In the epoch at which we have now arrived, certain *workshops*—for really this is the proper name to give them—acquired a remarkable importance, and their relations became of a much more extensive character. In several of the Belgian caves, flints have been found which must have come from the celebrated workshop of Grand-Pressigny, situated in that part of the present France which forms the department of Indre-et-Loire, and, from their very peculiar character, are easily recognisable. Commerce and manufacture had then emerged from their merely rudimentary state, and were entering into a period of activity implying a certain amount of civilisation.

The great principle of division of labour had already been put into practice, for there were special workshops both for the shaping and polishing of flints.

The most important of all the workshops which have been noticed in France is, unquestionably, that of Grand-Pressigny, which we have already mentioned. It was discovered by Dr. Léveillé, the medical man of the place; but, to tell the truth, it is not so much in itself a centre of manufacture as a series of workshops distributed in the whole neighbourhood round Pressigny.

At the time of this discovery, that is in 1864, flints were found in thousands imbedded in the vegetable mould on the surface of the soil, over a superficies of 12 to 14 acres. The Abbé Chevalier, giving an account of this curious discovery to the *Académie des Sciences* at Paris, wrote: "It is impossible to walk a single step without treading on some of these objects."

The workshops of Grand-Pressigny furnish us with a considerable variety of instruments. We find hatchets in all stages of manufacture, from the roughest attempt up to a perfectly polished weapon. We find, also, long flakes or flint-knives cleft off with a single blow with astonishing skill.

All these objects, even the most beautiful among them, are nevertheless defective in some respect or other; hence it may be concluded that they were the refuse thrown aside in the process of manufacture. In this way may be explained the accumulation of so many of these objects in the same spot.

There were likewise narrow and elongated points forming a kind of piercer, perfectly wrought; also scrapers, and saws of a particular type which seem to have been made in a special workshop. They are short and wide, and have at each end a medial slot intended to receive a handle.

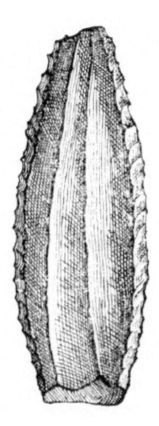

Fig. 105.—Nucleus in the Museum of Saint-Germain, from the Workshop of Grand-Pressigny.

But the objects which are the most numerous of all, and those which obviate any doubt that Pressigny was once an important centre of the manufacture of flint, are the *nuclei* (fig. 105), or the remnants of the lump of flint, from which the large blades known under the name of knives were cleft off. Some of these lumps which we have seen in the Museum of St. Germain were as much as 11 and 13 inches in length; but the greater part did not exceed 7 inches. The labourers of Touraine, who often turn up these flints with their plough-shares, call them *pounds of butter*, looking at the similarity of shape. At the present day these *nuclei* are plentiful in all the collections of natural history and geology.

A strange objection has been raised against the antiquity of the hatchets, knives, and weapons found at Pressigny. M. Eugène Robert has asserted that these flints were nothing else but the refuse of the siliceous masses which, at the end of the last century and especially at the beginning of the present, were used in the manufacture of gun-flints!

The Abbé Bourgeois, M. Penguilly l'Haridon, and Mr. John Evans did not find much difficulty in proving the slight foundation there was for this criticism. In the department of Loire-et-Cher, in which the gun-flint manufacture still exists, the residue from the process bears no resemblance whatever to the *nuclei* of Pressigny; the fragments are much less in bulk, and do not present the same constantly-occurring and regular shapes. Added to this, they are never chipped at the edges, like a great number of the flakes coming from the workshops of Touraine.

But another and altogether peremptory argument is that the flints of Pressigny-le-Grand are unfitted, on account of the texture, for the manufacture of gun-flints. Moreover, the records of the Artillery Depôt, as remarked by M. Penguilly l'Haridon, librarian of the Artillery Museum, do not make mention of the locality of Pressigny having ever been worked for this purpose. Lastly, the oldest inhabitants of the commune have testified that they never either saw or heard of any body of workmen coming into the district to work flints. M. Eugène Robert's hypothesis, which MM. Decaisne and Elie de Beaumont thought right to patronise, is, therefore, as much opposed to facts as to probability.

Very few polished flints are found in the workshops of Pressigny-le-Grand; it is, therefore, imagined that their existence commenced before the polished-stone epoch. According to this idea, the *nuclei* would belong to a transitional epoch between the period of chipped stone, properly so called, and that of polished stone. The first was just coming to an end, but the second had not actually commenced. In other words, most of the Pressigny flints have the typical shapes and style of cutting peculiar to the polished-stone age, but the polishing is wanting.

This operation was not practised in the workshops of Pressigny until some considerable period after they were founded, and were already in full operation. In the neighbourhood of this locality a number of polishers have been found of a very remarkable character. They are large blocks of sandstone (fig. 106), furrowed all over, or only on a portion of their surface, with grooves of various depths, in which objects might be polished by an energetic friction.

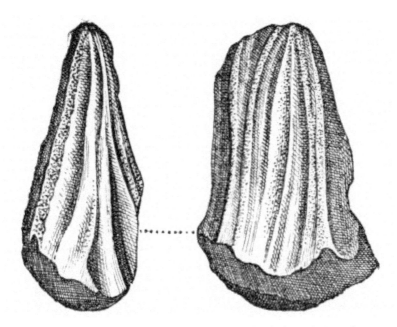

Fig. 106.—Polisher from Grand-Pressigny, both faces being shown.

Some polishers of the same kind, which have been found in various departments, are rather different from the one we have just named. Thus, one specimen which was found by M. Leguay in the environs of Paris, in the burial-places of Varenne-Saint-Hilaire, of which we give a representation further on, is provided not only with grooves but also hollows of a basin-like shape, and of some little depth.

The polishing of the flints was carried into effect by rubbing them against the bottom of these hollows, which were moistened by water, and no doubt contained siliceous dust of a harder nature than the stone which had to be polished.

We must here pause for a moment to remark that all these operations which were carried out by our ancestors in fashioning the flint could not fail to have presented certain difficulties, and must have required a remarkable development of intelligence and skill.

Working flints into shape, which appears at first sight a very simple matter, is, however, a rather complicated operation, on account of the properties of this mineral substance and the beds in which it lies.

In its natural state the flint presents itself in the shape of nearly round lumps, which are brittle, but nevertheless very hard, and which, like glass, can be split in any direction by a blow, so as to furnish scales with sharp edges. In consequence of this circumstance, all that would be requisite in order to produce sharp objects is to cleave off flakes in the shape of a knife or poniard, by striking a flint, held in the left hand, with another and harder flint or hammer. Instead of holding in the left hand the flint which was to be wrought, it might also be placed on a rest and, being held fast with the left hand, suitable blows might be applied to the stone.

We must not, however, omit to mention, that to enable the flint to be cut up into sharp splinters and to be broken in any desired direction, it is necessary for it to have been very recently extracted from the bosom of the earth; it must possess the humidity which is peculiar to it, with which it is impregnated when in its natural bed. If pieces of flint are exposed to the open air they cannot afterwards be readily broken with any degree of regularity; they then afford nothing but shapeless and irregular chips, of an entirely different character from that which would be required in fashioning them. This moisture was well known to the workmen who used to manufacture the gun-flints, and was called the *quarry damp*.

The necessity that the flint should be wrought when newly extracted from the earth, and that the stones should only be dug just in proportion as they were wanted, brought about as a proximate result the creation and working of mines and quarries, which are thus almost as ancient as humanity itself. Being unable to make use of flints which had been dried in the air, and consequently rendered unfit for being wrought, the workmen were compelled to make excavations, and to construct galleries, either covered or exposed to the open air, to employ wooden battening, shores, supports; in short, to put in use the whole plant which is required for working a stone-quarry. As, in order not to endanger the lives of the labourers, it was found necessary to prevent any downfalls, they were induced to follow out a certain methodical system in their excavations, by giving a sufficient thickness to the roofs of the galleries, by sinking shafts, by building breast-walls, and by adopting the best plan for getting out the useless *detritus*. When, as was often the case, water came in so as to hinder the miners, it was necessary to get rid of it in order that the workmen should not be drowned. It was also sometimes requisite that the galleries and the whole system of underground ways should be supplied with air.

Thus their labour in fashioning the flint must have led our ancestors to create the art of working quarries and mines.

It has been made a subject of inquiry, how the tribes of the Stone Age could produce, without the aid of any iron tool, the holes which are found in the flints; and how they could perforate these same flints so as to be able to fit in handles for the hatchets, poniards, and knives; in fact, lapidaries of the present day cannot bore through gun-flints without making use of diamond dust. We are of opinion that the *bow*, which was employed by primitive man in producing fire by rubbing wood against wood, was also resorted to in the workshops for manufacturing stone implements and weapons for giving a rapid revolving motion to a flint drill which was sufficient to perforate the stone. Certain experiments which have been made in our own day with very sharp arrow-heads which belonged to primitive man have proved that it is thus very possible to pierce fresh flints, if the action of the drill is assisted by the addition of some very hard dust which is capable of increasing the bite of the instrument. This dust or powder, consisting of corundum or zircon, might have been found without any great difficulty by the men of the Stone Age. These substances are, in fact, to be met with on the banks of rivers, their presence being betrayed by the golden spangles which glitter in the sand.

Thus the flint-drill, assisted by one of these powders, was quite adequate for perforating siliceous stones. When it is brought to our knowledge that the workmen of the Black Forest thus bore into Bohemian granite in less than a minute, we shall not feel inclined to call this explanation in question.[19]

Fig. 107 attempts to give a representation of the workshop at Pressigny for shaping and polishing flints—in other words, a manufacturing workshop of the polished-stone epoch.

Fig. 107.—The earliest Manufacture and Polishing of Flints.

In this sketch we have depicted the polisher found by M. Leguay, of which we give a representation in fig. 108. In this picture it was indispensable for us to show the operation of polishing, for the latter is a characteristic of the epoch of mankind which we are now describing, that is, the polished-stone period. It must, in fact, be remarked that during the epoch of the great bear and the mammoth, and the reindeer epoch, stone instruments were not polished, they were purely and simply flakes or fragments of stone. During the epoch at which we have now arrived, a great improvement took place in this kind of work, and stone instruments were polished. It is therefore essential to call attention to the latter operation.

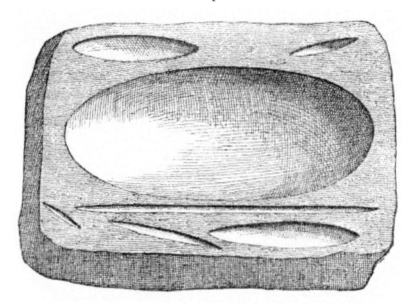

Fig. 108.—Polisher found by M. Leguay.

We think we ought to quote here the brief account M. Leguay has given of the polisher represented in our figure. In his 'Note sur une Pierre à polir les Silex trouvée en Septembre, 1860, à la Varenne-Saint-Hilaire (Seine),' M. Leguay thus writes:—

"Amongst the many monuments of the Stone Age which I have collected at Varenne-Saint-Hilaire, on the site of the ancient settlement which once existed there, there is one which has always struck me, not only by its good state of preservation, but also by the revelations which it affords us as to one of the principal manufactures of these tribes—the fabrication of flint weapons and utensils.

"This object is a stone for polishing and fashioning the finest kind of hatchets. I discovered it in September, 1860, at a spot called *La Pierre au Prêtre*, along with several other monuments of primitive art which I intend before long to make public. This stone is a rough sandstone of cubical shape, showing no trace whatever of having been hewn. It is 13 inches in its greatest thickness, and measures 37 inches long by 21 wide, and, just as in many boulders, one of its faces is well adapted to the use for which it was employed.

"This is the face which was used for many long years for rubbing and polishing the weapons made in the place, the remains of which are still found in small quantities in the neighbourhood, and abound in the burial-places, where they have been deposited as votive offerings.

"Almost the whole of its surface is occupied. In the centre is a basin presenting an oval surface 25 inches the long way, and 12 inches the narrow way. The stone, which has been considerably worn away in consequence of long use, has been rubbed off to a central depth of about 1 inch; this portion must have been used for rubbing the larger objects after they had been roughly shaped by chipping. The length of the basin allowed a motion of considerable length to be given to the stone which was being worked, at the same time giving facilities to the workman for the exercise of all his strength. Added to this, this cavity enabled the almond-like shape to be given to the objects—a form which they nearly all present.

"Either in front or to the right, according to the position in which the observer stands, and almost touching the edge of this basin, there is a hole deeply hollowed in the stone, being 30 inches long; it extends along almost the whole length of the sandstone, with the maximum breadth of about 1 inch, and presents the shape of a very elongated spindle hollowed out to a depth of something less than half an inch in the centre, which tapers off to nothing at the two ends.

"The wear of the stone and the shape of this groove point out its intention. It must have been used to reduce the edges or the sides of the hatchet, which after the chipping and flat polishing were left either too thick or too sharp for a handle to be easily fitted to them. Added to this, it smoothed down the roughnesses caused by chipping, which it replaced by a round form of no great thickness, which was again and again rubbed flatly on the stone to give it a square and sharp-edged level. This last operation took place in a basin, and it gave to the hatchet a curve in a lengthwise direction which is by no means ungraceful.

"The thinning off of the edges of the groove was not an immaterial matter. It not only assisted in forming the above-named curve, but also prevented the cutting edge being distorted, and avoided the need of subsequent repolishing, which spoiled the object by rubbing it away too much.

"It must not be for a moment imagined that the edge of the hatchet was made in this groove. Examination proves the contrary, and that it was done flatwise while polishing the rest of the object; and if sometimes its thickness did not allow this, it was preliminarily done, and then finished in the general polishing.

"But although this basin, and its accompanying groove, on account of their dimensions, acted very well for polishing the large hatchets, the case was different with the smaller ones. This is the reason why two other smaller basins, and also a small groove, were made on the flat part of the stone by the side of the others.

"These two basins were placed at two corners of the face of the stone, but still parallel to the larger basin and also to the larger groove, so as to be convenient for the requirements of the workman engaged in polishing without compelling him to shift his position; one is 10 inches, and the other 13 inches in length, with a mean breadth of about 2½ inches. They are both in the shape of a rather narrow almond, and end almost in a point, which seems to show that they also were used in polishing somewhat narrow objects—perhaps to set right the edges of hatchets, in which the rubbing in the larger basin had produced cavities prejudicial to the perfection of the faces.

"The small groove, placed very near the larger one, is 9 inches long. It is the same shape as the other, but is not so deep, and scarcely half an inch wide.

"Not far from the end of this latter groove, at the point where it approaches the larger one, there are traces of a groove scarcely commenced.

"Lastly, the flat portions of the stone which are not occupied by the basins and grooves, were sometimes used for touching up the polish, or even for smoothing various objects.

"Thus, as we see, this polishing-stone, which is one of the most complete in existence, has on it three basins of different sizes, two well-defined grooves, and one only just sketched out. It would serve for finishing off all the instruments that could be required; but, nevertheless, two other sandstones of moderate size were found near it; one round, and the other of a spindle-like shape; these, which were worn and rubbed all over their surfaces, must also have been used in polishing objects.

"Finding these stones was, however, a thing of frequent occurrence in several spots of this locality, where I often met with them; they were of all sizes and all shapes, and perfectly adapted for polishing small flints, needles, and the cutting edges of knives, deposited with them in the sepulchres.

"This polishing-stone, which is thickly covered with *dendrites* or incrustations, must have been in use at the time it was abandoned. I found it about 2 feet below the surface of the soil, in which it was turned upside down; that is, the basin lay next the earth. The few monuments that were with it—one among which I looked upon as an idol roughly carved in a block of sandstone—were all likewise turned upside down. There had been sepulchres in the neighbourhood, but they had been violated; and the displaced stones, as well as the bones themselves, only served to point out the presence of the former burial-place."

The polishing of stone instruments was effected by rubbing the object operated upon in a cavity hollowed out in the centre of the polisher, in which cavity a little water was poured, mixed with zircon or corundum powder, or, perhaps, merely with oxide of iron, which is used by jewellers in carrying out the same operation.

It is really surprising to learn what an enormous quantity of flints could be prepared by a single workman, provided with the proper utensils. For information on this point, it is requisite to know what could be done by our former flint-workers in the departments of Indre and Loire-et-Cher, who are, in fact, the descendants of the workmen of the Stone Age. Dolomieu, a French naturalist, desired at the beginning of the century to acquaint himself with the quantity which these workmen could produce, and at the same time to thoroughly understand the process which they employed in manufacturing gun-flints.

By visiting the workshops of the flint-workers, M. Dolomieu ascertained that the first shape which the workmen gave to the flint was that of a many-sided prism. In the next place, five or six blows with the hammer, which were applied in a minute, were sufficient to cleave off from the mass certain fragments as exact in shape, with faces as smooth, outlines as straight, and angles as sharp, as if the stone had been wrought by a lapidary's wheel—an operation which, in the latter case, would have required an hour's handiwork. All that was requisite, says Dolomieu, is that the stones should be fresh, and devoid of flaws or heterogeneous matter. When operating upon a good kind of flint, freshly extracted from the ground, a workman could prepare 1000 proper flakes of flint in a day, turning out 500 gun-flints, so that in three days he would perfectly finish 1000 ready for sale. In 1789, the Russian army was furnished with gun-flints from Poland. The manufactory was established at Kisniew. At this period, according to Dolomieu, 90,000 of these gun-flints were made in two months.

Besides those at Grand-Pressigny, some other pre-historic workshops have been pointed out in France. We may mention those of Charente, discovered by M. de Rochebrune; also those of Poitou, and lastly, the field of Diorières, at Chauvigny (Loire-et-Cher), which appears to have been a special workshop for polishing flint instruments. There is, in fact, not far from Chauvigny, in the same department, a rock on which twenty-five furrows, similar to those in the polishing-stones, are still visible; on which account the inhabitants of the district have given it the name of the "Scored Rock." It is probable that this rock was used for polishing the instruments which were sculptured at Diorières.

The same kind of open-air workshops for the working of flints have also been discovered in Belgium.

The environs of Mons are specially remarkable in this respect. At Spiennes, particularly, there can be no doubt that an important manufactory of wrought flints existed during the polished-stone epoch. A considerable number of hatchets and other implements have been found there; all of them being either unfinished, defective, or scarcely commenced. We here give a representation (fig. 109) of a spear-head which came from this settlement.

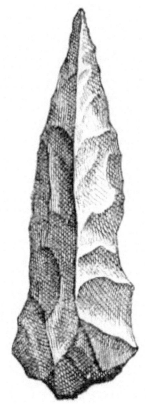

Fig. 109.—Spear-head from Spiennes.

Sometimes these workshops were established in caverns, and not in the open air. We are told this by M. J. Fournet, a naturalist of Lyons, in his work entitled, 'Influence du Mineur sur la Civilisation.'

"For a very long time past," says M. Fournet, "the caves of Mentone had been known to the inhabitants of the district, on account of the accumulation of *débris* contained in them, a boxful of which were sent to Paris, before 1848, by the Prince of Monaco; the contents of it, however, were never subjected to any proper explanation. Since this date, M. Grand, of Lyons, to whom I am indebted for a collection of specimens from these caves, carefully made several excavations, by which he was enabled to ascertain that the most remarkable objects are only to be met with at a certain depth in the clayey deposit with which the soil of these caves is covered. All the instruments are rough and rudimentary in their character, and must, consequently, be assigned to the first commencement of the art. Nevertheless, among the flints some agates were found, which, in my opinion, certainly came from the neighbourhood of Frejus; and with them also some pieces of hyaline quartz in the shape of prisms terminated by their two ordinary pyramids. We have a right to suppose that these crystals, which resembled the *Meylan diamonds* found near Grenoble, did not come there by chance, and that their sharp points, when fixed in a handle and acting as drills, were used for boring holes in stone."

Flint was not, however, the only substance used during this epoch in the manufacture of stone-hatchets, instruments and tools. In the caves of France, Belgium and Denmark a considerable number of hatchets have been found, made of gneiss, diorite, ophite, fibrolite, jade, and various other very hard mineral substances, which were well adapted to the purpose required and the use to which they were put.

Among the most remarkable we may mention several jade hatchets which were found in the department of Gers, and ornamented with small hooks on each side of the edge. One of these beautiful jade hatchets (fig. 110), the delineation of which is taken from the specimen in the Museum of Saint-Germain, was found in the department of Seine-et-Oise; it has a sculptured ridge in the middle of each face.

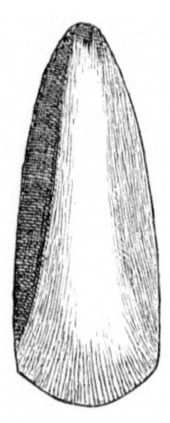

Fig. 110.—Polished Jade Hatchet in the Museum of Saint-Germain.

But neither flint, gneiss, nor diorite exist in every country. For these stones some less hard substance was then substituted. In Switzerland the instruments and tools were generally made of pebbles which had been drifted down by the streams. They were fashioned by breaking them with other stones, by rubbing them on sandstone, or by sawing them with toothed blades of flint according to their cohesive nature.

In some localities also objects of large size were made of serpentine, basalts, lavas, jades, and other rocks chosen on account of their extreme cohesiveness.

Manual skill had, however, attained such a pitch of perfection among the workmen of this period, in consequence of their being habituated to one exclusive kind of labour, that the nature of the stone became a matter of indifference to them. The hammer, with the proper use of which our workmen are almost unacquainted, was a marvellous instrument in the hands of our ancestors; with it they executed prodigies of workmanship, which seem as if they ought to have been reserved for the file and grindstone of the lapidary of the present day.

We shall not, perhaps, surprise our readers if we add that as certain volcanic lavas, especially obsidian, fracture with the same regularity and the same facility as the flint, obsidian was employed by the natives of America as a material for making sharp instruments. The ancient quarries whence the Indians procured this rock for the manufacture of instruments and tools, were situate at the *Cerro de Navajas*—that is, the *Mountain of Knives*—in Mexico. M. H. de Saussure, the descendant of the great geologist, was fortunate enough to meet with, at this spot, pieces of mineral which had merely been begun upon, and allowed a series of double-edged blades to be subsequently cut off them; these were always to be obtained by a simple blow skilfully applied. According to M. H. de Saussure, the first fashioning of these implements was confined to producing a large six-sided prism, the vertical corners of which were regularly and successively hewn off, until the piece left, or *nucleus*, became too small for the operation to be further continued.

Hernandez, the Spanish historian, states that he has seen 100 blades an hour manufactured in this way. Added to this, the ancient aborigines of Peru, and the Guanches of Teneriffe, likewise carved out of obsidian both darts and poniards. And, lastly, we must not omit to mention that M. Place, one of the explorers of Nineveh, found on the site of this ancient city, knives of obsidian, supposed to be used for the purpose of circumcision.

Having considered the flint instruments peculiar to the polished-stone epoch, we must now turn our attention to those made of stag's horn.

The valley of the Somme, which has furnished such convincing proof of the co-existence of man with the great mammals of extinct species, is a no less precious repository for instruments of stag's horn belonging to the polished-stone epoch. The vast peat-bogs of this region are the localities where these relics have been chiefly found. Boucher de Perthes collected a considerable number of them in the neighbourhood of Abbeville.

These peat-bogs are, as is well known, former marshes which have been gradually filled up by the growth of peat-moss (sphagnum), which, mixed with fallen leaves, wood, &c., and being slowly rotted by the surrounding water, became converted after a certain time into that kind of combustible matter which is called peat. The bogs in the valley of the Somme in some places attain to the depth of 34 feet. In the lower beds of this peat are found the weapons, the tools, and the ornaments of the polished-stone epoch.

Among these ancient relics we must mention one very interesting class; it is that formed by the association of two distinct component parts, such as stone and stag's horn, or stone and bone.

The hatchets of this type are particularly remarkable; they consist of a piece of polished flint half buried in a kind of sheath of stag's horn, either polished or rough as the case may be (fig. 111).

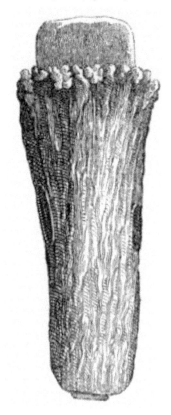

Fig. 111.—Polished Flint Hatchet, with a Sheath of Stag's Horn fitted for a Handle.

The middle of this sheath is generally perforated with a round or oval hole intended to receive a handle of oak, birch, or some other kind of wood adapted for such a use.

Fig. 112, taken from the illustration in Boucher de Perthes' work ('Antiquités Celtiques et Antédiluviennes'), represents this hatchet fitted into a handle made of oak.

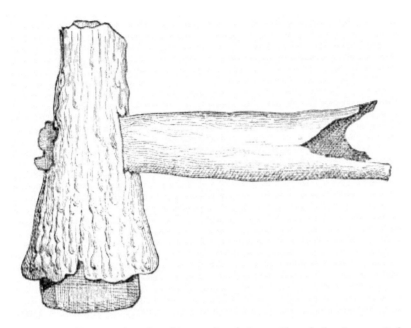

Fig. 112.—Flint Hatchet fitted into a Stag's-horn Sheath, having an Oak Handle, from Boucher de Perthes' illustration.

It is difficult to understand how it was that a hatchet of this kind did not fall out of its sheath in consequence of any moderately violent blow; for it seems as if there was nothing to hold it in its place. This observation especially applies to hatchets, the whole length of which—even the portion covered by the sheath—was polished; for the latter would certainly slide out of their casing with ease. The fact is, that complete specimens are seldom found, and, generally speaking, the flints are separated from their sheaths.

With regard to the handles, the nature of the material they were made from was unfavourable to their preservation through a long course of centuries; it is, therefore, only exceptionally that we meet with them, and even then they are always defaced.

Fig. 113 is given by Boucher de Perthes, in his 'Antiquités Celtiques,' as the representation of an oaken handle found by him.

A number of these sheaths have been found, which were provided at the end opposite to the stone hatchet with strong and pointed teeth. These are boar's tusks, firmly buried in the stag's horn. These instruments therefore fulfilled a double purpose; they cut or crushed with one end and pierced with the other.

Sheaths are also found which are not only provided with the boar's tusks, but are hollowed out at each end so as to hold two flint hatchets at once. This is represented in fig. 114 from one of Boucher de Perthes' illustrations.

Fig. 113.—Hatchet-handle made of Oak.

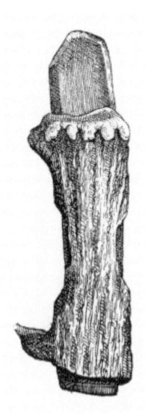

Fig. 114.—Stag's-horn Sheath, open at each end so as to receive two Hatchets.

The hatchet fitted into a sheath of stag's horn which we here delineate (fig. 115), was picked up in the environs of Aerschot, and is an object well worthy of note; it is now in the Museum of Antiquities at Brussels. Its workmanship is perfect, and superior to that of similar instruments found in the peat-bogs of the valley of the Somme.

Fig. 115.—Polished Flint Hatchet from Belgium, fitted into a Stag's-horn Sheath.

Stag's horn was often used alone as a material for the manufacture of tools which were not intended to endure any very hard work; among these were instruments of husbandry and gardening.

We here give representations (figs. 116, 117, 118) from Boucher de Perthes' illustrations, of certain implements made of stag's horn which appear to have had this purpose in view. It is remarked that they are not all perforated for holding a handle; in some cases, a portion of the stag's antler formed the handle.

Fig. 116.—Gardening Tool made of Stag's Horn (after Boucher de Perthes).

Fig. 117.—Gardening Tool made of Stag's Horn (after Boucher de Perthes).

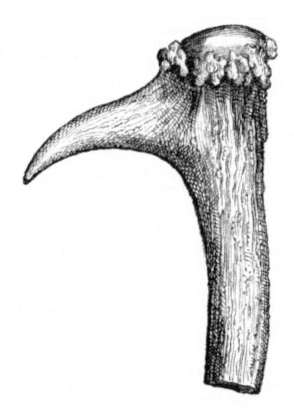

Fig. 118.—Gardening Tool made of Stag's Horn (after Boucher de Perthes).

In the course of his explorations in the peat-bogs of Abbeville, M. Boucher de Perthes found numerous flakes of flint of irregular shapes, the use of which he was unable to explain. But there have also been discovered in the same deposits some long bones belonging to mammals—tibia, femur, radius, ulna—all cut in a uniform way, either in the middle or at the ends; he was led to imagine that these bones might have been the handles intended to hold the flints. In order to assure himself that this idea was well founded, he took one of the bones and a stone which came out of the peat, and, having put them together, he found he had made a kind of chisel, well-adapted for cutting, scooping-out, scratching and polishing horn or wood. He tried this experiment again several times, and always with full success. If the stone did not fit firmly into the bone, one or two wooden wedges were sufficient to steady it.

After this, Boucher de Perthes entertained no doubt whatever that these bones had been formerly employed as handles for flint implements. The same handle would serve for several stones, owing to the ease with which the artisan could take one flint out and replace it with another, by the aid of nothing but these wooden wedges. This is the reason why, in the peat-bogs, flints of this sort are always much more plentiful than the bone handles. We must also state that it seems as if they took little or no trouble in repairing the flints when they were blunted, knowing how easy it would be to replace them. They were thrown away, without further care; hence their profusion.

These handles are made of extremely hard bone, from which we may conclude that they were applied to operations requiring solid tools. Most of them held the flint at one end only; but some were open at both ends, and would serve as handles for two tools at once.

Figs. 119 and 120 represent some of these flint tools in bone handles—the plates are taken from those in Boucher de Perthes' work.

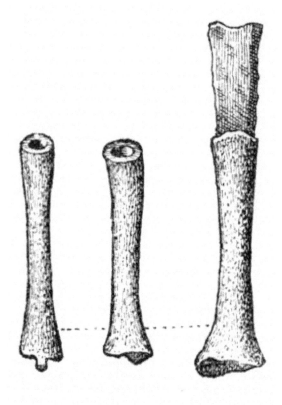

Fig. 119.—Flint Tool in a Bone Handle.

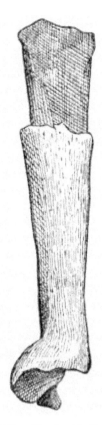

Fig. 120.—Flint Tool with Bone Handle.

Generally speaking, these handles gave but little trouble to those who made them. They were content with merely breaking the bone across, without even smoothing down the fracture, and then enlarging the medullary hollow which naturally existed; next they roughly squared or rounded the end which was intended to be grasped by the hand.

In fig. 121, we delineate one of these bone handles which is much more carefully fashioned; it has been cut off smooth at the open end, and the opposite extremity has been rounded off into a knob, which is ornamented with a design.

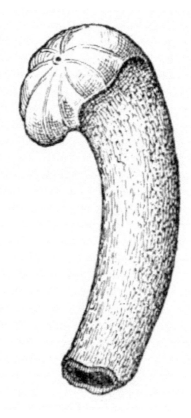

Fig. 121.—Ornamented Bone Handle.

During the polished-stone epoch, as during that which preceded it, the teeth of certain mammals were used in the way of ornament. But they were not content, as heretofore, with merely perforating them with holes and hanging them in a string round their necks; they were now wrought with considerable care. The teeth of the wild boar were those chiefly selected for this purpose. They were split lengthwise, so as to render them only half their original thickness, and were then polished and perforated with holes in order to string them.

In the peat-mosses of the valley of the Somme a number of boars' tusks have been found thus fashioned. The most curious discovery of this kind which has been made, was that of the object of which we give a sketch in fig. 122. It was found in 1834, near Pecquigny (Somme), and is composed of nineteen boars' tusks split into two halves, as we before mentioned, perfectly polished, and perforated at each end with a round hole. Through these holes was passed a string of some tendinous substance, the remains of which were, it is stated, actually to be seen at the time of the discovery.

A necklace of this kind must have been of considerable value, as it would have necessitated a large amount of very tedious and delicate work.

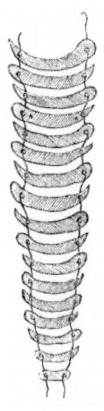

Fig. 122.—Necklace made of Boars' Tusks, longitudinally divided.

In the peat-bogs near Brussels polished flints have likewise been found, associated with animal bones, and two specimens of the human *humerus*, belonging to two individuals.

The peat-bogs of Antwerp, in which were found a human frontal bone, characterised by its great thickness, and its small surface, have also furnished fine specimens of flint knives (fig. 123), which are in no way inferior to the best of those discovered at Grand-Pressigny.

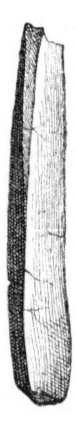

Fig. 123.—Flint Knife, from the Peat-bogs near Antwerp.

On none of the instruments of bone or horn, of which we have been speaking, are to be found the designs which we have described as being the work of man during the reindeer epoch. The artistic instinct seems to have entirely vanished. Perhaps the diluvial catastrophe, which destroyed so many victims, had, as one of its results, the effect of effacing the feeling of art, by forcing men to concentrate their ideas on one sole point—the care of providing for their subsistence and defence.

A quantity of remains, gathered here and there, bear witness to the fact that in the polished-stone epoch the use of pottery was pretty widely spread. Most of the specimens are, as we have said, nothing but attempts of a very rough character, but still they testify to a certain amount of progress. The ornamentation is more delicate and more complicated. We notice the appearance of open-work handles, and projections perforated for the purpose of suspension. In short, there is a perceptible, though but preliminary step made towards the real creations of art.

In the caves of Ariége, MM. Garrigou and Filhol found some remains of ancient pottery of clay provided with handles, although of a shape altogether primitive. Among the fragments of pottery found by these *savants*, there was one which measured 11 inches in height, and must have formed a portion of a vase 20 inches high. This vessel, which was necessarily very heavy, had been hung to cords; this was proved by finding on another portion of the same specimen three holes which had been perforated in it.

Agriculture.—We have certain evidence that man, during the polished-stone epoch, was acquainted with husbandry, or, in other words, that he cultivated cereals. MM. Garrigou and Filhol found in the caves of Ariége more than twenty mill-stones, which could only have been used in grinding corn. These stones are from 8 to 24 inches in diameter.

The tribes, therefore, which, during the polished-stone epoch, inhabited the district now called Ariége, were acquainted with the cultivation of corn.

In 1869, Dr. Foulon-Menard published an article intended to describe a stone found at Penchasteau, near Nantes, in a tomb belonging to the Stone Age.[20] This stone is 24 inches wide, and hollowed out on its upper face. It was evidently used for crushing grain with the help of a stone roller, or merely a round pebble, which was rolled up and down in the cavity. The meal obtained by this pressure and friction made its way down the slope in the hollowing out of the stone, and was caught in a piece of matting, or something of the kind.

To enable our readers to understand the fact that an excavation made in a circular stone formed the earliest corn-mill in these primitive ages, we may mention that, even in our own time, this is the mode of procedure practised among certain savage tribes in order to crush various seeds and corn.

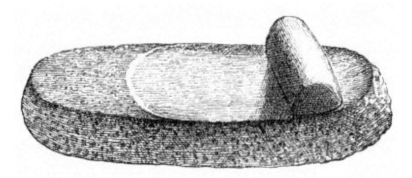

Fig. 124.—Primitive Corn-mill.

In the 'Voyage du Mississippi à l'Océan,' by M. Molhausen, we read:—

"The principal food of the Indians consisted of roasted cakes of maize and wheat, the grains of which had been pulverised *between two stones*."[21]

In Livingstone's Expedition to the Zambesi (Central Africa), it is stated that "the corn-mills of the Mangajas, Makalolos, Landines and other tribes are composed of a block of granite or syenite, sometimes even of mica-schist, 15 to 18 inches square by 5 or 6 inches thick, and a piece of quartz, or some other rock of equal hardness about the size of a half-brick; one of the sides of this substitute for a millstone is convex, so as to fit into a hollow of a trough-like shape made in the large block, which remains motionless. When the woman wants to grind any corn, she kneels down, and, taking in both hands the convex stone, she rubs it up and down in the hollow of the lower stone with a motion similar to that of a baker pressing down his dough and rolling it in front of him. Whilst rubbing it to and fro, the housewife leans all her weight on the smaller stone, and every now and then places a little more corn in the trough. The latter is made sloping, so that the meal as soon as it is made falls down into a cloth fixed to catch it."

Fig. 125.—The Art of Bread-making in the Stone Age.

Such, therefore, was the earliest corn-mill. We shall soon see it reappear in another form; two mill-stones placed one over the other, one being set in motion above the other by means of a wooden handle. This is the corn-mill of the bronze epoch. This type maintained its place down to historic times, as it constituted the earliest kind of mill employed by the Roman agriculturist.

In order to represent the existence of agriculture during the polished-stone epoch, we have annexed a delineation of a woman grinding corn into meal in the primitive mill (fig. 125).

In the same figure may be noticed the way of preparing the meal coming from the mill for making a rough kind of cake. The children are heating in the fire some flat circular stones. When these stones are sufficiently heated, they rapidly withdraw them from the fire, using for the purpose two damp sticks; they then place on the stones a little of the meal mixed with water. The heat of the stones sufficed to bake the meal and form a sort of cake or biscuit.

We may here state, in order to show that we are not dealing with a mere hypothesis, that it is just in this way that, in the poor districts of Tuscany, the *polenta* is prepared even in the present day. The dough made of chestnut-meal, moistened with water, is cooked between flat stones that are placed one over the other in small piles as portrayed in the annexed plate.

In the background of the same sketch we see animals, reduced to the state of domestic cattle, being driven towards the group at work. By this particular feature we have wished to point out that the polished-stone epoch was also that of the domestication of animals, and that even at this early period the sheep, the dog and the horse had been tamed by man, and served him either as auxiliaries or companions.

The traces of agriculture which we have remarked on as existing in the caves of Ariége, are also found in other parts of France. Round the hearths in the department of Puy-de-Dôme, M. Pommerol discovered carbonised wheat intermingled with pottery and flint instruments. The men of the period we are now considering no longer devoted themselves exclusively to the pursuits of hunting and fishing. They now began to exercise the noble profession of agriculture, which was destined to be subsequently the chief source of national wealth.

Navigation.—The first origin of the art of navigation must be ascribed to the polished-stone epoch. With regard to this subject, let us pay attention to what is said on the point by M. G. de Mortillet, curator at the Archæological and Pre-historic Museum of Saint-Germain—one of the best-informed men we have in all questions relating to the antiquity of man.

In M. de Mortillet's opinion, navigation, both marine and inland, was in actual existence during the polished-stone epoch.

Fig. 126.—The earliest Navigators.

The earliest boats that were made by man consisted simply of great trunks of trees, shaped on the outside, and hollowed out in the interior. They were not provided with any rests or rowlocks for the oars or paddles, which were wielded by both hands. In hollowing out the tree they used both their stone implements and also the action of fire.

In the earliest boats, the trunk of the tree, cut through at the two ends as well as their imperfect tools allowed, preserved its original outward form. The boat, in fact, was nothing but the trunk of a tree first burnt out and then chipped on the inside by some cutting instrument, that is, by the stone-hatchet.

Some improvement subsequently took place in making them. The outside of the tree was also chipped, and its two ends, instead of being cut straight through, were made to terminate in a point. In order to give it more stability in the water and to prevent it from capsizing, it was dressed equally all over, and the bottom of the canoe was scooped out. Cross-stays were left in the interior to give the boat more solidity, and perhaps, also, to serve as a support to the back, or, more probably, to the feet of the rowers, who sat in the bottom of the canoe.

Sails must soon have been added to these means of nautical progression. But it would be a difficult matter to fix any precise date for this important discovery, which was the point of transition between elementary and primitive navigation, and more important voyages. This progress could not have been made without the help of metals.

In an article entitled 'Origine de la Navigation et de la Pêche,' M. de Mortillet passes in review all the discoveries, which have been made in different countries, of the earliest boats belonging to pre-historic man.

After stating that the Museum of Copenhagen contains drawings of three ancient canoes, he goes on to say:—

"The first canoe is the half-trunk of a tree 17 inches wide, cut straight at the two ends, about 7 feet in length, and hollowed out in a trough-like shape. This canoe much resembles that of Switzerland.

"The second was about 10 feet in length, one end terminating in a point, the other more rounded. It was formed of the trunk of a tree hollowed out into two compartments, a kind of cross-stay or seat being left at a point about one-third of the length from the widest end.

"The third canoe, No. 295, likewise made of the trunk of a tree, was much longer, having a length of at least 13 feet, and was terminated by a point at both ends. At the sharpest end, the hollow is finished off squarely, and there is also a small triangular seat at the extremity. Two cross-stays were left in the interior.

"These three canoes are classed in the bronze series; a note of interrogation or doubt is, however, affixed to the two latter.

"Ireland, like Scandinavia, has a history which does not go back very far into the remote past; like Scandinavia, too, Ireland has been one of the first to collect with care not only the monuments, but even the slightest relics of remote antiquity and of pre-historic times. The Royal Irish Academy has collected at Dublin a magnificent Museum, and the praiseworthy idea has also been put in practice of publishing a catalogue illustrated with 626 plates.

"In these collections there are three ancient canoes. The first is about 23 feet long, 31 inches wide, and 12 inches deep, and is hollowed out of the trunk of an oak, which must have been at least 4½ feet in diameter. This boat, which came from the bogs of Cahore on the coast of Wexford, is roughly squared underneath. One of the ends is rounded and is slightly raised; the other is cut across at right angles, and closed with a piece let in and fitted into grooves which were caulked with bark. In the interior there are three cross-stays cut out of the solid oak.

"The interior, at the time the canoe was discovered, contained a wooden vessel, intended to bale out the boat, and two rollers, probably meant to assist in conveying it down to the sea.

"The second is a canoe made of one piece of oak, rather more than 23 feet long, about 12 inches wide, and 8 inches deep. It terminates in a point at both ends, and contains three cross-stays cut out of the solid wood, and a small terminal triangular seat.

"The third, likewise made of one piece, is rather more than 20 feet long and about 21 inches wide. On each side the wood is cut out so as to receive a seat. This boat appears less ancient than the others, although these may not have belonged to any very remote antiquity. In fact, Ware states that in his time there were still to be seen on some of the Irish rivers canoes hollowed out of a single trunk of oak.

"It is also well known that the lacustrine habitations constructed on the artificial islands called *Crannoges*, existed to a late period in Ireland. All the boats found round these island-dwellings are canoes made all in one piece and hollowed out of the trunks of large trees.

"The trough-shaped canoe, consisting merely of the trunk of a tree cut straight through at the two ends, and in no way squared on the outside, also exists in Ireland. A very singular variety has been found in the county of Monaghan;[22] at the two ends are two projections or handles, which were probably used for carrying the boat from one place to another, or to draw it up upon the beach after a voyage.

"According to Mr. John Buchanan, quoted by Sir C. Lyell,[23] at least seventeen canoes have been found in the low ground along the margin of the Clyde at Glasgow. Mr. Buchanan examined several of them before they were dug out. Five of them were found buried in the silt under the streets of Glasgow. One canoe was discovered in a vertical position, with the prow upwards, as if it had foundered in a tempest; it contained no small quantity of sea-shells. Twelve other canoes were found about 100 yards from the river, at the average depth of about 19 feet below the surface of the ground, or about 7 feet below high-water mark. A few only of them were found at a depth of no more than 4 or 5 feet, and consequently more than 20 feet above the present level of the sea. One was stuck into the sand at an angle of 45°; another had been turned over and lay keel upwards; the others were in a horizontal position, as if they had sunk in still water.

"Almost every one of these ancient boats had been formed of a single trunk of oak, and hollowed out with some blunt instrument, probably stone hatchets, assisted also by the action of fire. A few of them presented clean-made cuts, evidently produced by a metallic tool. Two of them were constructed of planks. The most elaborate of the number bore the traces of square metal nails, which, however, had entirely disappeared. In one canoe was found a diorite hatchet, and at the bottom of another, a cork bung, which certainly implies relations with southern France, Spain, or Italy.

"The Swiss lakes, with their lacustrine habitations, have furnished numerous specimens of canoes. Dr. Keller, in his fifth Report on Lake-Dwellings (plate X. fig. 23), represents a canoe from Robenhausen; it is the half trunk of a tree 12 feet long and 29 inches wide, hollowed out to a depth of from 6 to 7 inches only. Taking the centre as the widest part, this trunk has been chipped off so as to taper towards the two points which are rounded. It is, however, very probable that the whole of this work was executed with stone implements; for the primitive settlement of Robenhausen, situated in a peat-bog near the small lake Pfæffikon in the canton of Zurich, although very rich in many kinds of objects, has not, up to the present time, furnished us with any metal instruments.

"In his first report (plate IV. fig. 21), Dr. Keller had given the sketch of another canoe which came from the Lake of Bienne. Like the first, mentioned by M. Worsaae, it is the half of the trunk of a tree cut almost straight through, its two ends hollowed out inside in the shape of a trough, the exterior being left entirely unwrought.

"Professor Desor mentions several canoes found in the Lake of Bienne. One of them, near the island Saint-Pierre, was still full of stones. According to M. Desor the builders of the lacustrine habitations during the polished-stone epoch, in order to consolidate the piles which were intended to support their dwellings, were accustomed to bank them up with stones which they fetched in boats from the shore; the bottom of the lake being completely devoid of them. The canoe found at the isle of Saint-Pierre had therefore sunk to the bottom with its cargo, and thus may be dated back to the polished-stone epoch. M. Troyon[24] gives some still more circumstantial details as to this canoe. It is partly buried in the mud at the northern angle of the isle, and is made of a single piece of the trunk of an oak of large dimensions; it is not much less than 49 feet long with a breadth of from 3½ feet to 4 feet.

"M. Desor, in his *Palafittes*, informs us that the Museum of Neuchâtel has lately been enriched by the addition of a canoe which was discovered in the lake; unfortunately, it was dreadfully warped in drying.

"Also M. Troyon, in his 'Habitations Lacustres,' speaks of several canoes at Estavayer and Morges.

"Estavayer is situated on the Lake of Neuchâtel. There are two settlements near it, one of the Stone Age, and one of the bronze age. One canoe is still lying at the bottom of the lake, near these settlements. Another was brought out of the water by the fishermen some years ago; it was about 10 feet in length, and 2 feet in width. The end which had been preserved was cut to a point and slightly turned upwards.

"Morges is on the Lake of Geneva, in the Canton of Vaud. M. Forel discovered there two interesting settlements of the bronze age. Two canoes were found. According to M. Troyon, one of them which had been carried up on to the bank was not long before it was destroyed. It was formed of the trunk of an oak, hollowed out like a basin. The other still lay near some piles in 13 to 15 feet of water. One portion of it is buried in the sand, the other part, which is not covered, measures about 10 feet in length by 2 feet in width. It terminates in a point and has been cut out so as to provide a kind of seat, taken out of the thickness of the wood at the end, just as in the third canoe represented in the catalogue of the Copenhagen Museum.

"In France, too, several canoes have been found which date back to pre-historic times.

"On the 6th of January, 1860, the labourers who were working at the fortifications which the engineers were making at Abbeville found a canoe in the place called Saint-Jean-des-Prés, on the left bank of the canal; it was discovered in the peat, 36 feet below the road and about 220 yards from the railway station. It was made out of a single stick of oak and was about 22 feet in length; its ends were square and cut in a slope, so that its upper surface was 8 feet longer than its bottom, which was flattened off to a width of about 14 inches. The greatest width of its upper surface, the widest part being placed at about one-third of its length, measured nearly 3 feet; from this point the canoe contracted in width, and was not more than 18 inches in width at the furthest end. Now, as no tree exists which diminishes to this extent in diameter on so short a length, we must conclude that the trunk which formed the canoe must have been shaped outside.

"Two projections about 4 inches in thickness, placed 6½ feet from the narrowest end, and forming one piece with the sides and the bottom, which in this part are very thick, left between them an empty space which was probably intended to fit against the two sides of a piece of wood cut square at the bottom and meant to serve as a mast. The deepest internal hollow had not more than 10 inches in rise, and the side, which at the upper part was not more than an inch in thickness, followed the natural curve of the trunk, and united with the much thicker portion at the bottom. This canoe, although it was completely uncovered and still remained in a very good state of preservation, has not been got out from the place in which it lay.

"In 1834, another canoe was discovered at Estrebœuf, 33 feet long, about 21 inches wide, and 18 inches deep. The bottom was flat, the sides cut vertically both within and without, which gave it nearly the shape of a squared trough. In its widest part it bore some signs of having carried a mast. It was conveyed to the Museum at Abbeville and became completely rotten; nothing now is left but shapeless remains.

"The Abbé Cochet relates that between 1788 and 1800, during the excavation of the basin of *La Barre*, at Havre, at 11 feet in depth, a canoe was discovered, more than 44 feet in length, and hollowed out of one trunk of a tree. The two ends were pointed and solid, and the interior was strengthened with curved stays formed out of the solid wood. This canoe was found to be made of elm and was hollowed out to a depth of nearly 4 feet. It was in so good a state of preservation that it bore being carried to a spot behind the engineer's house on the south jetty; but when it was deposited there, it gradually wasted away by the successive action of the rain and sun.

"The same archæologist also mentions another canoe, with a keel of from 16 to 20 feet long, which was discovered in the year 1680, at Montéviliers, in the filled-up ditches known under the name of La Bergue.

"The Archæological Museum of Dijon also contains a canoe found in the gravel in the bed of the Loue, on the boundaries of the department of Jura, between Dôle and Salins. It is made of a single colossal trunk of oak, shaped, in M. Baudot's opinion, by means of fire. Its present length is 17 feet, and its width, 2 feet 4 inches; but it has become much less in the process of drying. Some iron braces which were fixed to keep the wood in position plainly showed that the width had diminished at least 6 inches. In the interior, the traces of two seats or supports, which had been left in the solid wood in order to give strength to the canoe, might be very distinctly seen. The first was about a yard from one end, the other 5½ feet from the other. Both extremities terminate in a point, one end being much sharper and longer than the other.

"At the Museum of Lyons there is a canoe which was found in the gravel of the Rhone, near the bridge of Cordon, in the department of Ain. It is 41 feet in length, and hollowed out of a single trunk of oak tapering off at the two ends. The middle of it is squared, and the interior is strengthened by two braces left in the solid wood.

"Lastly, we must mention the canoe that was dug out of the bed of the Seine in Paris, and presented by M. Forgeais to the Emperor. It is now in the Museum of Saint-Germain. It was made of a single trunk of oak and had been skilfully wrought on the outside, terminating in a point at both ends. This canoe was bedded in the mud and gravel at the extremity of the *Cité*, on the Notre-Dame side. Close by a worked flint was met with, and various bronze weapons; among others, a helmet and several swords were also found. In the beds of rivers objects belonging to different epochs readily get mixed up. This flint appears to have accidentally come thither; the bronze arms, on the contrary, seem to mark the date of the canoe."[25]

We have previously spoken of the *primitive workshop of human industry*, of which, indeed, we gave a design. In contrast to this peaceful picture, we may also give a representation of the evidences which have been preserved even to our own days of the earliest means of attack and defence constituting regular war among nations. War and battles must have doubtless taken their rise almost simultaneously with the origin of humanity itself. The hatred and rivalry which first sprung up between individuals and families—hatred and rivalry which must have existed from all time—gradually extended to tribes, and then to whole nations, and were outwardly expressed in armed invasions, pillage and slaughter. These acts of violence were, in very early days, reduced to a system in the art of war—that terrible expedient from which even modern nations have not been able to escape.

In order to find the still existing evidence of the wars which took place among men in the Stone Age, we must repair to that portion of Europe which is now called Belgium. Yes, even in the Stone Age, at a date far beyond all written record, the people of this district already were in the habit of making war, either among themselves or against other tribes invading them from other lands. This fact is proved by the fortified enclosures, or *entrenched camps*, which have been discovered by MM. Hannour and Himelette. These camps are those of Furfooz, Pont-de-Bonn, Simon, Jemelle, Hastedon, and Poilvache.

All these different camps possess certain characteristics in common. They are generally established on points overhanging valleys, on a mass of rock forming a kind of headland, which is united to the rest of the country by a narrow neck of land. A wide ditch was dug across this narrow tongue of land, and the whole camp was surrounded by a thick wall of stones, simply piled one upon another, without either mortar or cement. At the camp of Hastedon, near Namur, this wall, which was still in a good state of preservation at the time it was described, measured 10 feet in width, and about the same in height. When an attack was made, the defenders, assembled within the enclosure, rained down on their assailants stones torn away from their wall, which thus became at the same time both a defensive and offensive work (fig. 127).

Fig. 127.—The earliest regular Conflicts between Men of the Stone Age; or, the Entrenched Camp of Furfooz.

These entrenched positions were so well chosen that most of them continued to be occupied during the age which followed. We may mention, as an instance, the camp of Poilvache. After having been a Roman citadel it was converted in the middle ages into a strongly fortified castle, which was not destroyed until the fifteenth century.

The camps of Hastedon and Furfooz were likewise utilised by the Romans.

Over the whole inclosure of these ancient camps worked flints and remains of pottery have been found—objects which are sufficient to testify to the former presence of primitive man. The enormous ramparts of these camps also tend to show that pre-historic man must have existed in comparatively numerous associations at the various spots where these works are found.

If we were to enter into a detailed study of the vestiges of the polished-stone epoch existing in the other countries of Europe, we should be led into a repetition of much that we have already stated with regard to the districts now forming France and Belgium. Over a great portion of Europe we should find the same mode of life, the same manners and customs, and the same degree of nascent civilisation. From the scope, therefore, of our present work, we shall not make it our task to take each country into special consideration.

We will content ourselves with stating that the caves of Old Castille in Spain, which were explored by M. Ed. Lartet, have furnished various relics of the reindeer and polished-stone epochs. Also in the provinces of Seville and Badajos, polished hatchets have been found, made for the most part of dioritic rocks.

Numerous vestiges of the same epoch have, too, been discovered in various provinces of Italy.

We give in fig. 128 the sketch of a very remarkable arrow-head found in the province of Civita-Nova (the former kingdom of Naples). It is provided with a short stem with lateral grooves, so as to facilitate the point being fitted into a wooden shaft.

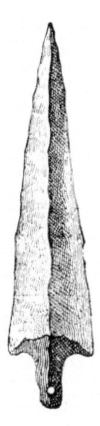

Fig. 128.—Flint Arrow-head, from Civita-Nova (Italy).

Elba, too, was surveyed by M. Raffaello Foresi, who found in this Mediterranean isle a large quantity of arrows, knives, saws, scrapers, &c., formed of flint, jasper, obsidian, and even rock crystal. There were also found in the Isle of Elba workshops for shaping flints. Great Britain, Wurtemburg, Hungary, Poland, and Russia all furnish us with specimens of polished stone instruments; but, for the reason which we stated above, it would be superfluous to dwell upon them.

We shall now pass on to an examination of the type of the human race which existed among the northern nations of Europe during the polished-stone age.

There is a cavern of Ariége which belongs to the polished-stone epoch, and has been explored by MM. Garrigou and Filhol—this is the cavern of *Lombrive*, or *des Echelles*; the latter name being given it because it is divided into two portions placed at such very different levels that the help of five long ladders is required in order to pass from one to the other. This cave has become interesting from the fact that it has furnished a large quantity of human bones, belonging to individuals of both sexes and every age; also two entire skulls, which M. Garrigou has presented to the Anthropological Society of Paris.

These two skulls, which appear to have belonged, one to a child of eight to ten years of age, the other to a female, present a somewhat peculiar shape. The forehead, which is high in the centre, is low at the sides; and the orbits of the eyes and also the hollows of the cheeks are deep.

We shall not enter into the diverse and contrary hypotheses which have been advanced by MM. Vogt, Broca, Pruner-Bey, Garrigou and Filhol, in order to connect the skulls found in the cave of Ariége with the present races of the human species. This ethnological question is very far from having been decided in any uniform way; and so it will always be, as long as scientific men are compelled to base their opinions on a limited number of skulls, which are, moreover, always incomplete; each *savant* being free to interpret their features according to his own system.

Neither in the Danish kitchen-middens nor in the lower beds of the peat-bogs have any human bones been discovered; but the tombs in Denmark belonging to the polished-stone epoch have furnished a few human skulls which, up to a certain point, enable us to estimate the intellectual condition and affinities of the race of men who lived in these climates. We may particularly mention the skull found in the *tumulus* at Borreby in Denmark, which has been studied with extreme care by Mr. Busk.

This skull (fig. 129) presents a somewhat remarkable similarity to that of Neanderthal, of which we have spoken in a previous chapter. The superciliary ridges are very prominent, the forehead is retiring, the occiput is short and sloped forward. It might, therefore, find its origin among the races of which the skulls of Neanderthal and Borreby are the representatives and the relics, and the latter might well be the descendants of the former.

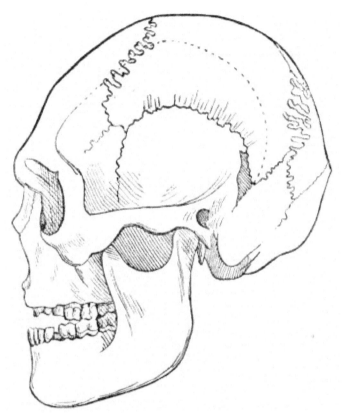

Fig. 129.—The Borreby Skull.

Anthropologists have had much discussion about the question, to what particular human race of the present time may the skulls found in the *tumulus* at Borreby be considered to be allied? But all these discussions are deficient in those elements on which any serious and definite argument might be founded. It would, therefore, be going beyond our purpose should we reproduce them here. If, in the sketch of the Borreby skull, we place, before the eyes of our readers the type of the human cranium which existed during the period of the Stone Age, our only object is to prove that the primitive Northerner resembles the present race of man, both in the beauty and in the regularity of the shape of his skull; also, in order once more to recall to mind how false and trivial must the judgment be of those short-sighted *savants* who would establish a genealogical filiation between man and the ape.

As we stated in the Introduction to this volume, a mere glance cast upon this skull is sufficient to bring to naught all that has been written and propounded touching the organic consanguinity which is asserted to exist between man and the ape, to say nothing of the objects produced by primitive man—objects which, in this work, we are studying in all necessary detail. An examination of the labours of primitive man is the best means of proving—every other consideration being set aside—that a great abyss exists between him and the animal; this is the best argument against our pretended *simial* origin, as it is called by those who seek to veil their absurd ideas under grand scientific phrases.

FOOTNOTES:

[18] 'Note sur un Amas de. Coquilles mélées à des Silex taillés, signalé sur les Côtes de Provence,' by M. A. Gory ('Revue Archéologique'). Quoted in the 'Matériaux de l'histoire positive de l'Homme,' by M. de Mortillet, vol. i. p. 535.

[19] See J. Evans, 'On the Manufacture of Stone Implements in Pre-historic Times,' in Trans. of the International Congress of Pre-historic Archæology (Norwich, 1868), p. 191; and C. Rau, 'Drilling in Stone without Metal,' in Report of Smithsonian Institution, 1868.

[20] 'Les Moulins Primitifs,' Nantes, 1869. Extract from the 'Bulletin de la Société Archéologique de Nantes.'

[21] 'Tour du Monde,' p. 374, 1860.

[22] Shirley's 'Account of the Territory of Farney.'

[23] J. Buchanan, 'British Association Reports,' 1855; p. 80. Sir C. Lyell, 'Antiquity of Man,' p. 48.

[24] 'Habitations Lacustres des Temps anciens et modernes,' pp. 119, 159, 166.

[25] 'Origine de la Navigation et de la Pêche,' pp. 11-21. Paris, 1867.

CHAPTER III.

Tombs and Mode of Interment during the Polished-stone Epoch—*Tumuli* and other sepulchral Monuments formerly called *Celtic*—Labours of MM. Alexandre Bertrand and Bonstetten—Funeral Customs.

HAVING in our previous chapters described and delineated both the weapons and instruments produced by the rudimentary manufacturing skill of man during the polished-stone epoch; having also introduced to notice the types of the human race during this period; we now have to speak of their tombs, their mode of interment, and all the facts connected with their funeral customs.

A fortunate and rather strange circumstance has both facilitated and given a degree of certainty to the information and ideas we are about to lay before our readers. The tombs of the men of the polished-stone epoch—their funeral monuments—have been thoroughly studied, described, and ransacked by archæologists and antiquarians, who for many years past have made them the subject of a multitude of publications and learned dissertations. In fact, these tombs are nothing but the *dolmens*, or the so-called *Celtic* and *Druidical* monuments; but they by no means belong, as has always been thought, to any historical period, that is, to the times of the Celts, for they go back to a much more remote antiquity—the pre-historic period of the polished-stone age.

This explanatory *datum* having been taken into account, we shall now study the *dolmens* and other so-called *megalithic* monuments—the grand relics of an epoch buried in the night of time; those colossal enigmas which impose upon our reason and excite to the very highest pitch the curiosity of men of science.

Dolmens are monuments composed of a great block or slab of rock, more or less flat in their shape according to the country in which they are situate, placed horizontally on a certain number of stones which are reared up perpendicularly to serve as its supports.

Fig. 130.—Danish *Dolmen*.

This kind of sepulchral chamber was usually covered by earth, which formed a hillock over it. But in the course of time this earth often disappeared, leaving nothing but the naked stones of the sepulchral monument.

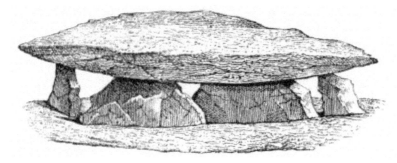

Fig. 131.—*Dolmen* at Assier.

These are the bare stones which have been taken for *stone altars*, being referred to the religious worship of the Gauls. The supposed Druidical altars are, in fact, nothing but ruined *dolmens*. The purpose, therefore, for which they were elevated was not, as has always been stated, to serve as the scene of the sacrifices of a cruel religion; for, at the present day, it is completely proved that the *dolmens* were the tombs of a pre-historic epoch.

These tombs were intended to receive several dead bodies. The corpses were placed in the chamber which was formed by the upper slab and the supports. Some of these chambers had two stages or stories, and then furnished a larger number of sepulchres.

Figs. 132 and 133 represent different *dolmens* which still exist in France.

Fig. 132.—*Dolmen* at Connéré (Marne).

Fig. 133.—Vertical Section of the *Dolmen* of Locmariaker, in Brittany. In the Museum of Saint-Germain.

Some *dolmens* are completely open to view, like that represented in fig. 132, nothing impeding a perfect sight of them; others, on the contrary, are covered with a hillock of earth, the dimensions of which vary according to the size of the monument itself.

This latter kind of *dolmen* more specially assumes the nature of a *tumulus*; a designation which conveys the idea of some mound raised above the tomb.

Figs. 134 and 135 represent the *tumulus-dolmen* existing at Gavr'inis (Oak Island), in Brittany, or, more exactly, in the department of Morbihan. It is the diminished sketch of an enormous model exhibited in the Museum of Saint-Germain. This model in relief has a portion cut off it which, by means of a cord and pulley, can be elevated or lowered at will, thus affording a view of the interior of the *dolmen*. It is composed of a single chamber, leading to which there is a long passage.

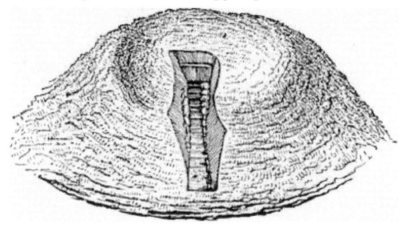

Fig. 134.—*Tumulus-Dolmen* at Gavr'inis (Morbihan).

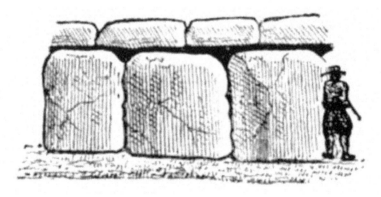

Fig. 135.—A portion of the *Dolmen* of Gavr'inis.

Were all these *dolmens* originally covered by earth? This is a question which still remains unsolved. M. Alexandre Bertrand, Director of the Archæological Museum of Saint-Germain, to whom we owe some very remarkable works on the primitive monuments of ancient Gaul, decides it in the affirmative; whilst M. de Bonstetten, a Swiss archæologist of great merit, is of the contrary opinion. The matter, however, is of no very great importance in itself. It is, at all events, an unquestionable fact that certain *dolmens* which are now uncovered were once buried; for they are noticed to stand in the centre of slightly raised mounds in which the supports are deeply buried. As we before stated, the action of time has destroyed the covering which the pre-historic peoples placed over their sepulchres in order to defend them from the injuries of time and the profanation of man. Thus, all that we now see is the bare stones of the sepulchral chambers— for so long a time supposed to be altars, and ascribed to the religious worship of the Gauls.

Fig. 136.—General Form of a covered Passage-Tomb.

In considering, therefore, the *dolmens* of Brittany, which have been so many times described by antiquarians and made to figure among the number of our historical monuments, we must renounce the idea of looking upon them as symbols of the religion of our ancestors. They can now only be regarded as sepulchral chambers.

Fig. 137.—Passage-Tomb at Bagneux, near Saumur.

Dolmens are very numerous in France; much more numerous, indeed, than is generally thought. It used to be the common idea that they existed only in Brittany, and those curious in such matters wondered at the supposed Druidical altars which were so plentifully distributed in this ancient province of France. But Brittany is far from possessing the exclusive privilege of these megalithic constructions. They are found in fifty-eight of the French departments, belonging, for the most part, to the regions of the south and south-west. The department of Finisterre contains 500 of them; Lot, 500; Morbihan, 250; Ardèche, 155; Aveyron, 125; Dordogne, 100; &c.
[26]

Fig. 138.—Passage-Tomb at Plouharnel (Morbihan).

The authors who have written on the question we are now considering, especially Sir J. Lubbock in his work on 'Pre-historic Times,' and Nilsson, the Swedish archæologist, have given a much too complicated aspect to their descriptions of the tombs of pre-historic ages, owing to their having multiplied the distinctions in this kind of monument. We should only perplex our readers by following these authors into all their divisions. We must, however, give some few details about them.

Fig. 139.—Passage-Tomb; the so-called *Table de César*, at Locmariaker (Morbihan).

Sir J. Lubbock gives the name of *passage grave*, to that which the northern archæologists call *Ganggraben* (tomb with passages); of these we have given four representations (figs. 136, 137, 138, 139), all selected from specimens in France. This name is applied to a passage leading to a more spacious chamber, round which the bodies are ranged. The gallery, formed of enormous slabs of stone placed in succession one after the other, almost always points towards the same point of the compass; in the Scandinavian states, it generally has its opening facing the south or east, never the north.

The same author gives the name of *chambered tumuli* (fig. 140) to tombs which are composed either of a single chamber or of a collection of large chambers, the roofs and walls of which are constructed with stones of immense size, which are again covered up by considerable masses of earth. This kind of tomb is found most frequently in the countries of the north.

Fig. 140 represents, according to Sir J. Lubbock's work, a Danish *chambered tumulus*.

Fig. 140.—A Danish *Tumulus*, or chambered Sepulchre.

Before bringing to a close this description of megalithic monuments, we must say a few words as to *menhirs* and *cromlechs*.

Menhirs (fig. 141) are enormous blocks of rough stone which were set up in the ground in the vicinity of tombs. They were set up either separately, as represented in fig. 141, or in rows, that is, in a circle or in an avenue.

Fig. 141.—Usual shape of a *Menhir*.

There is in Brittany an extremely curious array of stones of this kind; this is the range of *menhirs* of Carnac (fig. 142). The stones are here distributed in eleven parallel lines, over a distance of 1100 yards, and, running along the sea-shore of Brittany, present a very strange appearance.

Fig. 142.—The rows of *Menhirs* at Carnac.

When *menhirs* are arranged in circles, either single or several together, they are called *cromlechs*. They are vast circuits of stones, generally arranged round a *dolmen*. The respect which was considered due to the dead appears to have converted these enclosures into places of pilgrimage, where, on certain days, public assemblies were held. These enclosures are sometimes circular, as in England, sometimes rectangular, as in Germany, and embrace one or more ranks.

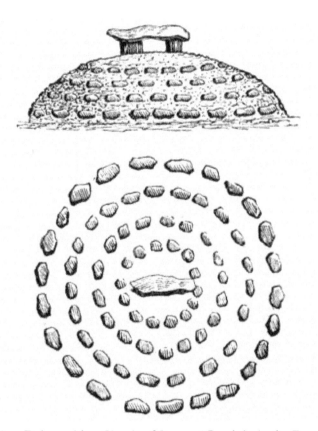

Fig. 143.—*Dolmen* with a Circuit of Stones (*Cromlech*), in the Province of Constantine.

Fig. 143 represents a *dolmen* with a circuit of stones, that is, a *cromlech*, which has been discovered in the province of Constantine; in fig. 144 we have a group of Danish *cromlechs*.

Fig. 144.—Group of Danish *Cromlechs*.

Among all these various monuments the "passage-tombs" and the *tumuli* are the only ones which will come within the scope of this work; for these only have furnished us with any relics of pre-historic times, and have given us any information with respect to the peoples who occupied a great part of Europe at a date far anterior to any traditionary record.

These stone monuments, as we have already stated, are neither Celtic nor Druidical. The Celts—a nation which occupied a portion of Gaul at a period long before the Christian era—were altogether innocent of any megalithic construction. They found these monuments already in existence at the time of their immigration, and, doubtless, looked upon them with as much astonishment as is shown by observers of the present day. Whenever there appeared any advantage in utilising them, the Celts did not fail to avail themselves of them. The priests of this ancient people, the Druids, who plucked from off the oak the sacred mistletoe, performed their religious ceremonies in the depths of some obscure forest. Now, no *dolmen* was ever built in the midst of a forest; all the stone monuments which now exist stand in comparatively unwooded parts of the country. We must, therefore, renounce the ancient and poetical idea which recognised in these *dolmens* the sacrificial altars of the religion of our ancestors.

Some *tumuli* attain proportions which are really colossal. Among these is Silbury Hill, the largest in Great Britain, which is nearly 200 feet high. The enormous amount of labour which would be involved in constructions of this kind has led to the idea that they were not raised except in honour of chiefs and other great personages.

On consulting those records of history which extend back to the most remote antiquity, we arrive at the fact that the custom of raising colossal tombs to the illustrious dead was one that was much in vogue in the ancient Eastern world. Traces of these monuments are found among the Hebrews, the Assyrians, the Greeks, the Egyptians, &c.

Thus Semiramis, Queen of Nineveh, raised a mound over the tomb of Ninus, her husband. Stones were likewise piled up over the remains of Laïus, father of Œdipus. In the 'Iliad,' Homer speaks of the mounds that were raised to the memory of Hector and Patroclus. That dedicated to Patroclus—the pious work of Achilles—was more than 100 feet in diameter. Homer speaks of the *tumuli* existing in Greece, which, even in his time, were considered very ancient, and calls them the tombs of the heroes. A *tumulus* was raised by Alexander the Great over the ashes of his friend Hephæstio, and so great were the dimensions of this monument that it is said to have cost 1200 talents, that is about £240,000 of our money. In Roman history, too, we find instances of the same kind. Lastly, the pyramids of Egypt, those costly and colossal funeral monuments, are the still visible representations of the highest expression of posthumous homage which was rendered by the generations of antiquity to their most illustrious and mighty men.

This, however, could not have been in every case the prevailing idea in the men of the Stone Age, in causing the construction of these *tumuli*. The large number of bodies which have been found in some of these monuments completely does away with the notion that they were raised in honour of a single personage, or even of a single family. They were often sepulchres or burial-places common to the use of all. Among this class we must rank the *tumuli* of Axevalla and of Luttra, situated not far from one another in Sweden. The first, which was opened in 1805, contained twenty tombs of an almost cubical form, each containing a skeleton in a crouching or contracted attitude. When the second was opened, the explorers found themselves in the presence of hundreds of skeletons placed in four rows one upon another, all in a contracted position like those at Axevalla; along with these human remains various relics of the Stone Age were also discovered.

Fig. 145.—Position of Skeletons in a Swedish Tomb of the Stone Age.

Fig. 145 represents the position in which the skeletons were found.

M. Nilsson has propounded the opinion that the "passage-graves" are nothing but former habitations, which had been converted into tombs after the death of those who had previously occupied them. When the master of the house had breathed his last—especially in the case of some illustrious individual—his surviving friends used to place near him various articles of food to provide for his long journey; and also his weapons and other objects which were most precious to him when in life; then the dwelling was closed up, and was only reopened for the purpose of bearing in the remains of his spouse and of his children.

Sir J. Lubbock shares in this opinion, and brings forward facts in its favour. He recites the accounts of various travellers, according to which, the winter-dwellings of certain people in the extreme north bear a very marked resemblance to the "passage-tombs" of the Stone Age. Of this kind are the habitations of the Siberians and the Esquimaux, which are composed of an oval or circular chamber placed a little under the surface of the ground, and completely covered with earth. Sir J. Lubbock thinks, therefore, that in many cases habitations of this kind may have been taken for *tumuli*—a mistake, he adds, all the more likely to be made because some of these mounds, although containing ashes, remains of pottery, and various implements, have not furnished any relics of human bones.

In his work on the 'Sépultures de l'Age de la Pierre chez les Parisii,' M. Leguay, a learned architect and member of the Archælogical Society, has called attention to the fact that the construction of these *dolmens* betrays, as existing in the men of this epoch, a somewhat advanced degree of knowledge of the elements of architecture:—

"The interment of the dead," says M. Leguay, "took place, during the polished-stone epoch, in vaults, or a kind of tomb constructed on the spot, of stones of various thicknesses, generally flat in shape, and not elevated to any very great height, being laid without any kind of cement or mortar. These vaults, which were at first undivided, were subsequently separated into compartments by stones of a similar character, in which compartments bodies were placed in various positions. They were covered with earth or with flat stones, and sometimes we meet with a circular eminence raised over them, formed of a considerable heap of stones which had been subsequently brought thither; this fact was verified by M. Brouillet in 1862 at the *Tombelle de Brioux* (Vienne).

"This kind of interment bears evidence of some real progress. Polished flint instruments are met with intermingled with worked stones which have been brought from a distance. Pottery of a very significant character approaches that of the epoch at which ornamentation commenced; and the *Tombelle de Brioux* has furnished two vessels with projecting and perforated handles formed in the clay itself. I met with specimens similar to these both in shape and workmanship in the cremation-tombs at Villeneuve-Saint-Georges, which, as I have previously stated, appeared to me to be later in date than the simple interment situated below them.

"The first element in the art of construction, that is, stability, is manifested in these latter monuments. They do not come up to the fine *dolmens*, or to the monuments which followed them, but the principle on which stones should be laid together is already arrived at. The slab forming the covering is the first attempt at the lintel, the primitive base of architectural science. By insensible degrees the dimensions of the monument increased, the nature of the materials were modified, and, from the small elementary monument to the grand sepulchral *dolmen*, but one step remained to be made—a giant step, certainly, but not beyond the reach of human intelligence.

"This step, however, was not accomplished suddenly and without transitional stages. We find a proof of this in the beautiful ossuary discovered in 1863, at Chamant near Senlis (Oise), on the property of the Comte de Lavaulx. This monument does not yet come up to the most beautiful of the class; but it possesses all the inspirations which suggested the form of its successors, of which, indeed, it is the type.

"Almost flat slabs of stone, of a greater height than those forming the vaults, and of rather considerable dimensions, are placed on edge so as to form a square chamber. A partition, formed of stones of a similar character, leaving a space or passage between them, separates the chamber into two unequal portions. Some arrangement of this kind has been observed in most of the finest *dolmens*; it is found at a spot not far from Chamant, in a covered way known under the name of the *Pierres Turquoises*, in the forest of Carnelle, near Beaumont-sur-Oise (Seine-et-Oise).

"At Chamant, however, the chamber was not more than 3 to 4 feet in height under the roof, which was formed of large flat stones, and was large enough to allow of a considerable number of bodies to be deposited within it, either in a recumbent or contracted position. Near them there were placed delicately-wrought flints, and also some fine-polished hatchets, one of which was of serpentine; another of large dimensions, sculptured after the fashion of the diluvial hatchets, appeared to me to have been prepared for polishing.

"The researches which have been made have brought to light but slight traces of pottery, and the small fragments that I have examined do not point out any very remote age for this monument. Nevertheless, the investigation of this sepulchre, in which I was guided by a somewhat different idea from that of merely studying the monument itself, was not carried out with the exact care that would be necessary for collecting all the indications which it might have furnished.

"Between the sepulchre of Chamant and the finest *dolmens*, the distinction is nothing more than a question of dimensions rather than any chronological point. The latter are formed of colossal stones, and when one examines them and seeks to realise the process which must have been employed for raising them, the mind is utterly perplexed, and the imagination finds a difficulty in conceiving how it was possible to move these immense masses, and, especially, to place them in the positions they now occupy; for at the present day, in order to arrive at similar results, it would be necessary to employ all the means which science has at command."[27]

The megalithic constructions do not all date back to the same epoch. Some were raised during the Stone Age, others during the Bronze Age. There is nothing in their mode of architecture which will enable us to recognise their degree of antiquity; but the relics which they contain afford us complete information in this respect. Thus, in France, according to M. Alexandre Bertrand, the *dolmens* and the *tumuli-dolmens* contain, in a general way, nothing but stone and bone articles; those of bronze and gold are very rare, and iron is never met with. In the *true tumuli*, on the contrary, bronze objects predominate, and iron is very abundant; this is an evident proof that these monuments are of less ancient origin than the *dolmens*. In the same way we ascertain that the Danish *dolmens* and the great sepulchral chambers of Scandinavia, all belong to the polished-stone epoch. When, therefore, we class the *dolmens* in this last-named epoch of man's history, we are deciding in full harmony with the great body of *data* which bear upon the point.

In order to fix the period with still greater accuracy, we might add that the *dolmens* belong to the latter portion of the polished-stone epoch and the commencement of the bronze age. But, as we before said, we do not attach any importance to these distinctions, which would only uselessly embarrass the mind of the reader.

An examination of the Danish *dolmens* has led the author of the 'Catalogue of Pre-historic Objects sent by Denmark to the Universal Exposition of 1867,' to sum up in the following words the details concerning these sepulchral monuments:—

"As regards the Danish *dolmens*, the number of skeletons contained in them varies much; in the largest, there are as many as twenty, and in the smallest there are not more than five or six; sometimes they are placed in stages one above the other.

"The bones are never found in natural order; the head lies close to the knees, and no limb is in its natural place. It follows from this, that in the course of interment the body was contracted into a crouching position.

"The bottom of the sepulchral chamber of a *dolmen* is generally covered with a layer of flints which have been subjected to fire; this is the floor on which the body was deposited; it was then covered with a thin coating of earth, and the tomb was closed. Yet, as we have just observed, it was but very rarely that *dolmens* contained only one skeleton. They must, therefore, have been opened afresh in order to deposit other bodies. It must have been on these occasions, in order to contend with the miasma of putrefaction, that they lighted the fires, of which numerous and evident traces are seen inside the *dolmens*. This course of action continued, as it appears, until the time when the *dolmen* was entirely filled up: but even then, the tomb does not, in every case, seem to have been abandoned. Sometimes the most ancient skeletons have been displaced to make room for fresh bodies. This had taken place in a *dolmen* near Copenhagen, which was opened and searched in the presence of the late King Frederick VII.

"A *dolmen* situated near the village of Hammer, opened a few years ago by M. Boye, presented some very curious peculiarities. In addition to flint instruments, human bones were discovered, which had also been subjected to the action of fire. We are, therefore, led to suppose, that a funeral banquet had taken place in the vicinity of the tomb, and that some joints of human flesh had formed an addition to the roasted stag. This is, however, the only discovery of the kind which has been made up to the present time, and we should by no means be justified in drawing the inference that the inhabitants of Denmark at this epoch were addicted to cannibalism.

"The dead bodies were deposited along with their weapons and implements, and also with certain vessels which must have contained the food which perhaps some religious usage induced them to leave close to the body. For a long time it was supposed that it was the custom to place these weapons by the side of *men* only. But in a *dolmen* at Gieruen, a hatchet was found near a skeleton which was evidently that of a woman.

"We now give the inventory of a 'find' made in a Danish *dolmen*, that of Hielm, in the Isle of Moen, which was opened in 1853. The sepulchral chamber was 16½ feet in length, 11½ feet in width, and 4½ feet in height.

"In it were discovered twenty-two spear-heads, the largest of which was 11 inches in length, and the smallest 5½ inches; more than forty flint flakes or knives from 2 to 5 inches in length; three flat hatchets, and one rather thicker; three carpenter's chisels, the longest of which measured 8 inches; a finely-made hammer 5 inches long; three flint nuclei exactly similar to those found in the kitchen-middens; and lastly, in addition to all these flint articles, some amber beads and forty earthen vessels moulded by the hand." [28]

What were the funeral customs in use among men during the polished-stone epoch? and what were the ceremonies which took place at that period when they buried their dead? These are questions which it will not be difficult to answer after a due investigation of the *dolmens* and *tumuli*.

In a great number of *tumuli*, animal bones have been found either broken or notched by sharp instruments. This is an indication that the funeral rites were accompanied by feasts just as in the preceding epochs.

The body which was about to be enclosed in the *tumulus* was borne upon boughs of trees, as is the case among some savage tribes of the present day. The men and women attending wore their best attire; necklaces of amber and shells adorned their necks. Men carrying torches walked in front of the procession, in order to guide the bearers into the dark recesses of the sepulchral chambers.

From these data fig. 146 has been designed, which gives a representation of *a funeral ceremony during the polished-stone epoch*.

Fig. 146.—A *Tumulus* of the Polished-stone Epoch.

If we may judge by the calcined human bones which are rather frequently met with in tombs, there is reason to believe that sometimes victims were sacrificed over the body of the defunct, perhaps slaves, perhaps even his widow—the custom of sacrificing the widow still being in practice in certain parts of India.

Sir J. Lubbock is, besides, of opinion that when a woman died in giving birth to a child, or even whilst she was still suckling it, the child was interred alive with her. This hypothesis appears a natural one, when we take into account the great number of cases in which the skeletons of a woman and child have been found together.

M. Leguay in his 'Mémoire sur les Sépultures des Parisii,' which we quoted above, expresses the opinion that after each interment, in addition to the funeral banquet, a fire was lighted on the mound above the *tumulus*, and that each attendant threw certain precious objects into the flames.

The objects which were most precious during the polished-stone epoch were flints wrought into hatchets, poniards, or knives.

"On to this burning hearth," says M. Leguay, "as numerous instances prove, those who were present were in the habit of casting stones, or more generally wrought flints, utensils and instruments, all made either of some kind of stone or of bone; also fragments of pottery, and, doubtless, other objects which the fire has destroyed.

"There are many of these objects which have not suffered any injury from the fire; some of the flints, indeed, seem so freshly cut and are so little altered by the lapse of time, that it might be readily imagined that they had been but recently wrought; these were not placed in the sepulchre, but are met with intermingled with the earth which covers or surrounds the hearth, and appear in many cases to have been cast in after the extinction of the fire as the earth was being filled in.

"Sometimes, indeed, when the archæologist devotes especial care to his digging, he comes across a kind of layer of wrought flints which are, in fact, to be looked upon as refuse rather than wrought articles. Their position appears to indicate the surface of the soil during that epoch, a surface which has been covered up by the successive deposits of subsequent ages; and although some of these flakes may have been due to some of the objects which had been placed in the sepulchre having been chipped on the spot, there are many others which have not originated in this way, and have come from objects which have been deposited in other places.

"All these stones, which are common to three kinds of burial-places, have fulfilled, in my opinion, a votive function; that is to say, that they represent, as regards this epoch, the wreaths and coronals of *immortelles*, or the other objects which we in the present day place upon the tombs of our relations or friends; thus following out a custom the origin of which is lost in the night of time.

"And let not the reader treat with ridicule these ideas, which I hold to be not far from the truth. Men, as individuals, may pass away, and generations may disappear; but they always hand down to their progeny and those that succeed them the customs of their epoch; which customs will undergo little or no change until the causes which have produced them also disappear. Thus it is with all that concerns the ceremonies observed in bearing man to his last resting-place—a duty which can never change, and always brings with it its train of sorrow and regret. Nowadays, a small sum of money is sufficient to give outward expression to our grief; but at these remote epochs each individual fashioned his own offering, chipped his own flint, and bore it himself to the grave of his friend.

"This idea will explain the diversity of shape in the flints placed round and in the sepulchres, and especially the uncouthness of many of the articles which, although all manufactured of the same material, betray a style of workmanship exercised by numerous hands more or less practised in the work.

"It may, however, be readily conceived that during an epoch when stones were the chief material for all useful implements, every wrought flint represented a certain value. To deprive themselves of these objects of value in order to offer them to the manes of the dead was considered a laudable action, just as was the case subsequently as regards still more precious objects; and this custom, which was observed during many long ages, although sometimes and perhaps often practised with the declining energy inherent in every religious custom, was the origin of a practice adopted by many of the nations of antiquity, that, namely, of casting a stone upon the tomb of the dead. Thus were formed those sepulchral heaps of stones called *gal-gals*, some of which still exist.

"It is, without doubt, to this votive idea that we must attribute the fact that so many beautiful objects which ornament our museums have been found deposited in these sepulchres; but we must remark that the large and roughly-hewn hatchets, and also the knives of the second epoch, are replaced, in the third epoch, by polished hatchets often even fitted with handles, and also by knives of much larger size and finer workmanship.

"As an additional corroboration of my ideas, I will mention a curious fact which I ascertained to exist in two sepulchres of this kind which I searched; the significance of this fact can only be explained by a hypothesis which any one may readily develop.

"Each of them contained one long polished hatchet, broken in two in the middle; the other portion of which was not found in the sepulchre.

"One is now in the Museum at Cluny, where I deposited it; the other is still in my own possession. It is beyond all dispute that they were thus broken at the time of the interment.

"Numerous hatchets broken in a similar way have been found by M. A. Forgeais in the bed of the Seine at Paris, and also in various other spots; all of them were broken in the middle, and I have always been of opinion that they proceeded from sepulchres of a like kind, which, having been placed on the edge of the river, had been washed away by the flow of water which during long ages had eaten away the banks."

At a subsequent period, that is, during the bronze epoch, dead bodies were often, as we shall see, reduced to ashes either wholly or in part, and the ashes were enclosed in urns.

FOOTNOTES:

[26] Alexandre Bertrand's 'Les Monuments Primitifs de la Gaule.'

[27] 'Des Sépultures à l'Age de la Pierre,' pp. 15, 16. 1865.

[28] 'Le Danemark à l'Exposition Universelle de 1867.' Paris. 1868.

THE AGE OF METALS.

I.
THE BRONZE EPOCH.

CHAPTER I.

The Discovery of Metals—Various Reasons suggested for explaining the Origin of Bronze in the West—The Invention of Bronze—A Foundry during the Bronze Epoch—Permanent and Itinerant Foundries existing during the Bronze Epoch—Did the knowledge of Metals take its rise in Europe owing to the Progress of Civilisation, or was it a Foreign Importation?

THE acquisition and employment of metals is one of the greatest facts in our social history. Thenard, the chemist, has asserted that we may judge of the state of civilisation of any nation by the degree of perfection at which it has arrived in the workmanship of iron. Looking at the matter in a more general point of view, we may safely say that if man had never become acquainted with metals he would have remained for ever in his originally savage state.

There can be no doubt that the free use of, or privation from, metals is a question of life and death for any nation. When we take into account the important part that is played by metals in all modern communities, we cannot fail to be convinced that, without metals civilisation would have been impossible. That astonishing scientific and industrial movement which this nineteenth century presents to us in its most remarkable form—the material comfort which existing generations are enjoying—all our mechanical appliances, manufactures of such diverse kinds, books and arts—not one of all these benefits for man, in the absence of metals, could ever have come into existence. Without the help of metal, man would have been condemned to live in great discomfort; but, aided by this irresistible lever, his powers have been increased a hundredfold, and man's empire has been gradually extended over the whole of nature.

In all probability, gold, among all the metals, is the first with which man became acquainted. Gold, in a metallic state, is drifted down by the waters of many a river, and its glittering brightness would naturally point it out to primitive peoples. Savages are like children; they love everything that shines brightly. Gold, therefore, must, in very early days, have found its way into the possession of the primitive inhabitants of our globe.

Gold is still often met with in the Ural mountains; and thence, perhaps, it originally spread all over the north of Europe. The streams and the rivers of some of the central countries of Europe, such as Switzerland, France, and Germany, might also have furnished a small quantity.

After gold, copper must have been the next metal which attracted the attention of men; in the first place, because this metal is sometimes found in a native state, and also because cupriferous ores, and especially copper pyrites, are very widely distributed. Nevertheless, the extraction of copper from the ores is an operation of such a delicate character, that it must have been beyond the reach of the metallurgic appliances at the disposal of men during the early pre-historic period.

The knowledge of tin also dates back to a very high antiquity. Still, although men might become acquainted with tin ores, a long interval must have elapsed before they could have succeeded in extracting the pure metal.

Silver did not become known to men until a much later date; for this metal is very seldom met with in the *tumuli* of the bronze epoch. The fact is, that silver is seldom found in a pure state, and scarcely ever except in combination with lead ores; lead, however, was not known until after iron.

Bronze, as every one knows, is an alloy of copper and tin (nine parts of copper and one of tin). Now it is precisely this alloy, namely bronze, which was the first metallic substance used in Europe; indeed the sole substance used, to the exclusion of copper. We have, therefore, to explain the somewhat singular circumstance that an alloy and not a pure metal was the metallic substance that was earliest used in Europe; and we must also inquire how it was that bronze could have been composed by the nations which succeeded those of the polished-stone epoch.

At first sight, it might appear strange that an alloy like bronze should have been the first metallic substance used by man, thus setting aside iron, deposits of which are very plentiful in Europe. But it is to be remarked, in the first place, that iron ores do not attract the attention so much as those of tin and copper. Added to this, the extraction of iron from its ores is one of the most difficult operations of the kind. When dealing with ferruginous ores, the first operation produces nothing more than rough cast iron—a very impure substance, which is so short and brittle that it possesses scarcely any metallic qualities, and differs but little from stone as regards any use it could be applied to. It requires re-heating and hammering to bring it into the condition of malleable iron. On the other hand, by simply smelting together copper and tin ores and adding a little charcoal, bronze might be at once produced, without any necessity for previously extracting and obtaining pure copper and tin in a separate state. This will explain how it came to pass that the earliest metal-workers produced bronze at one operation, without even being acquainted with the separate metals which enter into its composition.

We are left entirely to hypothesis in endeavouring to realise to ourselves how men were led to mix together copper and tin ores, and thus to produce bronze—a hard, durable and fusible alloy, and consequently well adapted, without much trouble, for the fabrication, by melting in moulds, of hatchets, poniards, and swords, as well as agricultural and mechanical instruments.

Bronze was endowed with all the most admirable qualities for aiding the nascent industrial skill of mankind. It is more fusible than copper and is also harder than this metal; indeed, in the latter respect, it may compete with iron. It is a curious fact that bronze has the peculiarity of hardening when cooled gradually. If it is made red-hot in the fire and is then suddenly cooled by plunging it into water, the metal becomes more ductile and may be easily hammered; but it regains its original hardness if it is again heated red-hot and then allowed to cool slowly. This, as we see, is just the contrary to the properties of steel.

By taking advantage of this quality of bronze they were enabled to hammer it, and, after the necessary work with the hammer was finished, they could, by means of gradual cooling, restore the metal to its original hardness. At the present day, cymbals and tom-toms are made exactly in this way.

All these considerations will perhaps sufficiently explain to the reader why the use of bronze preceded that of iron among all the European and Asiatic peoples.

On this quasi-absence of manufactured copper in the pre-historic monuments of Europe, certain archæologists have relied when propounding the opinion that bronze was brought into Europe by a people coming from the East, a more advanced and civilised people, who had already passed through their *copper age*, that is, had known and made use of pure copper. This people, it is said, violently invaded Europe, and in almost every district took the place of the primitive population; so that, in every country, bronze suddenly succeeded stone for the manufacture of instruments, weapons and implements.

By the side of these *savants*, who represent to some extent, in ethnological questions, the partisans of the great geological cataclysms or revolutions of the globe, there are others who would refer the appearance of bronze in Europe to a great extension of commercial relations. They utterly reject the idea of any conquest, of any great invasion having brought with it a complete change in manners, customs, and processes of industrial skill. In their opinion, it was commerce which first brought bronze from the East and introduced it to the men of the West. This is the view of Sir Cornewall Lewis, the archæologist and statesman, and also of Prof. Nilsson, who attributes to the Phœnicians the importation of bronze into Europe.

Without attaining any great result, Nilsson has taken much trouble in supporting this idea by acceptable proofs. We are called upon to agree with the Danish archæologist in admitting that the Phœnicians, that is, the inhabitants of Tyre and Sidon went *with their ships* to procure tin from Great Britain, in order to make an alloy with it in their own country, which alloy they subsequently imported into Europe.

This is nothing but historic fancy. To this romance of archæology we shall oppose the simple explanation which chemistry suggests to us. Our belief is that the bronze was fabricated on the spot by the very people who made use of it. All that was requisite in order to obtain bronze, was to mix and smelt together the ores of oxidised copper or copper pyrites, and tin ore, adding a small quantity of charcoal. Now, copper ore abounds in Europe; that of tin is certainly rare; and it is this rarity of tin ore which is appealed to in support of the conjecture against which we are contending. But, although tin ores are nowadays rare in Europe, except in England and Saxony, they are, nevertheless, to be met with in the centre and south of the Continent; and, doubtless, in the early ages of mankind the quantities were quite sufficient to supply the slender requirements of the dawning efforts of industrial skill. We may, perhaps, be permitted to allege that the cause of the supplies of tin ores being so poor in the centre and south of Europe, may be the fact that they were exhausted by the workings of our ancestors. Thus, at least, many of the deposits of copper, silver, and lead, have been exhausted by the Romans, and we now find nothing more than the mere remains of mines which were once very productive.

We may easily see that, in order to account for the presence of bronze in Europe during the primitive epochs of mankind, it was not necessary to build up such a framework of hypothesis as Prof. Nilsson has so elaborately raised.

To sum up the whole matter, we may say that the use of bronze preceded that of iron in the primitive industry of Europe and Asia; and that the people of our hemisphere were acquainted with bronze before they came to the knowledge of pure copper and tin; this is all that we can safely assert on the point.

It might of course have been the case that copper and tin were first used alone, and that the idea was subsequently entertained of combining the two metals so as to improve both. But the facts evidently show that, so far as regards Europe, things did not take place in this way, and that bronze was employed in the works of primitive industry before copper and tin were known as existing in a separate state.[29]

We must, however, state that in the New World the matter was different. The Indians of North America, long before they knew anything about bronze, were in the habit of hammering the copper which was procured from the mines of Lake Superior, and of making of it weapons, ornaments and implements.

After considering these general and theoretical points, we shall now pass on to the history of the employment of bronze among men of pre-historic ages, and shall endeavour to give some description of their works for the manufacture of metals.

Facts handed down by tradition evidently show that, among the peoples both of Europe and Asia, the use of bronze preceded that of iron.

Homer tells us that the soldiers of the Greek and Trojan armies were provided with iron weapons, yet he reserves for the heroes weapons made of bronze. It seems that bronze being the most ancient, was therefore looked upon as the more noble metal; hence, its use is reserved for chiefs or great warriors. Among all nations, that which is the most ancient is ever the most honourable and the most sacred. Thus, to mention one instance only, the Jews of our own times still perform the ceremony of circumcision with a knife made of stone. In this case, the stone-knife is an object consecrated by religion, because the antiquity of this instrument is actually lost in the night of time.

Bronze (or brass) is often mentioned in the Book of Genesis. Tubal-cain, the first metal-worker of the Scriptures, who forged iron for all kinds of purposes, also wrought in bronze (or brass). This alloy was devoted to the production of objects of ornament.

We read in the First Book of Kings (vii. 13, 14), "And King Solomon sent and fetched Hiram out of Tyre. He was a widow's son of the tribe of Naphtali, and his father was a man of Tyre, a worker in brass: and he was filled with wisdom, and understanding, and cunning to work all works in *brass*."

The word *brass* must be here understood as being synonymous with bronze, and certainly the Hebrew term had this signification.

As a specially remarkable object of bronze work, we may mention the "sea of brass" of the Hebrews, which contained 3000 measures of water.

Herodotus[30] speaks of another colossal basin made of bronze, which was sixty times the size of that which Pausanias, son of Cleobrontos, presented to the temple of Jupiter Orios, a temple which had been built near the Euxine, on the borders of Scythia. Its capacity was six hundred *amphoræ*, and it was six "fingers" in thickness. The Greeks used to employ these enormous basins in their religious ceremonies.

In Sweden and Norway, large receptacles of a similar kind were in primitive ages employed in sacrificial ceremonies; they used to receive the blood which flowed from the slaughtered animals.

In order to produce objects of this magnitude it was of course necessary to have at disposal large foundries of bronze. These foundries, which existed during historic periods, were preceded by others of less importance used during the pre-historic epochs which we are considering, that is, during the bronze epoch.

Vestiges of these ancient foundries have been discovered in Switzerland, at Devaine, near Thonon, and at Walflinger, near Wintherthur; especially also at Echallens, where objects have been found which evidently originated from the working of some pre-historic foundry.

At Morges, in Switzerland, a stone mould has been discovered, intended for casting hatchets. By running bronze into this ancient mould, a hatchet has been made exactly similar to some of those in our collections.

The casting was also effected in moulds of sand, which is the more usual and more easy plan.

From these *data*, it is possible to imagine what sort of place a foundry must have been during the bronze epoch.

In the production of bronze, they used to mix oxydated tin ore, in the proportions which experience had taught them, with oxydated copper ore or copper pyrites; to this mixture was added a small quantity of charcoal. The whole was placed in an earthen vessel in the midst of a burning furnace. The two oxides were reduced to a metallic state by means of the charcoal; the copper and tin being set free, blended and formed bronze.

When the alloy was obtained, all that was necessary was to dip it out and pour it into sand or stone moulds which had been previously arranged for the purpose.

The art of casting in bronze must have played a very essential part among primitive peoples. There was no instrument that they used which could not be made by casting it in bronze. The sword-blades were thus made; and, in order to harden the edge of the weapon, it was first heated and then cooled suddenly, being afterwards hammered with a stone hammer.

In fig. 147, we represent the workshop of a caster in bronze during the epoch we are considering. The alloy, having been previously mixed, has been smelted in a furnace, and a workman is pouring it into a sand-mould. Another man is examining a sword-blade which has just been cast.

Fig. 147.—A Founder's Workshop during the Bronze Epoch.

Bronze being precious, it is probable that in these ancient communities bronze weapons and implements were reserved for rich and powerful personages, and that stone weapons remained the attribute of the common people. The use of bronze could only become general after the lapse of time.

The high value of bronze would lead to its being economised as much as possible. The Pre-historic Museum at Copenhagen contains unquestionable proofs of this scarcity of the metal, and the means which were used for obviating it. Among the bronze hatchets in the Museum of Copenhagen, there are some which could only have served as ornaments, for they contained a nucleus of clay, and the metal of which they were composed was not thicker than a sheet of paper.

We must also add that worn-out instruments of bronze and utensils which were out of use were carefully preserved in order to be re-cast; the same material re-appearing in various forms and shapes.

We have just given a representation of the *workshop of a founder of bronze*; but we must also state that in addition to these fixed establishments there must have existed, at the epoch of which we are speaking, certain itinerant founders who travelled about, carrying all their necessary utensils on their backs, and offered their services wherever they were required.

Every one is acquainted with the travelling-tinkers who, at the present day, make their way down from the mountains of Auvergne, the Black Forest, the Alps, or the Cévennes, and are called *péirerous* and *estama-brazaïres* in the south of France, and *épingliers* in other districts. These men are in the habit of working at separate jobs in the villages and even in the public places of the towns. Of course they travel with no more of the utensils of their craft than strict necessity requires; but, nevertheless, what they carry is sufficient for every purpose. A hollow made in the ground is the furnace in which they place the nozzle of their portable bellows, and they hammer the iron on a small anvil fixed in the earth.

Aided by these merely rudimentary means they execute pieces of metal-work, the dimensions of which are really surprising. They make nails and tacks, and even worm screws, repair locks, clean clocks, make knives, mend skimmers, and restore umbrella-frames. They make bronze rings out of republican *décimes*, and sell these popular trinkets to the village beauties.

Incomparable in their line of business, these men are unequalled in patching or re-tinning vessels made of tin and wrought or sheet-iron. The mending of crockeryware also forms one of their numerous vocations; and the repairing of a broken plate by means of an iron rivet is mere play-work for their dexterous fingers. But melting down and re-casting—these are the real triumphs of their art. The village housewife brings to them her worn-out pewter vessel, and soon sees it reappear as a new, brilliant, and polished utensil. Lamps, cans, covers, and tin-plates and dishes are thus made to reappear in all their primitive brightness.

The fusion and casting of bronze does not perplex them any more than working in tin. They are in the habit of casting various utensils in brass or bronze, such as candlesticks, bells, brackets, &c. The crucible which they use in melting brass is nothing but a hole dug in the earth and filled up with burning charcoal, the fire being kept up with the help of their bellows, the nozzle of which is lengthened so as to open into the middle of the charcoal. On this furnace they place their portable crucible, which is a kind of earthen ladle provided with a handle.

Their system of casting is simple in the extreme. The pressed sand, which serves them for a mould, is procured from the ditch at the side of the road. Into this mould they pour the alloy out of the very crucible in which it has been melted.

These itinerant metallurgists, these *estama-brazaïres*, who may be noticed working in the villages of Lower Languedoc, whose ways we have just depicted (not without some degree of pleasant reminiscence), are nothing but the descendants of the travelling metal-workers of the pre-historic bronze epoch. In addition to the permanent establishment of this kind—the foundries, the remains of which have been found in Switzerland, the French Jura, Germany and Denmark, there certainly existed at that time certain workmen who travelled about singly, from place to place, exercising their trade. Their stock of tools, like the objects which they had to make or repair, was of a very simple character; the sand from the wayside formed their moulds, and their fuel was the dry wood of the forest.

The existence, at this remote epoch in the history of mankind, of the itinerant workers in metal is proved by the fact, that practitioners of this kind were known in the earliest *historic* periods who had already to some extent become proficients in the art. Moses, the Hebrew lawgiver, was able in the wilderness to make a brazen serpent, the sight of which healed the Israelites who had been bitten by venomous snakes; and, during the retirement of the prophet to Mount Sinai, Aaron seemed to find no difficulty in casting the golden calf, which was required of him by the murmurs of the people. Itinerant founders must therefore have accompanied the Jewish army.

We have been compelled to dwell to some extent on the general considerations which bear upon the introduction of bronze among the ancient inhabitants of Europe who succeeded the men of the Stone Age. In the chapters which follow we intend as far as possible to trace out the picture of that period of man's history, which is called *the Bronze Epoch*, and constitutes the first division of *the Age of Metals*.

FOOTNOTES:

[29] It must, however, be observed that the author's theory does not agree with the opinion of metallurgists, who do not consider the reduction of mixed copper and tin ore a practically effective process, and would favour the more usual view that the metals were smelted separately, and afterwards fused together to form bronze.—(*Note to Eng. Trans.*)

[30] Book iv. p. 81.

CHAPTER II.

The Sources of Information at our Disposal for reconstructing the History of the Bronze Epoch—The Lacustrine Settlements of Switzerland—Enumeration and Classification of them—Their Mode of Construction—Workmanship and Position of the Piles—Shape and Size of the Huts—Population—Instruments of Stone, Bone, and Stag's Horn—Pottery—Clothing—Food—*Fauna*—Domestic Animals.

IN endeavouring to trace out the early history of the human race we naturally turn our attention to all the means of investigation which either study or chance have placed at our disposal. Grottos and caves, the rock-shelters, the ancient camps, the centres of flint-working, the Scandinavian kitchen-middens, the *dolmens*, and the *tumuli*—all have lent their aid in affording those elements for the representation of the earliest epoch of the history of primitive man which we have already considered. The data which we shall resort to for delineating the bronze epoch will be of a different kind.

Among all the sources of authentic information as to the manners and customs of man in his earliest existence, none, certainly, are more curious than those ancient remains which have lately been brought to light and explored, and have received the name of *lacustrine dwellings*.

The question may be asked, what are these *lacustrine dwellings*, and in what way do they serve to elucidate the history of the bronze epoch? These are just the points which we are about to explain.

The most important discoveries have often depended on very slight causes. This assertion, although it has been made common by frequent repetition, is none the less perfectly correct. To what do we owe the knowledge of a multitude of curious details as to pre-historic peoples? To an accidental and unusual depression of the temperature in Switzerland. But we will explain.

The winter of 1853-1854 was, in Switzerland, so dry and cold that the waters of the lakes fell far below their ordinary level. The inhabitants of Meilen, a place situated on the banks of the Lake of Zurich, took advantage of this circumstance, and gained from the lake a tract of ground, which they set to work to raise and surround with banks.

In carrying out these works they found in the mud at the bottom of the lake a number of piles, some thrown down and others still upright, fragments of rough pottery, bone and stone instruments, and various other relics similar to those found in the Danish peat-bogs.

This extraordinary accumulation of objects of all kinds on the dried bed of the lake appeared altogether inexplicable, and every one was at fault in their remarks; but Dr. Keller of Zurich, having examined the objects, at once came to a right understanding as to their signification. It was evident to him that they belonged to pre-historic times. By an association of ideas which no one had previously dreamt of, he perceived that a relation existed between the piles and the other relics discovered in the vicinity, and saw clearly that both dated back to the same epoch. He thus came to the conclusion, that the ancient inhabitants of the Lake of Zurich were in the habit of constructing dwellings over the water, and that the same custom must have existed as regards the other Swiss lakes.

This idea was developed by Dr. Keller in five very remarkable memoirs, which were published in German.[31]

This discovery was the spark which lighted up a torch destined to dissipate the darkness which hung over a long-protracted and little-known period of man's history.

Previous to the discovery made on the dried-up bed of the Lake of Zurich, various instruments and singular utensils had been obtained from the mud of some of the lakes of Switzerland, and piles had often been noticed standing up in the depth of the water; but no one had been able to investigate these vestiges of another age, or had had any idea of ascribing to them anything like the remote antiquity which has since been recognised as belonging to them. To Dr. Keller the honour is due of having interpreted these facts in their real bearing, at a time when every one else looked upon them as nothing but objects of curiosity. It is, therefore, only just to pronounce the physician of Zurich to have been the first originator of pre-historic archæological science in Switzerland.

In 1854, after the publication of Dr. Keller's first article, the Swiss lakes were explored with much energy, and it was not long before numerous traces of human settlements were discovered. At the present day more than 200 are known, and every year fresh ones are being found.[32]

Thanks to the activity which has been shown by a great number of observers, magnificent collections have been formed of these archæological treasures. The fishermen of the lakes have been acquainted, for many years back, with the sites of some of these settlements, in consequence of having, on many occasions, torn their nets on the piles sticking up in the mud. Numerous questions were asked them, and they were taken as guides to the different spots, and ere long a whole system of civilisation, heretofore unknown, emerged from the beds of the Swiss lakes.

Among the lakes which have furnished the largest quantity of relics of pre-historic ages, we may mention that of Neuchâtel, in which, in 1867, no less than forty-six settlements were counted; in Lake Constance (thirty-two settlements); in the Lake of Geneva (twenty-four settlements); in the Lake of Bienne, canton of Berne (twenty settlements); in the Lake of Morat, canton of Fribourg (eight settlements).

Next come several other lakes of less importance. The Lake of Zurich (three settlements); the Lake of Pfæffikon, canton of Zurich (four settlements); the Lake of Sempach, canton of Lucerne (four settlements); the Lake of Moosseedorf, canton of Berne (two settlements); the Lake of Inkwyl, near Soleure (one settlement); the Lake of Nussbaumen, canton of Thurgau (one settlement); the Lake of Zug, &c.

Pile-work has also been discovered in former lakes now transformed into peat-bogs. We must place in this class the peat-bog of Wauwyl, canton of Lucerne (five settlements).

We will mention, in the last place, the settlement at the bridge of Thièle, on the water-course which unites the lakes of Bienne and Neuchâtel. This settlement must once have formed a portion of the Lake of Bienne, at the time when the latter extended as far as the bridge of Thièle.

The lacustrine villages of Switzerland do not all belong to the same period. The nature of the remains that they contain indubitably prove that some are far more ancient than others. The vestiges have been discovered of three successive epochs—the polished-stone epoch and the epochs of bronze and of iron.

The lacustrine settlements of Switzerland, when considered under the heads of the various pre-historical epochs to which they belong, may be divided in the following way:—

The Stone Age:—The Lake of Constance (about thirty settlements); the Lake of Neuchâtel (twelve settlements); the Lake of Geneva (two settlements); the Lake of Morat (one settlement); the lakes of Bienne, Zurich, Pfæffikon, Inkwyl, Moosseedorf, Nussbaumen, Wanger, &c.; the settlements of Saint-Aubin and Concise, the peat-bog of Wauwyl, and the settlement at the Bridge of Thièle.

The Bronze Epoch:—The Lake of Geneva (twenty settlements); the Lake of Neuchâtel (twenty-five settlements); the Lake of Bienne (ten settlements); also the lakes of Morat and Sempach.

The Iron Epoch:—The lakes of Neuchâtel and Bienne.

It may appear strange that the primitive inhabitants of Switzerland should have preferred aquatic dwellings to habitations built on *terra firma*, which could certainly have been constructed much more easily. Further on in our work we shall have something to say as to the advantages which men might derive from such a peculiar arrangement of their dwellings; but we may now remark that this custom was somewhat prevalent among the earliest inhabitants of Europe. Ancient history furnishes us with several instances of it. Herodotus, speaking of the Pæonians, of the Lake Prasias, in Thrace, says:—

"Their habitations are built in the following way. On long piles, sunk into the bottom of the lake, planks are placed, forming a floor; a narrow bridge is the means of access to them. These piles used to be fixed by the inhabitants at their joint expense; but afterwards it was settled that each man should bring three from Mount Orbelus for every woman whom he married. Plurality of wives, be it observed, was permitted in this country. On these planks each has his hut with a trap-door down into the lake; and lest any of their children should fall through this opening they took care to attach a cord to their feet. They used to feed their horses and beasts of burden on fish. In this lake fish was so abundant that if a basket was let down through the trap-door it might be drawn up a short time afterwards filled with fish."

Sir J. Lubbock, repeating the statement of one of his friends who resides at Salonica, asserts that the fishermen of the Lake Prasias still inhabit wooden huts built over the water, as in the time of Herodotus. There is nothing improbable in this, since the town of Tcherkask in Russia is constructed in a similar way over the River Don, and Venice itself is nothing but a lacustrine city built during historic times over a lagune of the Adriatic sea.

We may add that even in modern times this custom of building villages on piles still exists in some parts of the world. According to the evidence of Dampier and Dumont d'Urville, habitations built on piles are to be met with in New Guinea, Celebes, Ceram, Mindanao, the Caroline Islands, &c. The city of Borneo is, indeed, entirely built on this plan. In some of the isles of the Pacific Ocean there are several tribes of savages who likewise make their dwellings over water. The Indians of Venezuela have adopted this custom with the sole intention of sheltering themselves from the mosquitoes.

It is quite permissible to suppose that the need for security was the motive which induced the ancient inhabitants of Switzerland, and other countries, thus to make settlements and live upon the lakes. Surrounded as they were by vast marshes and impenetrable forests, they lived in dread of the attacks of numerous wild beasts. They therefore taxed their ingenuity to insure their safety as far as they possibly could, and no means appeared more efficacious than that of surrounding themselves with water. At a subsequent period, when men commenced to make war against one another, these aquatic habitations became still more valuable. They then constituted something in the nature of camps or fortification in which, being well-protected from all danger of sudden surprise, the people of the country could defy the efforts of their enemies.

We must, however, add, that in more recent times these buildings on piles were—according to M. Desor—used only as storehouses for utensils and provisions; the actual dwellings for men being built on *terra firma*.

These lacustrine dwellings are designated under various names by different authors. Dr. Keller, who was the first to describe them, gave them in German the name of *pfahlbauten* (buildings on piles) which the Italians have translated by the word *palafitta*. This latter appellation, when gallicized by M. Desor, becomes *palafitte*. Lastly, the name *ténevières* or *steinbergs* (mountains of stone) is given to constructions of a peculiar character in which the piles are kept up by masses of stone which have been brought to the spot. By Dr. Keller, this latter kind are called *packwerkbauten*.

When we examine as a whole the character of the lacustrine settlements which have hitherto been discovered, it may, in fact, be perceived that those who built them proceeded on two different systems of construction; either, they buried the piles very deeply in the bed of the lake, and on these piles placed the platform which was to support their huts; or, they artificially raised the bed of the lake by means of heaps of stones, fixing in these heaps somewhat large stakes, not so much for the purpose of supporting the habitations themselves as with a view of making the heaps of stones a firm and compact body.

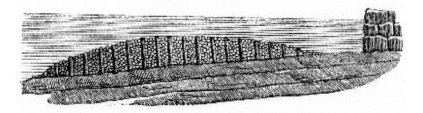

Fig. 148.—Section of the *Ténevière* of Hauterive.

This latter mode of construction is represented in fig. 148, taken from a design given by M. Desor in his remarkable work 'Les Palafittes.'[33]

One or the other of these modes of construction was employed according to the nature of the bed of the lake. In lakes with a muddy bottom, the first plan could be easily employed; but when the bed was rocky, it was necessary to have recourse to the second. This is the reason why on the northern shore of the Lake of Neuchâtel, where the banks of limestone come very close to the surface, a comparatively large number of *ténevières* may be observed.

These are the facts as generally noticed, especially in wide and deep lakes; the edifice, however, was not always constructed in this mode. In marshes and small lakes, which have now become peat-bogs, another system was frequently applied, a remarkable instance of which is furnished by the peat-moss at Wauwyl. In this locality were found several quadrangular spaces very distinctly enclosed by piles, between which were raised as many as five platforms one above the other. These piles are naturally very long, and some are buried as much as seven feet in the solid ground—an operation which must have required an enormous amount of labour. The intervals between the platforms are filled up with boughs of trees and clay, and the floors themselves are made in nearly the same way as those we have before mentioned. The lowest rested directly on the bed of the lake, and on the upper one the huts were placed.

It is sometimes the case that these heaps of stones rise above the water; they then form perfect artificial islands, and the habitations which covered them are no longer, properly speaking, dwellings on piles. Of this kind is the station on the Lake of Inkwyl in Switzerland; of this kind, also, are the *crannoges* of Ireland, of which we shall subsequently make special mention. Some of these artificial islands have braved the destructive action of ages, and are still inhabited at the present time. M. Desor mentions the Isle of Roses in the Lake of Starnberg (Bavaria) which has never been known to have been unfrequented by man; it now contains a royal residence.

Let us revert to the mode of construction of the aquatic dwellings of Switzerland.

In all probability the stones used were conveyed to the required spot by means of canoes made of hollowed-out trunks of trees. Several of these canoes may still be seen at the bottom of Lake Bienne, and one, indeed, is still laden with pebbles, which leads us to think that it must have foundered with its cargo. But it is very difficult to raise these canoes from the bottom, and it is, besides, probable that when exposed to the open air they would fall to dust. Nevertheless, one of them is exhibited in the Museum at Neuchâtel.

In the Museum at Saint-Germain there is a canoe very similar to that of Neuchâtel. It is made out of the trunk of a hollow tree. A second canoe, very like the first, but with the bark still on it, and in a bad state of preservation, lies in the entry of the same Museum of Saint-Germain. It was taken out of the Seine, as we stated when speaking in a previous chapter of the first discovery of the art of navigation during the Stone Age.

It may very easily be explained how the constructors went to work in felling the trees and converting them into piles. M. Desor has remarked that the pieces of wood composing the piles are cut cleanly through round their circumference only; the central part shows inequalities just like those which are noticed when a stick is broken in two by the hand after having been cut into all round the outside. The builders of the lacustrine villages, therefore, when they wanted to fell a tree must have acted much as follows: having cut all round it to a depth of 3 or 4 inches, they fixed a cord to the top, and broke the tree down by forcibly pulling at the upper part. They then cut it through in the same way with stone or bronze hatchets, giving it the requisite length, hewing it into a point at one end so that it should more easily penetrate the mud. Sometimes a fire applied to the base of the tree prepared for, and facilitated, the effect of the sharp instruments used. A great number of the piles that have been found still bear the marks of the fire and the cuts made by stone hatchets. In constructing the *ténevières*, the labour of pointing the piles was needless, as the latter were thoroughly wedged in by the accumulation of stones of which we gave a representation in fig. 148.

When the piles were prepared, they had to be floated to the spot fixed upon for the village, and to be fixed in the bed of the lake. If we consider that, in many cases, the length of these piles reached to as much as 16 or 20 feet, some idea may be formed of the difficulty of an undertaking of this kind. In the construction of the *ténevières* much thicker piles were used, and the labour was much less difficult. For instance, in the more ancient *ténevières* of the Lake of Neuchâtel piles are found made of whole trunks of trees which measure 10 to 12 inches in diameter.

The mind is almost confused when it endeavours to sum up the amount of energy and strong will which the primitive population of Switzerland must have bestowed on constructing, unaided as they were by metal implements, the earliest lacustrine settlements, some of which are of very considerable extent. The settlement of Morges, one of the largest in the Lake of Geneva, is not less than 71,000 square yards in area. That of Chabrey, in the Lake of Neuchâtel, measures about 60,000 square yards; another, in the same lake, 48,000 yards; and, lastly, a third, that of La Tène, 36,000 yards. There are many others which are smaller, although of respectable dimensions.

The number of piles which must have been used in some of these constructions is really surprising. M. Löhle has calculated that in the single lacustrine village of Wangen, in the Lake of Constance, at least 40,000 piles have been fixed, and that several generations must have been necessary to terminate the work. The more reasonable interpretation to give to a fact of this kind is that Wangen, which was very thinly populated at first, increased in size gradually as the numbers of inhabitants augmented. The same remark may be doubtless applied to all the important stations.

This was the plan employed in building a single habitation. When a whole village had to be built in the open water, a methodical course of action was adopted. They began by placing a certain number of piles parallel to the shore, and these they at once threw across the bridge which was intended to connect the village with the land, thus rendering the carriage of the materials much less difficult.

When the bridge was finished, and before fixing all the piles, the platform was commenced immediately; this constituted a base of operations, by the help of which the pile work could more easily be finished.

This platform was raised 3 or 4 feet above the surface of the water, so as to obviate any danger arising from the waves during a tempest. It was generally composed of branches and trunks of trees not squared, and bound horizontally to each other, the whole cemented together with clay; sometimes, also, they used thick rough slabs, which were obtained by splitting trunks of trees with wedges. The platform was fixed firmly on the pile-work, and in some cases wooden pegs were used to fasten together the largest pieces of timber, so that the cohesion and incorporation of the floor were rendered more complete. As soon as the esplanade was finished, they then proceeded to the construction of the huts.

The huts must have opened on to the platform by doors. Did they possess windows? Nothing is known as to this point. But in all probability there was an opening at the top of the roof, through which the smoke of the fire made its way. To avoid any fear of conflagration, a stone fire-place was placed in the middle of each dwelling. The daylight must have come in through the hole in the roof in a quantity almost sufficient to cause the absence of windows to be not much felt.

In each habitation, there was, no doubt, a trap-door in direct communication with the lake, such as those which existed in the dwellings of the Pæonians described by Herodotus. Under this trap-door there was a reservoir made of osiers, intended for the preservation of fish.

As the inhabitants of the lacustrine villages only lived upon the water with a view of increasing their security, it would be absurd to suppose that they would construct a large number of bridges between their aquatic settlement and the banks of the lake. There must have been, in general, but one bridge for each of these lake villages.

How were the huts constructed, and what were their shape and dimensions? These questions certainly seem difficult to answer, for, as may be well imagined, no specimen of these ancient dwellings has been preserved to our days. Nevertheless, a few relics, insignificant in appearance, enable us to reply to these inquiries in a way more or less satisfactory.

Everything seems to indicate that the huts were formed of trunks of trees placed upright, one by the side of the other, and bound together horizontally by interwoven branches. A coating of earth covered this wattling.

It has been fancied, from the imprint left by some of the branches which were used in building these huts, that it might be inferred that they were circular, like those which historians attribute to the ancient Gauls. This was Troyon's opinion, and at first Dr. Keller's also. This author has even sketched a circular hut in a plate representing a restored lacustrine habitation, which accompanies one of his memoirs. Sir C. Lyell, also, has reproduced this same plate in the frontispiece of his work on the 'Antiquity of Man.' But Dr. Keller has subsequently abandoned this idea, and in another of his memoirs he has supplied a fresh design showing nothing but huts with flat or sloping roofs.

From this latter plate, taken from Dr. Keller's work, we here give a representation of a Swiss lacustrine village (fig. 149).

Fig. 149—A Swiss Lake Village of the Bronze Epoch.

The suggestions for this reconstructive sketch were furnished to Dr. Keller not only by various scientific indications, but also and especially by a drawing made by Dumont d'Urville among the Papuans of New Guinea.

According to Dr. Keller, during the last century there still existed on the river Limmat, near Zurich, some fishermen's huts built in a similar way to those of the lacustrine villages.

What might have been the population of one of these settlements? This estimate M. Troyon endeavoured to make—an undertaking of a very interesting nature. He adopted as the base of his calculations the lacustrine village of Morges (Lake of Geneva), which, as we have already stated, had an area of 71,000 square yards. Allowing that only one-half of this area was occupied by huts, the other half being reserved for gangways between the dwellings, and assuming an average diameter of 16 feet for each hut, M. Troyon reckoned the number of dwellings in the pre-historic village of Morges at 311. Next, supposing that four individuals lived in each hut, the total amount of population he arrived at was 1244 inhabitants.

We might very justly be surprised if men of the bronze epoch, who were provided with metallic weapons, and were consequently in a much better position for resisting any violent attack, had continued to dwell exclusively in the midst of the water, and should not, to some extent, have dispersed over *terra firma*, which is man's natural standing-ground. It was, therefore, nothing more than might have been expected, when the discovery was made of the relics of dwellings upon land, containing remains of the bronze epoch. This discovery, in fact, took place, and those investigating the subject came to the conclusion that the valleys of Switzerland, as well as the lakes, were occupied during this period by an industrious and agricultural people.

At Ebersberg, canton of Zurich, there was discovered—which is a very curious fact—the remains of an ancient settlement situated on *terra firma*, and containing utensils similar to those found in the lacustrine settlements. In 1864, Dr. Clement searched several mounds composed of pebbles bearing the traces of fire; these mounds were situated in the neighbourhood of Gorgier (canton of Neuchâtel). One of these mounds has furnished various objects of bronze intermingled with fragments of charcoal, especially a bracelet and some sickles characterised by a projection or set-off at the spring of the blade.

On the plateau of Granges (canton of Soleure), Dr. Schild studied a certain spot which he considers to be the site of an ancient bronze foundry; for, besides finding there pebbles and calcined earth, he also discovered a number of reaping-hooks made with a shoulder, and also a fragment of a sword and four finely-made knives.

A hatchet-knife was likewise found in the gorge of the Seyon, near Neuchâtel; and a bracelet in the vicinity of Morges (canton of Geneva).

Some other bracelets, accompanied by calcined human bones, were discovered near Sion, in the Valais.

Lastly, M. Thioly obtained from a cave of Mont Salève, near Geneva, numerous fragments of pottery of the bronze epoch; and in a grotto on the banks of the Reuse, in the canton of Neuchâtel, M. Otz found relics of pottery of very fine clay, along with a quantity of bones.

Thus the people of this epoch did not dwell exclusively in settlements made over the water. They also were in the habit of building habitations on *terra firma*, and of furnishing them with everything which was necessary for existence.

All the facts which have been observed in Switzerland may, doubtless, be applied generally; and it may be said that during the bronze epoch the nature of man's habitation became decidedly fixed. The caves of the great bear and mammoth period, and the rock-shelters of the reindeer and polished-stone periods were now succeeded by dwelling-places which differ but little from those of the more civilised peoples who commence the era of historic times.

FOOTNOTES:

[31] 'Pfahlbauten,' Zurich, 1854-1856.

[32] Various distinguished *savants* have taken upon themselves the task of making known to the public the results of these unceasing investigations, and of bringing before the eyes of the present generation the ancient civilisation of the Swiss valleys. Among the works which have best attained this end, we must mention Troyon's 'Habitations Lacustres des Temps anciens et modernes,' Morlot's 'Etudes Géologico-archéologiques en Danemark et en Suisse,' and M. Desor's 'Palafittes, ou Constructions Lacustres du Lac de Neuchâtel.' These works, which have been translated into various languages, contain a statement of all the archæological discoveries which have been made in Switzerland.

[33] 'Les Palafittes, ou Constructions Lacustres du Lac de Neuchâtel.' Paris, 1865.

CHAPTER III.

Lacustrine Habitations of Upper Italy, Bavaria, Carinthia and Carniola, Pomerania, France, and England—The *Crannoges* of Ireland.

IT was difficult to believe that Switzerland alone possessed the monopoly of these pile-work-constructions. It was certainly to be supposed that the southern slopes of the Alps, which were all dotted over with large and beautiful lakes, must likewise contain constructions of a similar character; this, at least, was M. Desor's opinion. After the numerous pre-historic discoveries which had been made in Switzerland, the Zurich professor proceeded in 1860 to explore the lakes of Lombardy, being well convinced that there too he should find remains of lacustrine habitations.

The hopes he had formed were not deceived. Ere long, in fact, M. Desor obtained from the peat-bogs round Lake Maggiore piles and other objects similar to those found in the Swiss lakes. These researches were continued by MM. Gastaldi and Moro, who discovered in the peat-bogs round this lake several ancient villages built upon piles.

In the Lake of Varese, also in Lombardy, which was examined in 1863 by MM. Desor, G. de Mortillet, and the Abbé Stoppani, were discovered five settlements, some of which were of the Stone Age. Subsequently, the Abbé Ranchet pointed out four others, which raise to the number of nine the pile works found in this lake. In order to render due honour to MM. Keller and Desor, who have contributed so much to the investigation and popularity of lacustrine antiquities, the Abbé Stoppani gave the name of these *savants* to two of the settlements.

One of these isles is very curious, as it is inhabited up to the present day. It is called *Isoletta* ("small island"), and the Litta family possess a *château* upon it.

In the peat-mosses of Brianza, a portion of Lombardy situated to the north of Milan, the remains of lacustrine constructions have been discovered, together with bones, fragments of pottery, pieces of charcoal, and carbonised stone; also weapons, both of bronze and flint.

The Lake of Garda has been searched over by various explorers, who have discovered in it the sites of several lacustrine habitations. The authors of these discoveries are Dr. Alberti, of Verona, and MM. Kosterlitz and Silber, two Austrian officers, who presented all the objects which they collected to the antiquarian museums of Vienna and Zurich. The traces of pile-works were first perceived when the works were in progress which were excavated by the Austrians in 1855 round the fortress of Peschiera; which proves, at least, that fortresses may occasionally serve some useful purpose.

A settlement of the Stone Age, which was examined by M. Paolo Lioy, is situated in a small lake in Venetia, the length of which does not exceed half a mile, and the depth 30 feet; we allude to the Lake of Fimon, near Vicenza. M. Lioy discovered oaken piles partially charred, which proves that the village had at one time been burnt down; also slabs of timber roughly squared, a canoe hollowed out of a trunk of oak, cakes of clay which had come from the sides of huts, and still bore the imprint of the reed-stalks, and no doubt formed a kind of coating inside the huts; various instruments made of bone, flint, sandstone, granite, and stag's horn; rings or spindle-weights made of burnt earth, numerous fragments of rough pottery, merely dried in the sun, and, among all these remains, a dozen entire vessels.

There were also found stores of acorns, nuts, and water-chestnuts, the fruit of the sorb-tree, some sloe-stones, &c. A large quantity of animal bones certified to the existence of the bison, the stag, the wild boar, the fox, and several other doubtful species. All the long bones were broken, as is usually the case, for the extraction of the marrow, but not with the ordinary regularity; they had merely been cracked by blows with stones.

The investigation of lacustrine antiquities which had been inaugurated in Switzerland could hardly stop short in its path of progress. Attempts were made to discover *palafittes* in other countries, and these attempts met with success.

Thanks to the initiative action taken by M. Desor, and the liberality of the Bavarian Government, pile-works of ancient date have been discovered in six of the Bavarian lakes. Most of them go back to the Stone Age, but some belong to the bronze epoch. Among the latter we may mention the *Isle of Roses*, in the Lake of Starnberg, which is, in fact, an artificial island, like the Isoletta in the Lake of Varese. We have previously stated that this island has never ceased to be inhabited, and that a *château* now exists on it.

The movement spread from one place to another. Austria made it a point of honour not to remain in the rear of Bavaria, and Professor Hochstetter was commissioned by the Academy of Sciences at Vienna to undertake a search for *palafittes* in the lakes of Carinthia and Carniola.

These explorations were not without result. In four lakes of Carinthia, Dr. Hochstetter discovered piles, remains of pottery, bones, nuts, &c. In the Lake of Reutschach, which was the most closely investigated, he discovered shallows formed by stones, similar to the *steinbergs* of Switzerland. The marshes of Laybach have also furnished instruments of stag's horn, a perforated stone, and a canoe.

Next to Austria, Prussia took the matter up. Specimens of pile-work were discovered in several provinces of this kingdom; among these were Brandenburg and Pomerania, a district rich in marshes. In the environs of Lubtow the lacustrine constructions have the same characteristics as those of Robenhausen, on the Lake of Pfæffikon (Switzerland). Two distinct archæological strata may be distinguished; in the lower are found, all mingled together, bronze and stone instruments, fragments of pottery, wheat, barley, and charred peas; the upper stratum belongs to the iron age.

We have not as yet said anything about France; lacustrine dwellings have, however, been discovered in some of the departments which border on Switzerland.

The Lakes of Bourget and Annecy, in Savoy, contain several of them. The former of these lakes was thoroughly explored by M. Laurent Rabut, author of an article on the 'Habitations Lacustres de la Savoie,' which obtained a silver medal at the competition of the learned societies in 1863. In the Lake of Bourget, M. Rabut ascertained the existence of five or six settlements of the bronze epoch, three of which, those of Tresserve, Grésine and Châtillon, have been distinguished as furnishing numerous ancient relics.

The Lake of Paladru (Isère) which has been searched by M. Gustave Vallier, has afforded similar results. Pile-works are thought to exist in some other small lakes in the same district—those of Sainte-Hélène, on the left bank of the Isère, Saint-Martin-de-Belville, and Saint-Marcel, near Moutiers. Pile-works have also been discovered on the site of an ancient lake on the banks of the Saône; and in a totally different district, at the foot of the Pyrenees, as many as five have been pointed out.

Everything therefore leads us to believe that if we searched with care the peat-mosses and pools which are very common in a good many of the French departments, we should discover the vestiges of various pre-historic epochs.

In order to complete the enumeration of the lacustrine constructions of Europe, we may state that they have been found in Denmark in the Lake of Maribo, and in England in the county of Norfolk.

With these constructions we must also connect the *crannoges* or artificial islands of Ireland, the first of which was discovered in 1836 by Sir W. R. Wilde, a member of the Royal Academy of Dublin. Since this date various investigations have been made of these objects, and, at the present time, no less than fifty *crannoges* have been discovered, distributed among the various counties of Ireland.

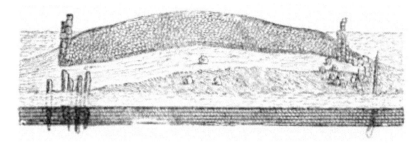

Fig. 150.—Vertical Section of a *Crannoge* in the Ardakillin Lake.

Most of these islets were composed of heaps of stones held together by piles, nearly in the same way as in the *ténevières* in Switzerland; but the *crannoges* differ from the latter in being raised above the water. Some of them, however, are formed by a collection of vertical piles and horizontal joists, constituting an external inclosure, and even internal compartments, inside which all kinds of remains were collected. This kind are called *stockaded* islands. They are generally of an oval or circular shape, and their dimensions are always kept within rather narrow limits. In his work on 'Prehistoric Times,' Sir John Lubbock gives the above sketch of a *crannoge* in the Ardakillin Lake.

Captain Mudge, of the Royal British Navy, has described a hut which he found at a depth of 16 feet, in the Drumkellin marsh. Its area was about 5 feet square, and its height 10 feet; it included two stories, each about 4½ feet high. The roof was flat, and the hut was surrounded by a fence of piles, doubtless intended to separate it from other adjacent huts, the remains of which are still to be perceived. The whole construction had been executed by means of stone instruments, a fact that was proved by the nature of the cuts that were still visible on some of the pieces of wood. Added to this, a hatchet, a chisel, and an arrow-head, all made of flint, were found on the floor of the cabin, and left no doubt whatever on this point. This, therefore, was in fact a habitation belonging to the Stone Age. Some nuts and a large quantity of broken shells were scattered over the ground. A large flat stone, perforated with a little hole in the middle, was found on the spot; it was probably used to break the nuts by means of round pebbles picked up outside.

From some of these settlements considerable masses of bones have been obtained, which have, alas, been utilised as manure. Sir John Lubbock tells us that the *crannoge* of Dunshauglin alone has furnished more than 150 cartloads of bones. These bones belong to the following species:—the ox, the pig, the goat, the sheep, the horse, the ass, the dog, the fox, the roe, the fallow-deer, and the great Irish stag, now extinct. If all other proof were wanting, the presence of the remains of this latter animal would be sufficient to indicate that certain *crannoges* date back to the Stone Age; but as in this case we evidently have to do with the polished-stone epoch, it is also proved that the gigantic antlered stag existed in Ireland at a much later date than on the continent.

Various historical records testify to the fact, that the *crannoges* were inhabited up to the end of the sixteenth century. They then constituted a kind of fortress, in which petty chiefs braved for a long time the royal power. After the definitive pacification of the country they were completely abandoned.

CHAPTER IV.

Palustrine Habitations or Marsh-Villages—Surveys made by MM. Strobel and Pigorini of the *Terramares* of Tuscany—The *Terramares* of Brazil.

HAVING described the *lacustrine* habitations which have been discovered in various parts of Europe, we must now mention the so-called *palustrine* habitations, as peculiar to the bronze epoch. This name has been given to that kind of village, the remains of which have been discovered round marshes and pools. Upper Italy is the locality in which these settlements have been pointed out.

The name of *palustrine settlements*, or *marnieras*, has been given to the sites of ancient villages established by means of piles on marshes or pools of no great size, which in the course of time have been filled up by mould of a peaty character, containing a quantity of organic and other *detritus*.

The discovery of those *palustrine settlements* is due to MM. Strobel and Pigorini, who have designated them by the name of *terramares*.

This term is applied by these *savants* to the accumulation of ashes, charcoal, animal bones, and remains of all kinds which have been thrown away by man all round his dwellings, and have accumulated there during the lapse of centuries. The name which has been given them was derived from the fact that they furnish a kind of earthy ammoniacal manure, known in the district by the name of *terra mare*.

These accumulations are the representatives of the Danish kitchen-middens; but with this difference, that instead of dating back to the Stone Age, the former belong to the bronze epoch.

Terramares are numerous in the districts of Parma and Modena; they are, however, almost entirely confined to the plain which extends between the Po, the Apennines, the Adda, and the Reno, forming an area of about 60 miles long, and 30 miles wide. In a general way, they form small mounds which rise from 6 to 12 feet above the level of the plain; as they go down some depth in the ground, their total thickness is in some places as much as 20 feet. Very few are seen having an area exceeding 9 acres.

Excavations which have been made in several spots enable a tolerably exact account to be given of the mode of construction adopted in these palustrine settlements. The *marniera* of Castione, in particular, has furnished us with valuable information on this point; and we shall describe this settlement as a type of the rest. Piles from 6 to 10 feet in length, and 4 to 6 inches in diameter (fig. 151), formed of trunks of trees, either whole or split, and pointed at the ends by some rough tool, were sunk to the depth of some inches in the bed of the hollow. Some of them still show on their tops the marks of the blows that they received when they were driven in. They were placed at intervals of from 18 inches to 6 feet; and connecting-beams from 6 to 10 feet in length, placed horizontally, and crossing one another, bound the piles together, and insured the solidity of the whole construction. On these cross-beams rested a floor (fig. 152) formed of joists 1 to 3 inches thick, 6 to 12 inches wide, and 5 to 7 feet long.

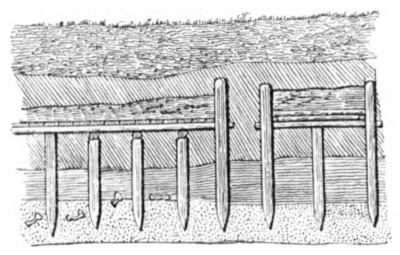

Fig. 151.—Vertical Section of the *Marniera* of Castione.

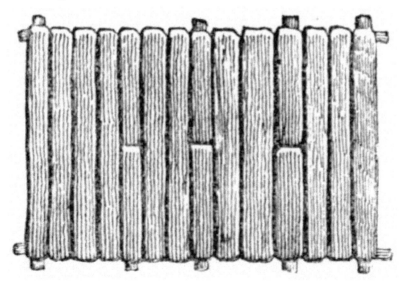

Fig. 152.—Floor of the *Marniera* of Castione.

Fig. 153 gives the plan of the tie-beams and piles of the *marniera* of Castione, taken from the author's work.[34] These slabs or joists were not fixed in any way; at least, no trace now exists of any fastening. They seemed to have been provided by splitting trunks of trees by means of wooden wedges, a number of these wedges having been found in the peaty earth. Neither the saw nor the gimlet appear to have been employed; but the square holes have been cut out by means of the chisel. The timber that was used was principally ash and oak.

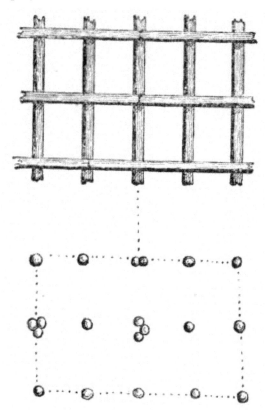

Fig. 153.—Plan of the Piles and Cross-beams in the *Marniera* of Castione.

The floor was covered with beaten earth to a thickness of 10 to 12 inches. Fragments of this kind of paving were found scattered about in two sandy heaps, almost entirely devoid of other *débris*, whilst the adjacent earth, of a blackish colour, contained a large quantity of relics of all kinds. It is probable that the huts of the inhabitants of the *marniera* were situated upon these sandy heaps, and that the dark-coloured earth is the final result of the accumulation of refuse and various kinds of *detritus* on the same spot.

It is not known whether the layer of beaten earth extended over the whole surface of the floor, or was confined to the interior of the habitations. In the former case, it is probable that it was rammed down with less care on the outside than on the inside of the huts, as is shown by the discovery of a storehouse for corn, the floor of which is formed by nothing but a layer of sandy earth placed upon the planks. This storehouse, which, from the use to which it was put, could not have been used as a dwelling by any one, measured 13 feet in length, and 10 feet in width. It contained carbonised beans and wheat, spread in a layer of about 4 inches thick.

MM. Strobel and Pigorini found no remains of huts in the *marniera* of Castione: probably because, having been built entirely of wood, they were completely destroyed by fire, numerous traces of which may still be detected. In addition to the carbonised corn and fruit already mentioned, many other objects bearing the evident marks of fire were, in fact, collected at Castione. The floor-slabs, the tie-beams, and the tops of the piles were often found to be half consumed.

But although at Castione there is no evidence forthcoming in respect to huts, information which bears upon this point has been obtained at other spots. MM. Strobel and Pigorini have ascertained that the palustrine dwellings bore a great similarity to those on the Swiss lakes. The sides were lined with boughs, and the interior was daubed with clay. In Italy, just as in Switzerland, certain fragments of the clayey coating which have been hardened and preserved by fire have enabled us to draw these inferences.

At Castione several beds of ashes and charcoal containing remains of meals, pointed out the sites of the domestic hearths, round which they, doubtless, assembled to eat their food. Another bed of charcoal, mixed with straw, wheat, and pieces of burnt pottery, was found in a peculiar situation—it was embedded in a bank of calcareous pebbles vitrified on the surface; this bank was about 5 feet wide, and about 8 inches in thickness. The explorers thought that it was, perhaps, a place which had been devoted to the fusion of metals.

On the edge of the basin of the marsh, a kind of rampart or defensive work was discovered, composed of slabs as much as 16 feet in length, laid horizontally one over the other. These slabs were tied down by stakes driven in obliquely, and likewise placed one above the other, their ends being inserted between the slabs.

This last discovery, added to other indications, led MM. Strobel and Pigorini to the supposition that the pile-work of Castione, and doubtless also those in all the *marnieras*, were in the first place constructed as places of defence, and were subsequently converted into fixed and permanent residences. The basin of the marsh having been gradually filled up by the accumulations of *débris* resulting from the presence of man, the habitations were built on a solid foundation, and a great portion of the former floor was done away with, which would account for so little of it now remaining.

The objects discovered in the *terramares* and *marnieras* do not essentially differ from those found in the pile-works of Switzerland. They are almost all worn or broken, just as might be expected from finding them in rubbish heaps. There are a great quantity of fragments of pottery of a greyish or dark-coloured clay mixed with grains of quartz, imperfectly baked, and made without the aid of a potter's wheel. The ornamentation is, in general, of a very simple character, but the shapes of the ears, or handles, are very varied. Some of the vessels are furnished with a spout or holes for the liquid to flow out. The *terramares* also contain supports for vessels with round or pointed bottoms.

In the *marniera* of San Ambrogio a slab of pottery was found, elliptical in shape, and about half an inch in thickness, concave on one side and convex on the other, and pierced with seventeen circular holes about a quarter of an inch in diameter. The idea was entertained that this object was used as a kind of fire-grating, for it bore traces of the long-continued action of fire.

The other objects most commonly found were weights made of baked earth, and perhaps used for the weaving-loom, much worn in the place where the cord passed through on which they were hung; *fusaiolas*, or spindle-whorls, very varied both in shape and size, likewise made of baked earth; large mill-stones with a polished surface. Next, we have poniards or spear-heads, hatchets, and hair-pins, all made of bronze. The *marniera* of San Ambrogio has furnished a mould indicating that bronze was melted and cast in this district.

An attentive study of the bones of animals contained in the *terramares* has led to the following information being obtained as to the *fauna* of Upper Italy during the bronze epoch.

With respect to the mammals which lived in a wild state, the existence has been ascertained of a species of stag of much greater size than the present variety, and about equal to that of the lacustrine settlements of Switzerland (fig. 154); also of a wild-boar, much more powerful than that of Sardinia or even of Algeria, the roe, the bear, the rat, and the porcupine. In different spots have been found stags' horns and bones, and also sloe-stones which have retained the impression of the teeth of some small rodent. The bear, the wild-boar, the stag and the roe, have, at the present day, disappeared from the country. The porcupine, too, has migrated into regions further south, which leads to the supposition that the temperature of the provinces of Parma and Modena is a little lowered since the date of the bronze epoch.

Fig. 154.—The Chase during the Bronze Epoch.

It is to be remarked that in these settlements, contrary to what has been noticed in Switzerland, in the lacustrine habitations belonging to the Stone Age, the remains of wild animals are met with much more rarely than those of domestic animals; this must be consequent on a superior and more advanced stage of civilisation having existed in Italy. Among the domestic species found we may mention the dog, two breeds of which, of different sizes, must have existed; the pig of the peat-bogs, the same variety as that of which the bones were discovered in Switzerland; the horse, the remains of which, although rare, testify to the existence of two breeds, one large and bulky, the other of slighter and more elegant proportions; the ass, of which there are but few bones, could not, therefore, have been very common; the ox, the remains of which are on the contrary very abundant, like the dog and the horse, is represented by two distinct breeds, the more powerful of which appears to have descended from the *Bos primigenius* or *Urus*; lastly, the sheep and the goat, the remains of which can scarcely be clearly distinguished on account of their great anatomical resemblance.

When we compare the present *fauna* with that of which we have just given the details, we may perceive several important modifications. Thus the pig of the peat-bogs, one breed of oxen, and a breed of sheep (the smallest) have become entirely extinct; and the common sheep, the goat, the horse, and the ass have assumed much more important dimensions. With regard to the wild species of mammals, we have already said that some have become less in size, and others have disappeared. Hence results one proof of a fact which is beyond dispute, although often called in question, namely, that the intelligent action of man working by means of domestication on wild natures, will ultimately succeed in ameliorating, reclaiming, and perfecting them.

The skulls and the long bones found in the *terramares* are almost always broken for the purpose of extracting the brain and the marrow, a very ancient usage which had endured to this comparatively late epoch. But instead of being split longitudinally, as was the case in preceding epochs, they are generally broken across at one end. The *terramares* and the *kitchen-middens* have this peculiarity in common—that all the dogs' skulls found in them have been intentionally broken; a fact which proves that in Italy, as in Denmark, this faithful guest or servant of man was occasionally, in default of some better food, and doubtless with much regret, used as an article of subsistence.

No remains of fish have been found in these *marnieras*; from this, MM. Strobel and Pigorini have justly concluded that the inhabitants of these pile-works were not fishermen, and that, at all events, the water which surrounded them was shallow and of limited extent.

The species of birds, molluscs and insects, the remains of which have been found in the *terramares*, are likewise determined. The existence of the domestic fowl and the duck, no doubt living in complete liberty, has been duly recognised; but it is thought that the appearance of these species must not be dated further back than the *end* of the bronze epoch, and perhaps even the beginning of that of iron.

The examination of the insect remains has enabled us to ascertain that the refuse food and rubbish must have lain for some little time in front of the doors of the habitations before it was pushed into the water; for in it, flies, and other insects of the kind, found time to be born, to mature, and to undergo their whole series of metamorphoses; a fact which is proved by the perforated and empty envelopes of their chrysalides.

We mention this last fact as one of the most curious instances of the results which science and inference may, in combination, arrive at when devoted to the novel and interesting study of some of the earlier stages in man's existence. But, on the other hand, it gives us but a poor idea of the cleanliness of the Italian race during the bronze epoch. It would seem to us that a feeling of the dignity inherent in the body of man, and the cares that it so imperiously claims, would have been now more strongly developed than at a period when men dwelt confined in caves. This, however, is not the case. But have we, in the present day, any right to be astonished when we see, even now, the prevalence, in some of the great cities of America, of certain practices so disgusting in character and so opposed to the public health? Osculati, an Italian traveller, relates that at all the street corners in the city of Guayaquil, in the republic of Ecuador, heaps of filth are to be seen which exhale an insupportable odour. Similar heaps exist at the very gates of Mexico, where, at the present time, they form small hills. These facts ought to render us indulgent towards the neglect of cleanliness by our ancestors during the bronze epoch.

Such were the animal remains collected in the *terramares*. The vegetable remains consisted of grains of carbonised corn, broken nuts, acorns, halves of burnt apples, stones of the dog-berry, plums and grapes.

In concluding our consideration of the palustrine settlements, we may add, that some have recently been discovered in Moravia and Mecklenburg. At Olmutz, a city of Moravia, M. Jeitteler, a learned Viennese, has found piles sunk into the peat, along with various bronze and stone objects, ornamented pottery, charcoal, charred wheat, numerous animal bones, and a human skeleton of a brachycephalous race. All the facts lead to the belief that this will not be the last discovery of the kind.

We must also state that the *terramares*, or deposits of the remains of habitations on the edge of marshes, are not peculiar to Europe exclusively. On the coast of Africa (at San Vicente) M. Strobel found remains of an exactly similar nature; and Dr. Henrique Naegeli, a distinguished naturalist of Rio Janeiro, has testified to the existence on the coast of Brazil of like deposits, which he proposes to subject to a thorough examination.[35]

FOOTNOTES:

[34] 'Les Terramares et les Pilotages du Parmesan;' Milan, 1864. (Extract from the 'Atti della Società Italiana di Scienze naturali.')

[35] 'Matériaux pour l'histoire positive et philosophique de l'Homme,' by G. de Mortillet. Paris, 1865: vol. i. p. 397.

CHAPTER V.

Weapons, Instruments, and Utensils contained in the various Lacustrine Settlements in Europe, enabling us to become acquainted with the Manners and Customs of Man during the Bronze Epoch.

WE have just spoken of the discovery and investigation of the *lacustrine habitations* found in various parts of Europe, and also of the *palustrine villages* of Northern Italy. These rich deposits have thrown a considerable light on the primitive history of the human race. With the elements that have been thus placed at our disposal, it will be possible to reconstruct the domestic life of the tribes of the bronze epoch, that is, to describe the weapons, instruments, and utensils which were proper to the every-day proceedings of this period.

In order to give perspicuity to our representation or account, we have classed the lacustrine habitations under the head of the *bronze* epoch. But we must by no means forget that these lacustrine villages contained other objects besides those belonging to the bronze epoch; there were also found in them a number of articles which must be referred to the preceding period, that is, the polished-stone epoch.

It is a question indifferent to our purpose, whether the lacustrine villages were constructed during the Stone Age, as inferred from the presence in some settlements of stone objects only, or whether the habitations were built during the bronze epoch, some of the articles made of stone and dating back to the preceding period being still preserved in use. For it is certain that the larger number of lacustrine settlements do not go back beyond the bronze epoch. But as certain objects made of stone form a portion of the implements found in these ancient habitations, we must commence by describing these relics of the Stone Age; although we shall considerably abridge this description, so as to avoid repeating those details which we have already given in the preceding chapters.

The stone weapons and instruments are found to consist, in Switzerland as elsewhere, of hatchets, spear-heads and arrow-heads, hammers, saws, knives and chisels.

The hatchets and hammers are made of various materials, as flint, quartzite, diorite, nephrite, jade, serpentine, &c. But the other weapons and implements are, nearly all of them, of flint.

The hatchet was in continual use, not merely as a weapon but as a tool; thus, very numerous specimens of it are found in the Swiss lakes.

The hatchets, however, are generally speaking, small in size. Their length varies from 2 to 8 inches, and their width, at the cutting edge, from 1½ to 2 inches. Fig. 155 represents one of the flint hatchets. They are the same shape as the Danish hatchets during the polished-stone epoch.

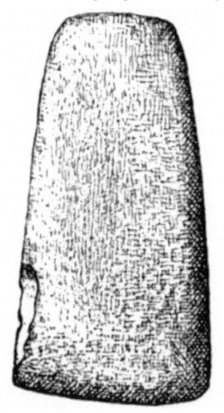

Fig. 155.—Stone Hatchet from the Lacustrine Habitations of Switzerland.

The most simple plan of fixing a handle to the small-sized hatchets, which were in fact chisels, consisted in inserting them into a piece of stag's horn, hollowed out for this purpose at one end. In this way they obtained a kind of chisel which was very ready of use. Fig. 156 represents this kind of handle.

Fig. 156.—Stone Chisel with Stag's-horn Handle from the Lacustrine Habitations of Switzerland.

There was also another mode of fixing handles to these instruments. The shaped flint was previously fixed in a holder of stag's horn. This holder was itself perforated through the middle with a round hole, in order to receive a wooden handle. It then became a complete hatchet.

Fig. 157 represents one of these hatchets fitted with a handle, in a way similar to many of the specimens in the Museum of Saint-Germain.

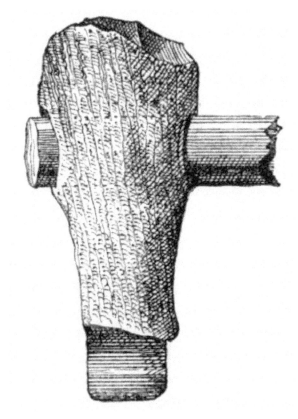

Fig. 157.—Flint Hammer, fitted with a Stag's-horn Handle.

This mode of insertion into a handle is frequently met with during the polished-stone epoch, as we have already stated upon the authority of Boucher de Perthes (see fig. 112).

There was also another way of adapting for use the stone chisels and hammers. The following is the mode employed. The flint was inserted into a short holder of stag's horn, hollowed out at one end for this purpose, the other end of the piece of horn being cut square. This squared end, which was thinner than the rest of the holder, was fitted into a wooden handle, which had been perforated with a hole of the same shape and size.

M. Desor, in his 'Mémoire sur les Palafittes,' supplies the following sketch (fig. 158), as representing these double-handled hatchets.

Fig. 158.—Stone Hatchet, with double Handle of Wood and Stag's Horn.

It is very seldom that hatchets of this type are met with in a complete state in the lacustrine habitations of Switzerland; the handles have generally disappeared. In other localities, where the hatchets are very plentiful, very few holders are found. Is it not the case that in these spots the stone was the special object of work and not the handles? There were, in fact, in Switzerland, as in France and Belgium, workshops devoted to the manufacture of these articles. The large number of hatchets, either just commenced or defective in workmanship, which have been found in some of the principal lacustrine settlements leave no doubt on this point.

The finest and most carefully-wrought instruments are the hammers and double, or hatchet-hammers. Most of them are made of serpentine. One of the ends is generally rounded or flattened, whilst the other tapers off either into a point or a cutting edge, as represented in figs. 159 and 160, taken from M. Desor's work. They are perforated with a round hole intended to receive a handle of wood. This hole is so sharply and regularly cut out, that it is difficult to believe it could have been made with nothing better than a flint tool. Metal alone would appear to be capable of effecting such finished work. This is one of the facts which tend to the idea that the lacustrine settlements, which have been ascribed to the Stone Age, belong rather to the bronze epoch.

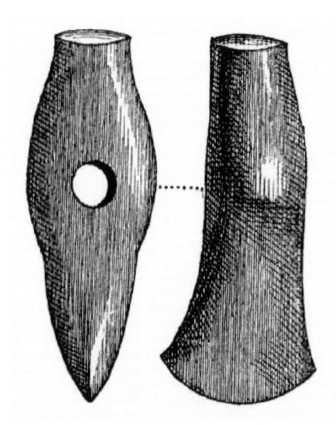

Fig. 159-160.—Serpentine Hatchet-hammers, from the Lacustrine Habitations of Switzerland.

Fig. 161 represents another hatchet-hammer obtained from the Swiss lakes.

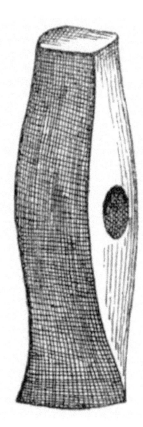

Fig. 161.—Another Hatchet-hammer, from the Lacustrine Habitations of Switzerland.

The knives and saws have nothing remarkable about them. They are mere flakes of flint, long and narrow in shape, the cutting edge or teeth being on the widest side. There are some which are fitted into handles of stag's horn, as represented in fig. 162, taken from M. Desor's work.

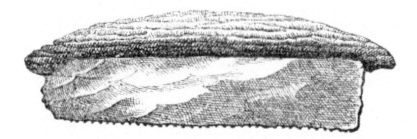

Fig. 162.—Flint Saw fitted into a piece of Stag's Horn.

They must have been fastened into the handles by means of bitumen, for traces of this substance have been found on some of the handles. The same plan was adopted in order to fix the hatchets in their holders.

The spear-heads (fig. 163) are very skilfully fashioned; their shape is regular, and the chiselling very perfect, although inferior to that observed in Denmark. They are made level on one side, and with a longitudinal middle ridge on the other.

Fig. 163.—Flint Spear-head from the Lacustrine settlements of Switzerland.

The arrow-heads are very varied in shape (fig. 164). In delicacy of workmanship they are in no way inferior to the spear or javelin-heads.

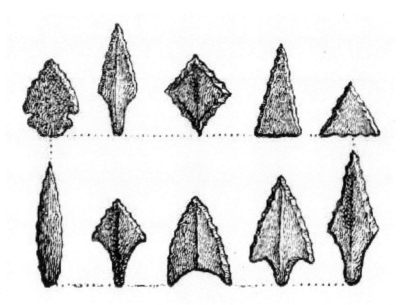

Fig. 164.—Various shapes of Flint Arrow-heads, from the Lacustrine settlements of Switzerland.

The cutting of these small objects must have required much labour and skill. Some are toothed on the edges, which must have rendered the wounds inflicted by them much more dangerous. The greater part of these arrow-heads are made of flint, but some have been found the material of which is bone, and even stag's horn.

The arrow-heads were fixed into the shafts by means of bitumen. This plan is represented in figs. 165 and 166, which are given by M. Mortillet in his 'Promenades préhistoriques à l'Exposition Universelle.'

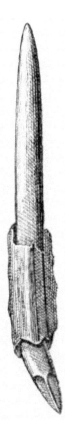

Fig. 165.—Arrow-head of Bone fixed on the Shaft by means of Bitumen.

Fig. 166.—Stone Arrow-head fixed on the Shaft by means of Bitumen.

Sometimes they were merely attached to the shaft by a ligature of string (fig. 167).

Fig. 167.—Arrow-head fixed on the Shaft by a Ligature of String.

A few relics have been discovered of the bows which were used to impel these arrows. They were made of yew, and roughly cut.

Tools and instruments of bone seem, like those made of flint, to have been much in use. In addition to the arrow-heads which we have just mentioned, there have also been found piercers, or bodkins of various shapes (figs. 168 and 169), chisels for working in wood (fig. 170), pins with lenticular heads (fig. 171), needles perforated sometimes with one eye and sometimes with two, and occasionally hollowed out round the top in a circular groove, so as to attach the thread.

Figs. 168, 169, 170 and 171 are given by M. Desor in his 'Mémoire sur les Palafittes.'

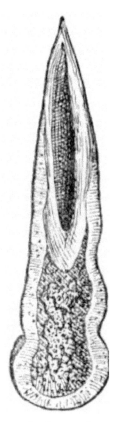

Fig. 168.—Bone Bodkin, from the Lacustrine Habitations of Switzerland.

Fig. 169.—Bone Bodkin, from the Lacustrine Habitations of Switzerland.

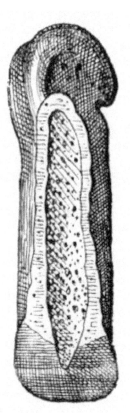

Fig. 170.—Carpenter's Chisel, from the Lacustrine Habitations of Switzerland.

Fig. 171.—Bone Needle.

It is probable that, as during the reindeer epoch, garments were sewn by means of the needle and the bodkin, the latter piercing the holes through which the needle passed the thread.

That kind of needle which has a hole in the middle and is pointed at the two ends, which is found in large numbers in the lacustrine settlements, must doubtless have been used as a hook for fishing. When the fish had swallowed the bait, the two points stuck into the flesh, and it was then easy to pull out the captive. Some of these fish-hooks are carved out of boars' tusks.

Stag's horn was likewise employed for several other purposes. A kind of pick-axe was sometimes made of it (fig. 172); also harpoons (fig. 173), harpoons with a double row of barbs (fig. 174), and small cups of conical shape (fig. 175), perforated with a hole in the upper part so that they could be suspended if required.

Fig. 172.—Pick-axe of Stag's Horn.

Fig. 173.—Harpoon made of Stag's Horn, from the Lacustrine Habitations of Switzerland.

Fig. 174.—Harpoon made of Stag's Horn, from the Lacustrine Habitations of Switzerland.

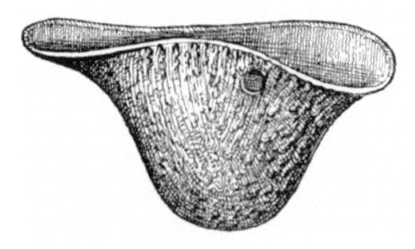

Fig. 175.—Vessel made of Stag's Horn.

The taste for personal adornment was not foreign to the nature of the primitive people of Switzerland. Canine teeth and incisors of various animals, rings and beads made of bone or stag's horn, all united in a necklace, formed one of their most usual adornments.

They also made use of hair-pins and bone combs. These pins were finished off with a knob, and combined elegance and simplicity in their shape; they would, indeed, be no disfigurement to the *coiffure* of the women of modern times.

Such were the instruments, utensils and tools, used for the purpose of domestic life, which have been found in the lacustrine habitations of Switzerland belonging to the Stone Age. We will now pass on to the objects of the same character, peculiar to the bronze epoch.

The quantity of bronze objects which, up to the present time, have been collected from the Swiss lakes is very considerable. The finest collection in the country, that of Colonel Schwab, contained in 1867, according to a catalogue drawn up by Dr. Keller, no less than 4346 specimens.

Most of these objects have been cast in moulds, as is evident from the seams, the traces of which may be observed on several of the specimens.

Among the most remarkable of the relics of the bronze epoch which have been recovered from the Swiss lakes, the hatchets or celts are well deserving of mention. They are from 4 to 8 inches in length, and weigh from 10 to 15 pounds. Their shapes are varied; but all possess the distinctive characteristic of being adapted to fit longitudinally on their handles, and not transversely, as in the Stone Age. It is but seldom that they are not furnished with a hole or ear, so as to furnish an additional means of attachment.

We have in the first place the hatchet with wings bent round on each side of the blade, so as to constitute a kind of double socket, intended to receive a handle divided in the middle and bent into an elbow. This is the most prevalent type. Sometimes, as may be noticed in fig. 176, the upper end is pierced with an eye, doubtless intended to hold a band for fixing firmly the curved handle. This arrangement is peculiar to the hatchets of large size, that is, to those which had the most strain put upon them.

Another type which is very rare in Switzerland—only one specimen of it existing in the Museum of Neuchâtel—is that (fig. 177) in which the wings, instead of bending back upon the blade perpendicularly to the plane of the cutting edge, turn back in the same plane with it, or in the thickness of the blade.

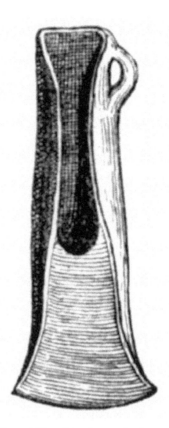

Fig. 176.—Bronze Winged Hatchet, from the Lacustrine Habitations of Switzerland.

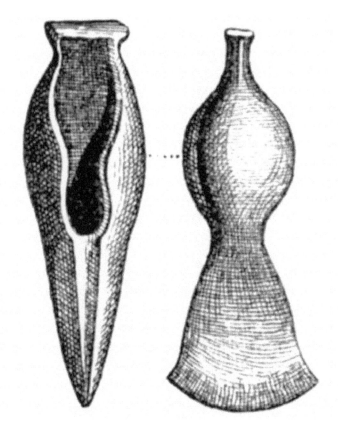

Fig. 177.—Winged Hatchet (front and side view), from the Lacustrine Habitations of Switzerland.

There is also the hatchet with the ordinary socket, either cylindrical (fig. 178) or angular. This shape is very common in France, where they are known by the name of *celts*.

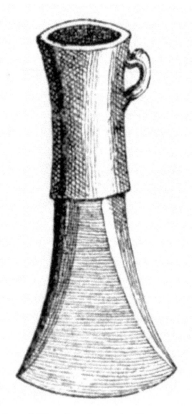

Fig. 178.—Socketed Hatchet from the Lacustrine Habitations.

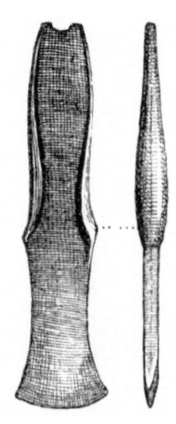

Fig. 179.—Knife Hatchet (front and side view), from the Lacustrine Habitations

M. Morlot has given the name of *knife-hatchets* (fig. 179), to those instruments, the perforated ears of which are scarcely, if at all developed, and could by no means serve to give firmness to a handle. It is probable that these instruments were grasped directly by the hand; and that the mere rudiments of wings which may be noticed, were merely intended to substitute a rounded surface for a sharp ridge. Figures 176, 177, 178 and 179, are taken from M. Desor's 'Mémoire sur les Palafittes.'

Next to the hatchets we must mention the chisels for wood-work (fig. 180), which are cut out to a great nicety, and in no way differ from our present chisels, except in the mode of fitting to the handle, which is done by means of a socket.

Fig. 180.—Carpenter's Chisel, in Bronze.

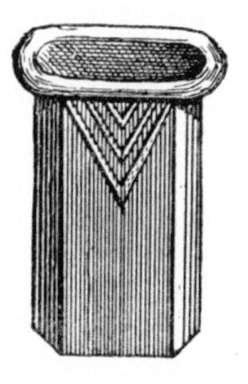

Fig. 181.—Hexagonal Hammer.

Fig. 182.—Knife with a tang to fit into a Handle, from the Lacustrine settlements of Switzerland.

There has also been discovered a kind of prismatically shaped hexagonal hammer (fig. 181), likewise provided with a socket, the length of which is about 3 inches. This hammer forms a portion of the collection of Colonel Schwab.

The knives are the most numerous of all the sharp instruments. The workmanship of them is, in general, very skilfully executed, and their shape is very elegant. Some of them have a metallic handle; but the greater part terminate in a kind of tang intended to fit into a handle of wood or stag's horn, as represented in fig. 182, taken from M. Desor's 'Mémoire sur les Palafittes.'

We also find knives furnished with a socket (fig. 183). The blade measures from 4 to 8 inches in length, and is often adorned with tracings; in some instances the back of the blade is very much thickened.

Fig. 183.—Socketed Knife, from the Lacustrine settlements of Switzerland.

Together with the knives we must also class the sickles or reaping hooks. These implements have been collected in somewhat large quantities in the settlements of Auvernier and Cortaillod (Lake of Neuchâtel). They are of good workmanship, and frequently provided with ridges or ribs in the metal of the blade. Fig. 184, given by M. Desor in his work, represents a sickle of this kind which was found by the author at Chevroux.

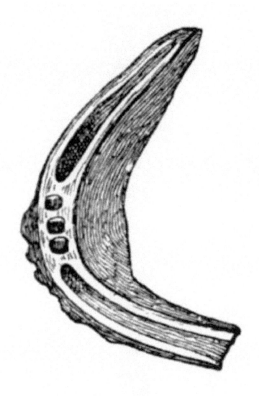

Fig. 184.—Bronze Sickle, found by M. Desor at Chevroux.

The largest of these sickles does not exceed 6 inches in length. They were fitted into a wooden handle.

We cannot of course describe all the bronze objects which have been recovered from the Swiss lakes. After having mentioned the preceding, we shall content ourselves with naming certain saws of various shapes—razors, actual razors, indicating no small care given to personal appearance—bodkins, or piercers—needles, with eyes either at the end or some distance from the end, articles of fishing tackle, such as single and double fishing-hooks (figs. 185 and 186), with a plain or barbed point—harpoons, various small vessels, &c.

Fig. 185.—Bronze Fish-hook, from the Lacustrine settlements of Switzerland.

Fig. 186.—Double Fish-hook, from the Lacustrine settlements of Switzerland.

We shall dwell, although briefly, on the various objects of personal ornament which have been found in the Swiss lacustrine settlements of the bronze epoch.

We will mention, in the first place, the hair-pins, &c. which have been recovered from the various lakes. The most curious fact about them is, that no one has ever found two exactly alike both in shape and dimensions. We borrow from M. Desor's work the four following figures representing various shapes of pins. Some have a round head (fig. 187), and others a flat (fig. 188), or cylindrical head (fig. 189); others, again, are finished off with a twisted end to which is attached a movable end (fig. 190).

Fig. 187.—Hair-pin, found by M. Desor in one of the Swiss Lakes.

Fig. 188.—Hair-pin, found by M. Desor in one of the Swiss Lakes.

Fig. 189.—Hair-pin with cylindrical Head.

Fig. 190.—Hair-pin with curled Head.

The round-headed pins are sometimes massive in shape and unornamented, that is, exactly similar to the bone pins of the Stone Age; sometimes, and even more frequently, they are perforated with one or more round holes and adorned with a few chasings.

The flat-headed pins differ very much in the diameter of the button at the end, which is sometimes of considerable size. There are some, the head of which is nothing more than a small enlargement of the pin, and others, in which there are two or three of these enlargements, placed a little way apart and separated by a twist. Their sizes are very various, and in some cases are so exaggerated, that it is quite evident that the objects cannot have been used as hair-pins. In Colonel Schwab's collection, there is one 33 inches long, and M. Troyon has mentioned some 20 and 24 inches long.

At the *Exposition Universelle* of 1867, in the collection sent by M. Desor, the visitors' admiration might have been called forth by some of the pins which had been repolished by the care of the learned Swiss naturalist. They were certainly very elegant, and ladies of the present day might well have decorated themselves with these ornaments, although they dated back to an era so many thousands of years ago.

Among many savage tribes, the dressing of the hair, especially among the men, is carried to an excessively elaborate pitch. The head of hair of an Abyssinian soldier forms a species of lofty system of curls which is meant to last a whole lifetime. He carries with him a long pin, furnished with a thick button, owing to the impossibility of reaching his skin through his *coiffure* with the extremities of his fingers.

In the same way the New Zealanders wear an enormous "chignon," 2 feet high and ornamented with ribbons.

The Chinese and the Japanese also devote excessive attention to the dressing of their hair.

It is, therefore, probable that the inhabitants of the lacustrine villages, both men and women, devoted an immense amount of care to the cultivation of their *coiffure*. In the tombs of the bronze epoch, pins have been found 2½ feet in length, with large knobs or buttons at the end, similar to those used by the Abyssinian soldiers of our own day. The combs, which resembled those of the present New Zealanders, although 6 inches long, had only six to eight teeth, and must have been better fitted to scratch their heads than to dress their hair.

Bracelets, too, have been found in some considerable numbers in the Swiss lakes. They are very varied in their shapes, decidedly artistic in their workmanship, and often set off with carved designs.

Some (fig. 191) are composed of a single ring of varying width, the ends of which almost meet and terminate by a semi-circular clasp; others (fig. 192), are a combination of straight or twisted wires ingeniously joined to one another.

Fig. 191.—Bronze Bracelet, found in one of the Swiss Lakes.

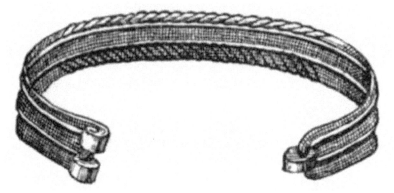

Fig. 192.—Another Bronze Bracelet.

We also find certain rings, cylindrical in shape, and made all in one piece (fig. 193), which were probably placed round the legs.

Fig. 193.—Bronze Ring.

Some of these ornaments remain, even up to the present day, in a perfect state of preservation. In an urn which was recovered from the settlement of Cortaillod, six specimens were discovered, the designs of which appeared quite as clearly as if they had only just been engraved. There is one point which must be remarked, because it forms an important *datum* in respect to the size of the Swiss people during the bronze epoch; this is, that most of the bracelets are so small that they could scarcely be worn nowadays. They must, therefore, have been adapted to very slender wrists—a fact which naturally leads us to believe that all the other limbs were small in proportion. This small size in the bracelets coincides with the diminutiveness of the sword-hilts which have been found in the lacustrine habitations of Switzerland.

Earrings, also, have been found in great numbers in the Swiss lakes. They are either metallic plates, or wires differently fashioned; all, however, testifying to a somewhat developed degree of taste.

Next after these trinkets and objects of adornment we must class certain articles of a peculiar character which must have been pendants or appendages to bracelets.

All these ornaments are, in fact, perforated at the top with a circular hole, intended, no doubt, to have a thread passed through it, by which it was hung round the neck. Some of them (fig. 194) are small triangular plates of metal, frequently ornamented with engraved designs; others (fig. 195), are in open-work, and include several branches, each terminated by a hole similar to that at the top. Some, again, assume the form of a ring not completely closed up (fig. 196), or rather, perhaps, of a crescent with wide and almost contiguous horns. In the same class may be placed the rings (fig. 197) to which were suspended movable ornaments in the shape of a double spiral.

Fig. 194.—Bronze Pendant, from the Lacustrine Habitations of Switzerland.

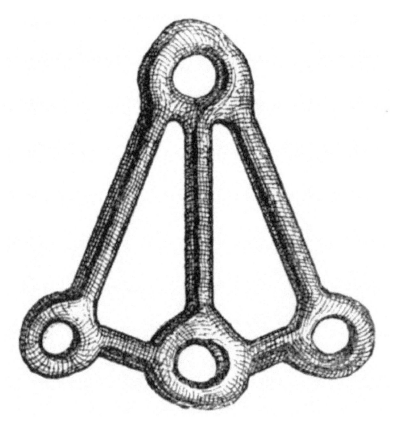

Fig. 195.—Another Bronze Pendant, from the Lacustrine Habitations of Switzerland.

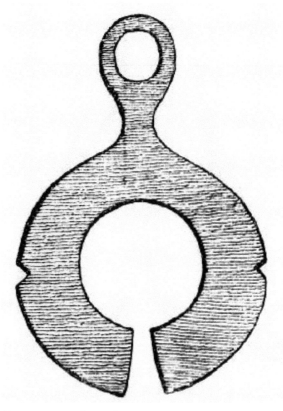
Fig. 196.—Bronze Ring, from the Lacustrine Habitations of Switzerland.

Fig. 197.—Another Ornamental Ring.

The four bronze objects, representations of which we have just given, are designed from the sketches supplied by M. Desor in his 'Mémoire sur les Palafittes.'

Some few trinkets of gold have been found in the lacustrine settlements of the bronze epoch; but this sort of "find" is very rare. They are in the form of earrings, and may be seen in the collection of Colonel Schwab.

CHAPTER VI.

Industrial Skill and Agriculture during the Bronze Epoch—The Invention of Glass—Invention of Weaving.

THE manufacture of pottery, which appears to have remained stationary during the Stone Age, assumed a considerable development during the bronze epoch. The clay intended for making pottery was duly puddled, and the objects when moulded were baked in properly formed furnaces. At this date also commences the art of surfacing articles of earthenware.

The specimens of pottery which have been found in the settlements of man of this period are both numerous and interesting; entire vessels have indeed been discovered. We notice indications of very marked progress beyond the objects of this kind manufactured in the preceding age. They are still fashioned by the hand and without the aid of the wheel; but the shapes are both more varied in their character and more elegant. In addition to this, although in the larger kind of vessels the clay used is still rough in its nature and full of hard lumps of quartz like the material employed in the Stone Age, that of the smaller vessels is much finer, and frequently covered with a black lead coating.

Most of these vessels are characterised by a conical base, a shape which we had before occasion to point out in the stag's-horn vessels of the Stone Age. If, therefore, it was requisite to place them upright, the lower ends of them had to be stuck into the earth, or to be placed in holders hollowed out to receive them.

Some of these supports, or holders, have been discovered. They are called *torches*, or *torchères*, by French archæologists.

Figs. 198 and 199 give a representation of a bronze vessel from the lacustrine habitations of Switzerland with its support or *torchère*.

Fig. 198.—Earthenware Vessel with Conical Bottom, from the Lacustrine Habitations of Switzerland.

Fig. 199.—Earthen Vessel placed on its support.

In a general way, the vessels made with conical bases have no handles; but others, on the contrary, are provided with them (fig. 200). They are nearly always ornamented with some sort of design, either mere lines parallel to the rim, triangles, chevrons, or rows of points round the handle or the neck. Even the very roughest specimens are not altogether devoid of ornamentation, and a stripe may often be observed round the neck, on which the fingers of the potter have left their traces.

Fig. 200.—Fragments of an Earthen Vessel with a Handle.

These vessels were intended to contain beverages and substances used for food. Out of one of them M. Desor took some apples, cherries, wild plums, and a large quantity of nuts. Some of these vessels, perforated with small holes, were used in the manufacture of cheese. Dishes, porringers, &c., have also been found.

Relics of the pottery of the Stone Age are very frequently recovered from the Swiss lakes; but vessels in an entire state are seldom met with. It is, however, stated as a fact, that considerable accumulations of them once existed; but, unfortunately, the importance of them was not recognised until too late. An old fisherman of the Lake of Neuchâtel told M. Desor that in his childhood he had sometimes amused himself by pushing at *these old earthen pots* with a long pole, and that in certain parts of the lake there were *real mountains* of them. At the present day, the "old earthen pots" are all broken, and nothing but pieces can be recovered.

These relics are, however, sufficient to afford a tolerably exact idea of the way in which the primitive Swiss used to fashion clay. They seem to denote large vessels either cylindrical (figs. 201 and 202) or bulbous-shaped with a flat bottom, moulded by the hand without the aid of a potter's wheel. The material of which they are composed is rough, and of a grey or black colour, and is always mingled with small grains of quartz; the baking of the clay is far from satisfactory.

Fig. 201.—Vessel of Baked Clay, from the Lacustrine Settlements of Switzerland.

Fig. 202.—Vessel of Baked Clay, from the Lacustrine Settlements of Switzerland.

The ornamentation is altogether of an ordinary character. It generally consists of mere lines traced out in the soft clay, either by the finger, a pointed stick, or sometimes a string was used. There are neither curves nor arabesques of any kind; the lines are almost always straight.

A few of the vessels are, however, decorated in a somewhat better style. Some are provided with small projections perforated with holes, through which might be passed a string for the purpose of hanging them up; there are others which have a row of studs arranged all round them, just below the rim, and others, indeed, in which hollows take the place of the studs. Several have been met with which are pierced with holes at different heights; it is supposed that they were used in the preparation of milk-curd, the holes being made to let out the whey. The vessels of this period are entirely devoid of handles; this ornament did not appear until the bronze age.

Mill-stones, or stones for crushing grain, are not unfrequently found in the Swiss lakes.

At some date during the period we are now discussing we must place the discovery of glass. Glass beads of a blue or green colour are, in fact, found in the tombs of the bronze epoch. What was their origin? Chemistry and metallurgy combine to inform us that as soon as bronze foundries existed glass must have been discovered. What, in fact, does glass consist of? A silicate with a basis of soda and potash, combined with some particles of the silicates of iron and copper, which coloured it blue and green. As the scoria from bronze foundries is partly composed of these silicates it is indubitable that a kind of glass was formed in the earliest metal-works where this alloy was made. It constituted the slag or dross of the metal works.

Thus, the classic tradition which attributes the invention of glass to certain Phœnician merchants, who produced a mass of glass by heating on the sand the *natron*, that is *soda*, brought from Egypt, ascribe too recent a date to the discovery of this substance. It should properly be carried back to the bronze epoch.

The working of amber was carried out to a very great extent by these peoples. Ornaments and objects of this material have been discovered in great abundance in the lacustrine settlements of Switzerland.

On the whole, if we compare the industrial skill of the bronze age with that of the preceding age, we shall find that the later is vastly superior to the earlier.

The art of weaving seems to have been invented during the stone age. We have positive and indisputable proofs that the people who lived during this epoch were acquainted with the art of manufacturing cloth.[36] All the objects which we have thus far considered do not, in fact, surpass those which might be expected from any intelligent savage; but the art of preparing and manufacturing textile fabrics marks out one of the earliest acquisitions of man's civilisation.

In the Museum of Saint-Germain we may both see and handle some specimens of woven cloth which were met with in some of the lacustrine settlements in Switzerland, and specially at Robenhausen and Wangen. This cloth, which is represented in fig. 203, taken from a specimen in the Museum of Saint-Germain, is formed of twists of interwoven flax; of rough workmanship, it is true, but none the less remarkable, considering the epoch in which it was manufactured. It is owing to the fact of their having been charred and buried in the peat that these remains of pre-historic fabrics have been kept in good preservation up to the present time.

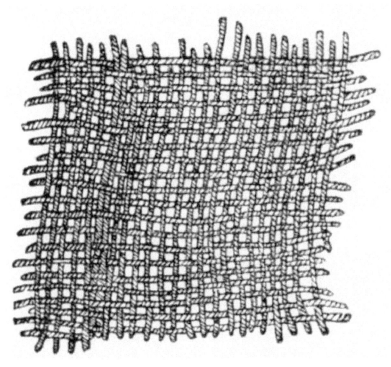

Fig. 203.—Cloth of the Bronze Age, found in the Lacustrine Settlements of Switzerland.

Balls of thread and twine have also been found; likewise ends of cord, and ropes made of bark, nets with large and moderately-sized meshes, which we have previously represented, and lastly some fragments of a basket of straw or osier.

Ribs of animals, split through and tapering off at one end, have been considered to be the teeth of the cards or combs which were used for unravelling the flax. The whole comb was formed of several of these bones joined firmly together with a band.

Fig. 204.—The First Weaver.

There were also found in the Swiss lakes a large number of discs made of baked earth perforated with a hole in their centre, of which we here give a representation (fig. 205), taken from one of the numerous specimens in the Museum of Saint-Germain. These are ordinary spindle-whorls.

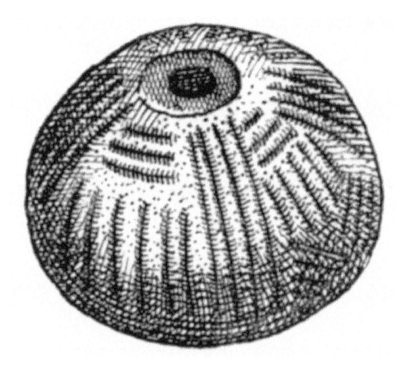

Fig. 205.—Spindle-whorls made of baked Clay, found in the Lacustrine Settlements of Switzerland.

Also, terra cotta weights pierced with a hole through the centre were intended to support the thread of flax in the weaving loom. The thread passed through the hole and was stopped by a knot at its extremity. We think that this interpretation of the use of these objects can hardly be called in question.

We also find in the lacustrine settlements woven fabrics, threads, strings, combs used for carding the flax, and spindle-whorls; the co-existence of all these objects proves that the invention of the art of weaving may be fixed at this date. The loom of the weaver may, therefore, be traced back to the most remote ages.

Acting upon this idea we have given a representation of *weaving in pre-historic times*.

The weaving-loom is so simple a matter that the men of the bronze age were enabled to produce it in nearly the same form as that in which it exists in the present day for the manufacture of plain kinds of cloth in various districts of the world where the art is still in a barbaric condition. The loom being upright, not horizontal as with us, the terra cotta weights just mentioned were used to keep the threads of the warp stretched. This seems to be the only difference. But, as we again repeat, the weaver's loom, on the whole, must have differed but very slightly from that of the present day. Its productions bear testimony to the fact.

Metal weapons and implements were at first obtained by means of exchange. But very soon the art of manufacturing bronze became prevalent in Switzerland, and foundries were established there. No doubt can be entertained on this point, as a mould for celts or hatchets has been found at Morges and also a bar of tin at Estavayer.

During this epoch the shape of the pottery became more advanced in character, and ornamentation was the rule and not the exception. After the indispensable comes the superfluous. Taste in ornamentation made its appearance and soon developed itself in ceramic objects of an elegant style. Articles of pottery now assumed more pleasing outlines, and were ornamented with various designs. Progress in artistic feeling was evidently manifested.

The simplicity and monotony of ornamentation during this epoch is especially remarkable. Art was then confined to the mere representation of a certain number of lines and geometrical figures. They were similar to those represented in fig. 206, and were applied to all kinds of objects—weapons, vases, utensils and trinkets. None of them attempt any delineation of nature; this idea does not seem to have entered into the head of man during the bronze epoch. In this respect they were inferior to their predecessors, the inhabitants of the caves of Périgord, the contemporaries of the mammoth and the reindeer.

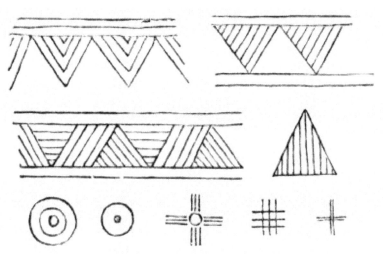

Fig. 206.—Principal Designs for the ornamentation of Pottery during the Bronze Epoch.

During the period we are now considering, commercial intercourse had assumed an activity of a totally different character from that manifested during the Stone Age. It became necessary to procure tin, which was indispensable for the manufacture of bronze. As no tin ore could be found in Switzerland, the inhabitants, doubtless, went to Saxony in order to obtain it. The traffic must have been carried out by means of barter, as is customary among all infant nations.

Flint, which likewise did not exist in Switzerland, was necessarily procured from the surrounding countries which were more fortunate in this respect. No country was more favoured on this point than France; commerce must, therefore, have existed between the two countries.

At Concise, in Switzerland, some pieces of white coral were found, and at Meilen, on the banks of the Lake of Zurich, some fragments of amber; from this we may conclude that during the bronze epoch the inhabitants of Switzerland traded with the inhabitants of the shores of the Mediterranean and the Baltic.

Among the other specimens of foreign productions, we must not omit to mention graphite, which was used to surface pottery, amber beads, and even a few glass trinkets suitable for female adornment.

We will now pass on to the system of food adopted by man during the bronze epoch.

Researches made in various lacustrine settlements have furnished us with very circumstantial information upon the system of food customary among the earliest inhabitants of Switzerland. From them we learn that these men did not live solely upon the products of fishing and hunting, but that they possessed certain ideas of agriculture, and also devoted themselves to the breeding of cattle. We shall enter into a few details as to this eminently interesting aspect of their history, taking as our guides Professors Heer and Rütimeyer, the first of whom has carefully examined the vegetable remains, and the second the animal relics which have been found in the lacustrine settlements of Switzerland.

At Meilen, Moosseedorf, and Wangen, some charred cereals have been found, viz., barley and wheat. The latter was the most abundant, and, at Wangen in particular, there were several bushels of it, either in ears or in thrashed corn collected in large heaps. These grains are almost the same shape and size as the wheat of the present time. Several ears of six-rowed barley (*Hordeum hexastichon*) were found, which differ from our common barley in having smaller grains arranged in six rows. De Candolle is of opinion that this is the species which was cultivated by the ancient Greeks, Egyptians, and Romans.

This corn was preserved in large earthen vessels, as may be gathered from the contents of some of them, still in an entire state.

What preparation did the corn undergo in order to render it fit for human food? On this subject we have tolerably exact data to go upon.

The grain was bruised by hand, either between two stone discs or millstones, or in a mortar by means of a round pestle. In almost all of the lacustrine villages, some of these mill-stones made of granite or sandstone have been met with, a few of which are as much as 2 feet in diameter. M. Heer is of opinion that the grain was parched before being pounded, and then placed in vessels and slightly soaked. In this state it was fit for eating.

At the time of the conquest of the Canary Islands by the Spaniards, it was remarked that the natives prepared their corn in this manner; and in the present day the inhabitants of the same regions still feed on parched grain.

Nevertheless, the earliest inhabitants of western Switzerland also made real bread, or rather wheat-cakes, for leaven was not then known. Charred fragments of these loaves have been found, the grain of which is badly ground, thus affording us the opportunity of recognising the species of corn of which they are composed. These fragments are flat, and indicate that the whole cake was of a circular form. No doubt, after being bruised and wetted, the grain was made into a sort of dough, which was baked between two heated stones—a process we have previously described as having been practised in the Stone Age.

In order to cultivate cereals, it was, of course, necessary for the ground to undergo some preliminary preparation. It was at least necessary to break it up so as to mellow it, and to make furrows in which to sow the seed. We are reduced to mere conjecture as to all the details of these operations, for no agricultural implements have been discovered in any of the settlements of man belonging to the bronze epoch. Perhaps, as M. Heer suggests, they made use of the stem of a tree with a projecting crooked branch, and adapted it so as to perform the functions of the plough.

Wild fruits and berries formed a considerable portion of the food of the earliest lacustrine peoples; and, from certain indications which have been brought to our notice, we have reason to believe that several varieties of trees were the objects of their intelligent culture; in short, that they were cultivated in orchards and gardens. The settlement of Robenhausen on the Lake of Pfæffikon, has furnished us with the most valuable information on this point. The lacustrine villages of Wangen (Lake of Constance), and Concise (Lake of Neuchâtel) have also been the scenes of curious discoveries.

In all of these settlements a large number of charred apples have been met with, cut in two, and sometimes four pieces, and evidently stored up for the winter. These apples are no larger than walnuts, and in many of the Swiss forests a species of apple still exists which appears to be the same sort as those found in the lacustrine settlements. Pears have been discovered only in the settlement of Wangen; they were cut up and dried just like the apples.

In the mud of the lakes, stones of the wild plum and the bird-cherry, or Sainte-Lucie plum, were found; also the seeds of blackberries and raspberries, the shells of beech-nuts and hazel-nuts, and several species of the water-chestnut, which is now only to be met with at two points of the Swiss Alps.

We must also add that M. Gilliéron collected in the settlement of the Isle of Saint-Pierre, oats, peas, lentils, and acorns, the latter evidently having been intended for the food of swine. This discovery is an important one, because oats had, hitherto, never been met with anywhere.

We shall complete this list of names by enumerating the other vegetables which have been ascertained to have existed in the lake settlements, the berries and seeds of some of which were used as food, &c. They are the strawberry, the beech, the yew, the dog-rose, which is found in hedges, the white and yellow water-lily, the rush, and the forest and the marsh pine. There are no traces of the vine, rye, or hemp.

Fig. 207, representing *the cultivation of gardens during the bronze epoch*, is intended to sum up and delineate materially all the ideas we have previously suggested concerning the agricultural and horticultural knowledge possessed by man during the bronze epoch. A gardener is tilling the ground with a horn pick-axe, a representation of which we have previously given. Others are gathering fruit from trees which have been planted and cultivated with a view of increasing the stock of food.

Fig 207.—The Cultivation of Gardens during the Bronze Epoch.

The sheep and oxen which may be noticed in this figure indicate the domestication of these animals and of their having been reared as tame cattle. The dog, the faithful companion of man, could scarcely have been omitted in this assemblage of the auxiliary or domestic animals of the bronze epoch.

The bones which have been found in the lacustrine settlements of Switzerland have enabled us to reconstruct with some degree of accuracy the *fauna* of this epoch, and to ascertain what species of animals were then in subjugation to the yoke of man.

Professor Rütimeyer is of opinion that the whole of these bones may be referred to about seventy species of animals—ten of which are fish, three reptiles, twenty birds, and the rest mammiferous animals.

The remains most commonly met with are those of the stag and the ox, the former wild, and the latter domestic. Next in order comes the pig, remains of which are also very abundant; then follows the roe, the goat, and the sheep, all of which are much less common. The remains of the fox are met with almost as often as those of the latter species, and in spite of the fœtid smell of this animal it certainly was used for food—a fact which is proved by its bones having been split open and notched with knives. It is, however, very probable that this kind of sustenance was turned to as a last resort only in cases when no other more suitable food could be obtained.

The long bones which have been found in lakes, like those met with in caves and kitchen-middens, have been split in order to extract the marrow.

Just as in the kitchen-middens, the softer parts are always gnawed, which shows us that the dog had been there.

The repugnance which is felt by so many nations for the flesh of the hare is a very curious fact, and shows us how difficult it is to root out certain prejudices. This repugnance may be traced back as far as pre-historic ages. Neither the diluvial beds, the caves, the kitchen-middens, nor the lacustrine settlements have, in fact, furnished us with any traces of the hare. Even in the present day, the Laplanders and Greenlanders banish this animal from their alimental list.

Among the Hottentots the women eat it but not the men. The Jews, too, look upon it as unclean, and many years have not elapsed since the Bretons would hardly endure to hear it spoken of.

The antipathy which is thus shown by certain modern nations to the flesh of the hare has, therefore, been handed down to them from the primitive ages of mankind.

The researches of Prof. Rütimeyer have led to the conclusion that there existed in Switzerland during the Stone Age six species of domestic animals—the ox, the pig, the goat, the sheep, the dog, and the horse, the latter being very rare. There were, also, three specimens of the bovine race; the two wild species of the ox genus, namely, the urus and the bison, both very anciently known, had been increased by a third, the domestic ox.

The bones belonging to the Stone Age seem to point to the existence of a larger proportion of wild beasts than of domestic animals; and this is only what might be expected, for the art of domesticating animals was at this epoch still in its infancy, but a commencement had been made, and the practice continued to spread rapidly during the following age.

In fact, agriculture and the breeding of cattle made considerable progress during the bronze epoch. There were brought into use various new breeds of cattle. The ox became a substitute for the bison; the sheep was bred as well as the goat; and all these animals were devoted to the purpose of providing food for man.

Fig. 208.—A Feast during the Bronze Epoch.

We may here pause for a moment and contemplate, with just pride, this marvellous resuscitation of an era long ago buried in the darkness of bygone ages.

By means of the investigations of science, we know that the primitive inhabitants of Switzerland dwelt in wooden villages built on lakes; that they were hunters, fishers, shepherds, and husbandmen; that they cultivated wheat, barley, and oats; that they brought into a state of servitude several species of animals, and devoted to the requirements of agriculture the sheep and the goat; that they were acquainted with the principal rudiments of the baker's art; that they stored up apples, pears, and other fruits or berries for the winter, either for their own use or that of their cattle; that they understood the art of weaving and manufacturing flaxen fabrics; that they twisted up cord and mats of bark; and, lastly, that as a material for the manufacture of their implements and weapons they availed themselves of stone, bronze, animals' bones, and stag's horn.

It is equally certain that they kept up some kind of commercial intercourse with the adjacent countries; this must have been the case, if it were only for the purpose, as before mentioned, of procuring flints, which are not found in Switzerland; also amber and white coral, numerous relics of which have been met with in the settlements of Meilen and Concise.

Though there may still remain many an obscure page in the history of mankind during the bronze epoch, it must, nevertheless, be confessed that, as far as Switzerland is concerned, a bright light has of late years been thrown on that branch of the subject which refers to man's mode of existence in these regions during the bronze epoch.

FOOTNOTE:

[36] See 'The Lake Dwellings of Switzerland,' &c. p. 323, by Dr. F. Keller. Translated and edited by Dr. J. E. Lee. London, 1866.

CHAPTER VII.

The Art of War during the Bronze Epoch—Swords, Spears, and Daggers—The Bronze Epoch in Scandinavia, in the British Isles, France, Switzerland, and Italy—Did the Man of the Bronze Epoch entertain any religious or superstitious Belief?

THE Swiss lakes have furnished us with elements which afford us some knowledge of the state of man's industrial skill during the bronze epoch, and also enable us to form a due estimation of the manners and customs of the people of these remote ages. But if we wish to become acquainted with all the details which concern the art of war at the same date, we must direct our attention to the north of Europe, that is to say, to the Scandinavian peoples.

Nevertheless, before we touch upon the important pre-historic relics found in Denmark, we must say a few words concerning the traces of the art of war which have been furnished by the investigations made in the Swiss lakes.

The warlike accoutrements of the bronze epoch are, like those of the Stone Age, composed of spear-heads and arrow-heads, poniards and, in addition, swords. Swords are, however, but rarely met with in the Swiss lakes. The few which have been found are straight, short, double-edged, and without hilts. In the Museum of Neuchâtel there is a sword (fig. 209) which was discovered forty years ago at Concise, at a time when no one suspected the existence of any such thing as lacustrine settlements; M. Desor has supplied a sketch of it in his 'Mémoire sur les Palafittes.' This sword measures 16 inches in length, and has on its surface four grooves which join together on the middle ridge of the blade. The handle, which is terminated by a double volute, is remarkably small, being only 3 inches in length.

Daggers (fig. 210), too, like the swords, are but rarely found in the Swiss lakes. From a specimen found in the lake of Bienne, we see that the blade was fixed to the handle by means of a series of rivets arranged in a single line. This dagger is, like the sword found at Concise, ornamented with grooves symmetrically placed on each side of the projecting ridge which divides the blade into two equal portions.

Fig. 209.—Bronze Sword, in the Museum of Neuchâtel.

Fig. 210.—Bronze Dagger, found in one of the Swiss Lakes.

In the collection of Colonel Schwab, there are two daggers of an extraordinary character, having hilts enriched with silver.

The spear-heads (fig. 211) are not inferior either to the swords or the daggers in the skill and finish of their workmanship. They are formed of a nearly oval blade, strongly consolidated in the middle by a rounded ridge, which is prolonged so as to form a socket intended to hold a thick wooden handle. The length of the daggers varies from 4 to 7 inches.

Fig. 211.—Bronze Spear-head, found in one of the Swiss Lakes.

The arrow-heads (fig. 212) are, except in their material, identical with those of the preceding age. They are triangular, with more or less pointed barbs, and provided with a stem, by which they were fastened to the stick. A few have, however, been found which are made with sockets. They do not exceed 1 to 2 inches in length.

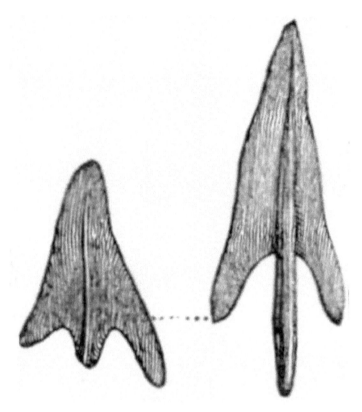

Fig. 212.—Bronze Arrow-heads, found in a Lacustrine Settlement of Switzerland.

We shall now pass on to the consideration of the relics found in the tombs of Scandinavia, Great Britain, Ireland and France; which remains will throw some light on the subject of the weapons and warlike instruments belonging to the bronze epoch.

The Scandinavian States (Denmark, Sweden, and Norway) are very rich in instruments belonging to the bronze epoch. The workmanship of the swords and other weapons of war is much more elaborate here than anywhere else, on account of the tardy introduction of metal into these countries. These weapons are nearly always adorned with somewhat complicated designs, among which curved lines and spiral scrolls are the most prevalent.

The Danish swords of the bronze epoch (figs. 213, 214) are of quite a peculiar shape. The hilt is firmly fixed to the blade by means of two or more rivets. The daggers and poniards only differ from the swords in the smallness of their dimensions.

Fig. 213.—Scandinavian Sword.

Fig. 214.—Hilt of a Scandinavian Sword.

Some of the hatchets seem to have been copied from models belonging to the Stone Age; these are probably the most ancient, and their ornamentation is of a very scanty character. Others are winged or with sockets, and a few have been found perforated with a transverse hole, like those which have long been used by civilised nations. In this hole a wooden handle was inserted, which was fixed by means of a strap, or merely forcibly driven in. The rarely-found specimens of this kind are sharply defined in shape and splendidly ornamented.

Figs. 215 and 216, taken from Sir J. Lubbock's work, represent the probable way in which handles were fitted to the various kinds of hatchets used in the North.

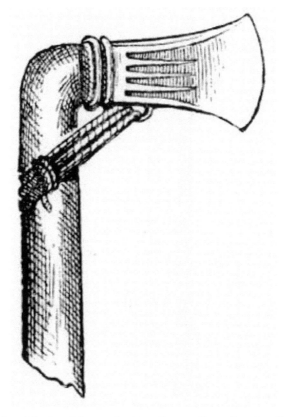

Fig. 215.—Mode of fixing the Handle to a Scandinavian Hatchet.

Fig. 216.—Another mode of fixing the Handle to a Scandinavian Hatchet.

The blades of the bronze knives found in Scandinavia are, like those of Switzerland, somewhat curved in their shape, but the handles are much more richly ornamented. Two of these knives have furnished us with the only examples known of any representation of living beings during the bronze epoch. We may notice that on one of these knives, which is represented in fig. 217, taken from Sir J. Lubbock's work, a swan is roughly carved at the offset of the blade.

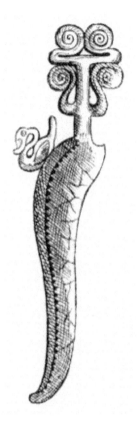

Fig. 217.—Danish Bronze Knife, of the Bronze Epoch.

In another knife, which is represented in fig. 218, taken from the same work, the handle is formed by a human figure, executed with some degree of fidelity. The figure is in a standing position, and holds in front of it a nearly cylindrical-shaped vessel; the individual is represented as wearing large earrings. There is every reason to believe that this last-mentioned article belongs to the end of the bronze epoch, or else to a transitionary epoch between this and the following, for the blade is straight, like those of all the knives belonging to the iron age.

Fig. 218.—Danish Bronze Knife of the Bronze Epoch.

The same thing may, doubtless, be said of several razors (fig. 219) with straight blades, which appear even overloaded with ornaments; among these embellishments is an attempt to represent a sort of vessel.

Fig. 219.—Blade of a Danish Razor of the Bronze Epoch.

These designs evidently point to some very advanced period in the bronze epoch; and perhaps these objects may belong to the commencement of the iron age.

What, we may ask, was the wearing apparel of man during the period we are describing?

A very important discovery, made in 1861, in a *tumulus* in Jutland (Denmark), has lately supplied us with the most accurate *data* respecting the way in which the inhabitants of the north of Europe were clothed during the bronze epoch. In this *tumulus* MM. Worsaae, and Herbst found three wooden coffins, one of which was smaller than the two others, and was no doubt that of a child. One of the two larger coffins was minutely examined by these *savants*, and measured inside 7 feet in length and 20 inches in width. It was closed up by means of a movable lid. By an extremely rare chance the soft parts of the body had been to some extent preserved, and had become converted into a black greasy substance. The bones were decomposed, and had decayed into a kind of blue powder. The brain had preserved its normal conformation. They found it at one end of the coffin (where the head had lain); it was still covered with a woollen cap, about 6 inches high, to which several black hairs were adhering.

Several woollen garments, in which the body had been buried, were also found in different parts of the coffin. We add a description of these garments.

There was in the first place a coarse cloak (fig. 220) which appeared shaggy in the inside, and was scalloped out round the neck. This cloak was 3 feet 4 inches long, and wide in proportion. Next there were two shawls nearly square in shape (fig. 221), ornamented with a long fringe, and measuring 4½ feet in length, and 3½ feet in width. Afterwards came a shirt (fig. 222), also scalloped out round the neck, and drawn in at the waist by means of a long narrow band. Lastly, at the feet of the body, two pieces of woollen material were found, which were 14 inches long, by 4 inches wide, and bore the appearance of having been the remains of gaiters. Close to the latter were also found vestiges of leather, evidently belonging to feet-coverings of some kind.

Fig. 220.—Woollen Cloak of the Bronze Epoch, found in 1861, in a Tomb In Denmark.

Fig. 221.—Woollen Shawl found in the same Tomb.

Fig. 222.—Woollen Shirt, taken from the same Tomb.

The whole body had been wrapped up in the skin of an ox.

The coffin also contained a box, tied up with strips of osier or bark, and in this box was a smaller one, in which were found two woven woollen caps (fig. 223, 224), a comb (fig. 225), and a bronze razor.

Fig. 223.—First Woollen Cap found in the same Tomb.

Fig. 224.—Second Woollen Cap found in the same Tomb.

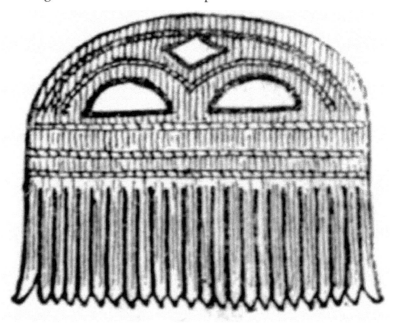

Fig. 225.—Bronze Comb found in the same Tomb.

We must not forget to mention a bronze sword, placed on the left side of the body, in a wooden sheath; this sword measured about 26 inches in length.

There is no doubt that all these relics were those of a warrior of the bronze epoch; there is the less reason to doubt this, owing to the fact, that the objects taken from the two other coffins most certainly belonged to that period. These were a sword, a knife, a bodkin, an awl, a pair of tweezers, a double button, and a small bronze bracelet; also a double tin button, a ball of amber and a flint spear-head.

Fig. 226.—Warriors during the Bronze Epoch.

The shape of the swords and knives shows that this burial-place in Jutland must be referred to the latter part of the bronze epoch—to a time, perhaps, when iron was first used.

Following out the *data* afforded by these records, and all the discoveries which have been made in other tombs, we have given in fig. 226, a representation of *warriors of the bronze epoch*.

The accoutrements of the horseman of pre-historic ages are composed of a bronze sword, like those found in the tombs in Denmark, and a bronze hatchet and sword-belt. His horse is decked with round bronze discs, which, in after times, formed among the Romans the chief ornament of this faithful and intrepid auxiliary of man in all his combats. The horseman's head is bare; for no helmet or metallic head-covering has ever, at least, to our knowledge, been discovered in the tombs of the bronze epoch. The spear and bronze hatchet are the weapons of the foot-soldiers.

Next to the Scandinavian regions, Great Britain and Ireland occupy an important place in the history of the civilisation of the bronze epoch. The same type of implements are found in these countries as in Denmark and Switzerland.

Hatchet-moulds (fig. 227) are also found there—a circumstance which proves that the founder's art was known and practised in these countries. The Dublin Museum contains a beautiful collection of various objects belonging to the bronze epoch.

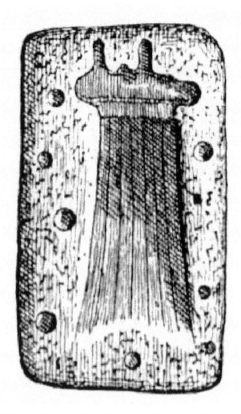

Fig. 227.—Bronze Hatchet-mould found in Ireland.

Some of the departments of France have also furnished objects belonging to the same period; but there is nothing peculiar among them which deserves mention.

Did any kind of religious worship exist among the men of the bronze epoch? Nothing would be more interesting than any discovery bearing on this point; but up to the present time no vestiges of anything in the shape of an idol have been found, nor anything whatever which authorizes us unhesitatingly to answer this question in the affirmative. The only thing which might prove the existence of any religious feeling, is the discovery, in various lacustrine settlements, of a certain number of crescent-shaped objects, most of them made of very coarse baked earth and some of stone.

The dimensions of these crescents vary considerably; there are some which measure as much as 16 inches from one point to the other. They are ornamented with perfectly primitive designs, as shown in fig. 228, drawn at the Museum of Saint-Germain from one of the numerous specimens of this class of objects.

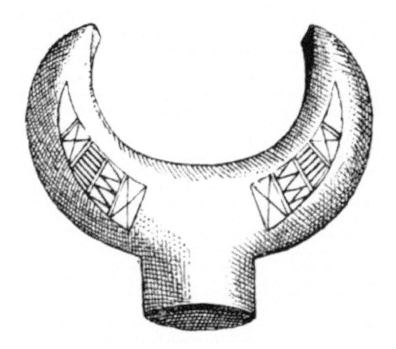

Fig. 228.—Stone Crescent found in one of the Swiss Lakes

Several archæologists consider these crescents to have been religious emblems or talismans which were suspended either outside or inside the habitations. Dr. Keller is of opinion that they bear some relation to the worship of the moon—an hypothesis which is not at all an impossible one; for all nations who have not attained to a certain degree of moral and intellectual culture adore the heavenly bodies as the sources of light and heat.

M. Carl Vogt, in considering the crescents which have been discovered in such large quantities in the lacustrine habitations, cannot admit that they indicate that any religious belief existed among these ancient nations. He attributes to these objects a very different kind of use, and, as we shall presently show, rather an odd one.

In the lectures on *pre-historic man* which were delivered by Prof. Carl Vogt at Antwerp, in 1868, and have been reported by the Belgian journals,[37] when speaking on the subject of the crescents belonging to the bronze epoch, he expresses himself as follows:—

"My opinion is that these crescents were used as resting-places for the head during the night. Among many savage tribes we find the attention paid to the dressing of the hair carried to a high pitch, especially among the men; it was not until a later period that woman also devoted her cares to the culture of her *coiffure*. Now this care is, by many nations, carried out to a really curious extent. They inflict the most severe tortures on themselves in order to satisfy their vanity. Everyone has seen, in the 'Magasin Pittoresque' and other illustrated journals, the strange head-dresses of the Abyssinian soldiers. They really seem to form a kind of fleece, and it may be noticed that each soldier carries in this hairy construction a large pin.

"Well, all this tends to explain the use of these crescents. In Abyssinia, as soon as a young girl is married it becomes her duty to devote herself to her husband's head of hair. This head of hair is made to assume a certain shape, which it has to retain during his whole lifetime. The labour which this process necessitates lasts for three years. Each hair is twisted round a stem of straw, and remains so until the straw perishes. The man's head is thus covered with a whole system of spirals, the top of which is a foot from the surface of his head. During the whole remainder of his life this *coiffure* must never be again disturbed. When asleep, the Abyssinian rests the nape of his neck on a triangle which he carries about everywhere with him. He has also a long pin, as it would be impossible for him to reach the skin of his head with the end of his finger.

"The same custom exists among the New Zealanders, who also have an apparatus upon which they rest their necks, in order, when asleep, to save their *coiffures*. They wear an enormous chignon, two feet high and ornamented with ribbons, of which they are very proud. The only difference between this chignon and certain others which I need not mention is, that the former cannot be removed at will. This object, thus adorned, rests, during the sleep of its owner, on a sort of framework.

"The Chinese and Japanese sleep, in the same way, on a bedstead bevelled off at the head; and in the Egyptian hieroglyphical drawings we find instruments evidently meant for the same use.

"It is very probable that during the bronze epoch great attention was devoted to the hair, and this is the more probable as in every tomb belonging to this period we find pins from 2 feet to 2½ feet in length, furnished with large knobs, and of the same shape as the pins used by the Abyssinian soldiers; and also, because during the Stone Age, as well as the Bronze Age, a kind of comb is found which is similar to that which is now used by the New Zealanders to scratch, rather than to comb, their heads. The heads of the pins are often very richly ornamented; they are of the most varied shapes, and are extremely common both in the tombs and also in the lacustrine dwellings.

"We have the less right to be astonished at our ancestors sleeping with their heads resting on such a machine as we have just described, knowing, as we do, that the hussars of Frederick the Great used to spend the whole night in arranging their *coiffures*!"

Thus, while Dr. Keller and many other archæologists ascribe the *crescents* found in the Swiss lakes to some kind of religious worship, M. Vogt, whose idea is of a much more prosaic character, does not attribute them to any other worship but that of *self* as represented by the hair! The reader can take his choice between these two explanations. We shall only remark, in corroboration of Dr. Keller's opinion, that certain Gallic tribes used for a religious symbol this very crescent which M. Vogt would make out to be a pillow—a stone pillow which, as it seems to us, must have been very hard, even for primitive man.

Various objects found in the dwellings of man belonging to the bronze epoch appear to have been religious symbols. Such, for instance, are the designs so often met with on swords, vases, &c. These drawings never represent objects in nature; they seem rather to be cabalistic signs or talismans. Most of them bear some relation to a circle; sometimes they are single circles, and sometimes combinations of circles. Many authors have had the idea of attributing them to the worship of the sun.

Another sign was still more often used, and it was known even as early as the Stone Age—we speak of the cross. It is one of the most ancient symbols that ever existed. M. G. de Mortillet, in a work entitled 'La Croix avant le Christianisme,' has endeavoured to establish the fact, that the cross has always been the symbol of a sect which contended against fetishism. This much is at least certain, that it is one of the most ancient symbolical signs; for it is found depicted on objects belonging to the Stone Age, and on some of the earliest relics of the Bronze Age. At the time of the Etruscans the cross was generally prevalent as a sign. But at a later period Christianity exclusively monopolized this religious symbol.

A third figure is sometimes found on various objects belonging to the bronze epoch; this figure is the triangle.

It is, on the whole, very probable that all these signs which are not connected with any known object, bear some relation to certain religious or superstitious ideas entertained by the men of the bronze epoch; and, as a consequence of this, that their hearts must have been inspired with some degree of religious feeling.

FOOTNOTE:

[37] *Indépendance Belge*, November and December, 1868.

CHAPTER VIII.

Mode of Interment and Burial-places of the Bronze Epoch—Characteristics of the Human Race during the same Period.

THE question naturally arises—what was the mode of interment, and what was the nature of the burial-places employed by man during the bronze epoch?

In the early part of this period the dead were still buried in those sepulchral chambers which are now called by the name of *dolmens*; Nilsson and Lubbock have drawn somewhat confused and arbitrary distinctions in discussing these burial-places; but it may be positively asserted that towards the conclusion of this period the practice of burning dead bodies was commenced.

In a work, published in 1869, and entitled 'Le Danemark à l'Exposition Universelle,' being a sort of catalogue of the objects which were exhibited in the galleries devoted to the *History of Labour*, in the Exhibition in the Champ de Mars, in 1867, we find several pages which we shall quote, as they seem to recapitulate pretty clearly the ideas which are now current among scientific men concerning the burial-places and funeral customs of the bronze epoch:—

"The study which, during the last few years, has been devoted by M. Worsaae to the tombs belonging to the bronze epoch, has thrown much light," says M. Valdemar Schmidt, "on the commencement of the bronze age in Denmark. It appears that at the first beginning of the bronze epoch the dead were buried in a manner similar to that practised during the stone age, that is to say, the bodies of the defunct were deposited in sepulchral chambers made of stone, and covered by *tumuli*; the only difference is, these chambers are rather small, and generally contain but one skeleton. But to make up for this, several of these small sepulchral chambers, or rather stone coffins, are sometimes found in the same *tumulus*.

"These chambers present, however, in some respects, great similarities with those of the Stone Age; thus, beds of flint which have been subjected to the action of fire are often found spread over the ground, and on these beds skeletons are met with which appear to have been placed in a contracted position before they were buried, exactly following the practice of the Stone Age.

"After this class of tombs, we have another, in which the sepulchral chamber, though always made of stone, is not covered with a stone slab but with a *wooden roof*. Elsewhere, skeletons have been found along with bronze weapons deposited in a sort of *wooden framework*, which has in many cases entirely perished except a few minute fragments. These cases were covered with small stones, which now seem to lie immediately upon the skeleton.

"Lastly, in all the Danish provinces large oak coffins are found, formed of hollowed-out trunks of trees; these also contain human bodies, which seem to have been buried in woollen garments.

"With regard to the funeral rites observed, these tombs do not appear to have differed much. The bodies were deposited in them with their implements, weapons, and utensils, either of bronze or stone; but, in addition, at the bottom of the tomb, animal skins, generally those of oxen, were often spread.

"Next, a new period succeeded, when the bodies were burned, and the remains collected together. All the ancient customs were not, however, at once given up. Thus, as the dead were formerly buried in woollen garments, the *débris* of the bones were now wrapped in pieces of cloaks made of the same material. Subsequently, however, this custom also disappeared, and the ashes and remains of bones were simply collected together in urns. This custom was observed until the bronze epoch, and characterises, so to speak, its second and last period—which was, however, the longest of that age.

"There were, then, in short, two distinct epochs in the bronze age; firstly, that *in which the dead were quite simply interred*, either in small sepulchral chambers or wooden coffins, and, secondly, that *in which the bodies of the dead were incinerated*.

"One of the most remarkable 'finds,' as regards the first period of the bronze epoch, was made in 1861, in the two mounds known by the names of Treenhöi and Kengehöi, and situated near Kongeaa, in Jutland. In each of these *tumuli* two people had been buried, both having a double coffin, made of magnificent trunks of oak-trees. The skeletons had been almost entirely destroyed by the damp which, on the contrary, had preserved the garments. These individuals seem to have been dressed almost like the Scotch; at least they must have worn a sort of woollen petticoat, and bands by way of trousers, very like those worn by the warriors depicted in the Carlovingian miniatures, and, in addition, a cloak, a cap, and also perhaps a shawl. With these garments were found some bronze swords in wooden sheaths; also some bronze knives, a comb, some boxes, cups, small wooden coffers, a tin ball, and, lastly, in one of the coffins, a small flint arrow-head. A fragment of the cloak was to be seen in the Palace of the Champ de Mars (No. 596).

"Another 'find' made a few miles from this *tumulus*, at Höimp, in North Schleswig, has also brought to light skeletons in oak coffins together with bronze implements.

"Discoveries of no less interest have been made in Zealand. Thus, in 1845, in a *tumulus* at Höidegaard, near Copenhagen, a tomb belonging to the first period of the bronze epoch was found; it was searched in the presence of some of the principal Danish archæologists. The tomb was placed at a distance of more than 10 feet below the summit of the *tumulus*, and was built of stones; it was more than 6 feet in length, and its width on the eastern side was about 2 feet, and on the western side 19 inches. The bottom was lined with a layer of small flint stones, on which was found, in the first place, a skin, doubtless that of an ox, and above it, besides a piece of tissue containing remains of human bones, a bronze sword with a wooden sheath, covered with leather, and in a perfect state of preservation; lastly, a box containing the following articles:—1st, a fragment of an amber bead; 2nd, a piece of reddish stone; 3rd, a small shell, which can be none other than the *Conus mediterraneus*; it is perforated so as to be worn as a pendant for the neck; 4th, a fragment of a flint point, doubtless an amulet; 5th, the tail of a serpent (*Coluber lævis*); 6th, a small cube of pine or fir-wood, and 7th, a bronze knife with a convex blade and ornamented handle.

"According to the investigations of various savants, these bones belong to a man, who, to judge from the objects placed by his side in his tomb, must have been some distinguished personage, and perhaps combined the functions of a warrior and a sorcerer. The cube of pine-wood leads us to conjecture that that tree had not then completely disappeared, and from this fact we may infer that the period at which the sorcerer in question lived was very remote. It is, however, possible that this piece of pine-wood, as well as the shell, were introduced from some other country. The existence of the *Conus mediterraneus* seems to establish the fact that Denmark had already formed some kind of connection with the Mediterranean.

"*The second period of the bronze epoch* is characterised by the custom of the cremation of the dead, which generally took place in the following way: the body of the defunct was usually placed, together with his weapons and ornaments, on the funeral pile, which was built on the exact spot which was destined to form the centre of the *tumulus*; the fire was then lighted, and, after the body was consumed, the remains of the bones were collected together in an urn. The rubbish that resulted was left on the spot, surrounded with stones, and covered with earth till the *tumulus* was complete. The urn which contained the ashes was then placed in another part of the *tumulus*. This course of procedure was not the only one employed; in some cases the weapons and other articles of adornment were not placed upon the funeral-pile, but were afterwards brought and placed round the urn.

"The number of tombs of the bronze epoch which have been discovered in Denmark is very considerable. There are thousands of *tumuli*, and many of them contain a large number of funeral urns. A great many of these *tumuli* have been searched at various times and have produced a number of different bronze articles. The Museum of Copenhagen possesses no less than 600 swords dating back to the bronze epoch."[38]

Twenty years ago, however, a very curious discovery was made at Lübeck (Pomerania), for it exhibited, so to speak, in the same tomb, the three modes of interment belonging to the pre-historic epochs of the stone, bronze, and iron ages.

At Waldhausen, near Lübeck, a *tumulus* was found, which was 13 feet 9 inches in height. This *tumulus* was pulled down in horizontal layers, and the following details were successively brought to light.

At the top was a very ancient burial-place, evidently belonging to the iron age; for the skeleton it contained was accompanied by an object made of rusty iron and several earthenware articles. It was buried in loose earth.

Underneath this, and half way down the *tumulus*, there were some small enclosures composed of uncemented walls, each one containing a sepulchral urn filled with calcined bones, as well as necklaces, hair-pins, and a bronze knife.

Lastly, at the base of the *tumulus*, there was a tomb belonging to the Stone Age. It was formed of large rough blocks of stone, and contained, in addition to the bones, some coarse specimens of pottery, with flint hatchets.

It is evident that the first inhabitants of the country began by building a tomb on the bare ground, according to the customs of the age, and then covered it up with earth. During the bronze epoch another burial-place was made on this foundation, and a fresh heap of earth doubled the height of the mound. Lastly, during the iron age, a dead body was buried in a grave hollowed out on the top of the same mound. Here, then, we have a clear delineation of the three different modes of interment belonging to the three pre-historic periods.

In short, during the bronze epoch, the dead were generally buried in sepulchral chambers, and sometimes, exceptionally, they were burned. The custom of funeral feasts still remained in full force. The pious practice of placing by the side of the dead body the instruments or weapons which the individual had been fond of during his lifetime, was likewise still kept up;

and it is, moreover, owing to this circumstance that archæological science is now enabled to collect numerous vestiges of the ancient customs of these remote ages.

But we must call attention to the fact that, at the end of and after this epoch, the hatchets and instruments which were placed in the tombs were often of much smaller dimensions than those employed for every-day use. They were small and delicately-made hatchets, intended as *votive* offerings. Some might, perhaps, conclude from this that the heirs, animated by a feeling of economy, had contented themselves with depositing very diminutive offerings in the tombs of the dead. The human race was already becoming degenerate, since it curtailed its homage and its offerings to the dead!

In order to bring to a conclusion all the details which concern the bronze epoch, the question will naturally arise, what was the human type at this epoch, and did it differ from that of the preceding age? Unfortunately, the positive information which is required for the elucidation of this question is entirely wanting; this deficiency is owing to the extreme rarity of human bones, both in the lacustrine settlements of Switzerland, and also in the tombs belonging to that epoch which have been searched in different European countries. The whole of the lacustrine settlements of Switzerland have furnished no more than some seven skeletons, one of which was found at Meilen, two at Nidau, one at Sutz, one in the settlement of Bienne, and two at Auvernier. The first, that is the skeleton found at Meilen, near lake Zurich, is the only one which belongs to the Stone Age; the six others are all of the Bronze or Iron Ages.

The skeleton found at Meilen is that of a child; the skull, which is in a tolerable state of preservation, although incomplete, occupies, according to the observations of MM. His and Rütimeyer, a middle place between the long and short heads.

Figs. 229 and 230, representing this skull, are taken from M. Desor's work, entitled 'Mémoire sur les Palafittes.' From the mere fact that it is a child's skull, it is almost impossible to make any use of it in ascertaining the characteristic features of the race to which it belongs; for these features are not sufficiently marked at such an early age. The skull is of a very elongated shape, that is to say, it belongs to the *dolichocephalous* type. The upper part of the skull is flattened, and it has an enormous occipital development; but, on the other hand, there is scarcely any forehead. If these special features might be generally applied, they would not prove much in favour of the intellectual capacity of the Helvetic nation, or of its superiority over the races of anterior ages; it represents, in fact, a very low type of conformation, which, however, harmonises perfectly with the rough manners and cruel practices of the Gallic tribes.

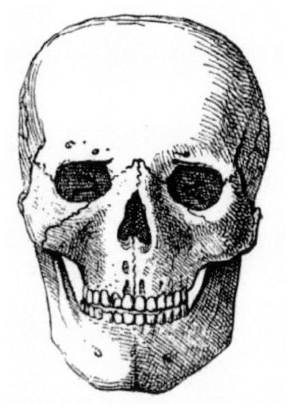

Fig. 229.—Skull found at Meilen, front view.

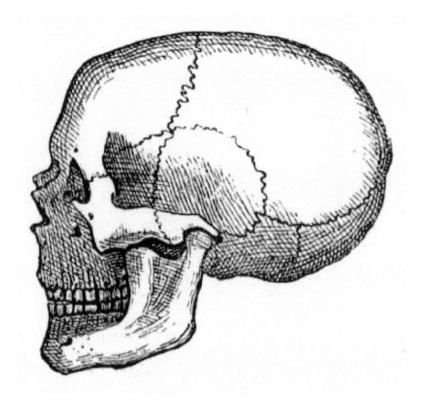

Fig. 230.—Skull found at Meilen, profile view.

At the time of the discovery, this skull was accompanied by various bones belonging to the body and limbs, which show by their extraordinary bulk that their owners were men of very large size. We have already remarked upon the large size of the men existing in the Stone Age, that is to say, at the time of the first appearance of mankind. Thus, the human type had changed but little since its first appearance on the globe.

The settlement of Auvernier, in the lake of Neuchâtel has, as we have before said, contributed two skulls. One belonged to a child about eight years of age, and the other to an adult. The child's skull differs very slightly from the one found at Meilen. It is small, elongated, and has a low and narrow forehead. That of the adult presents the same characteristics, and, in addition, an extraordinary development of the occiput, a feature which is not observable in the former, probably, on account of the youth of the subject. These two skulls seem, therefore, to show that the population of the lacustrine settlements had not at all changed at the beginning of the bronze epoch.

A discovery made in the neighbourhood of Sion has confirmed these first ideas. At this spot, in tombs of rough stone, there were found some bodies bent into a contracted position, and accompanied by certain bronze objects. According to MM. His and Carl Vogt, the skulls found at Sion agree tolerably well with those discovered at Meilen and Auvernier; and, in addition to this, the same shape is perpetuated down to our own days in German Switzerland, where it strongly predominates, and constitutes what is called the Helvetic type.

The *data* which have been collected up to the present time are not sufficient to enable us to make any positive assertion respecting the development of the intelligence of man during the bronze epoch. The few skulls which have been recovered are always in an incomplete state, and do not justify us in forming any exact opinion on this matter. But when we are considering the degree of intelligence possessed by our ancestors at this period of man's development, there are things which will enlighten us far better than any fragments of bones or any remains of skeletons; these are the works which have been executed by their hands. The fine arts had already begun to throw out promising germs, industrial skill had become an established fact, agriculture was in full practice, and bronze was made to adapt itself to all the caprices and all the boldest ideas of the imagination. What more can be necessary to prove that man, at this epoch, was already comparatively far advanced in intellectual culture?

In concluding our account of the bronze epoch, the question naturally arises whether it is possible to form any estimate of the exact space of time embraced by this period of man's history. We shall endeavour here to give, not the solution of the problem, but merely an idea of the way in which scientific men have entered on the question.

Morlot, the Swiss archæologist and naturalist, who has written a great deal upon the subject of the lacustrine settlements, was the first to endeavour to estimate the duration of the Stone Age, as well as that of the Bronze Epoch, and the following is the way in which he set about it.

In the neighbourhood of Villeneuve there is a cone or hillock formed of gravel and *alluvium*, slowly deposited there by the stream of the Tinière which falls at this spot into the lake of Geneva. This cone was cut in two, to lay down the railway which runs along the side of the lake. Its interior structure was thus laid bare, and appeared to be perfectly regular, a proof that it had been gradually formed during a long course of ages. There were three layers of vegetable earth placed at different depths between the deposits of *alluvium*, each of which double layers had in its turn formed the outer surface of the cone.

The first layer was found at a depth of 3 feet 6 inches from the top, and was 4 to 6 inches thick. In it were found some relics of the Roman epoch.

The second, situated 5 feet 3 inches lower, measured 6 inches in depth, and was recognised as belonging to the bronze age; it contained a pair of bronze pincers and some fragments of unglazed earthenware.

The lower bed lay at a depth of 18 feet from the top, and varied in thickness from 6 to 7 inches. It contained some rough earthenware, charcoal, and animal bones, all pointing to the Stone Age, but to the latest times of that period.

After having carefully examined these different beds and ascertained the regular structure of the cone, Morlot fancied that he could calculate approximately the age of each of them. He took for his base of operations two historical dates; that of the entrance of the Romans into Helvetia, fifty-eight years before Christ, and that of their decisive expulsion towards the end of the fifth century of the Christian era. By comparing these two dates, he came to the conclusion that the Roman layer was at the most eighteen and at the least thirteen centuries old. Then remarking that since that epoch the cone had increased 3 feet 6 inches, and always going upon the hypothesis that the increase was the same as in subsequent ages, he came to the conclusion that the bed corresponding with the bronze epoch was at least 2900 and at the most 4200 years old; and that the layer belonging to the Stone Age, forming the entire remainder of the cone, was from 4700 to 10,000 years old.

Another calculation, the conclusions of which agree tolerably well with these, was made by M. Gilliéron, professor at the college of Neuveville. We have already said that the remains of a pile-work belonging to the Stone Age was discovered near the bridge of Thièle, between the lakes of Bienne and Neuchâtel. It is evident that the valley, the narrowest part of which was occupied by the lacustrine settlement, was formerly almost entirely under water, for below this point it suddenly widens out and retains these proportions as far as the lake of Bienne. The lake must, therefore, have retired slowly and regularly, as may be ascertained from an examination of the mud deposited by it. If, therefore, we know its annual coefficient of retreat, that is to say, how much it retired every year, we should be able to estimate with a sufficient degree of approximation the age of the settlement of the bridge of Thièle.

Now there is, not far from the lake, at about 1230 feet from the present shore, an old abbey, that of Saint-Jean, which is known to have been built about the year 1100. A document of that time mentions that the cloister had the right of fishing in a certain part of the lake; and there is some likelihood that it was built on the edge of the lake; a supposition which naturally presents itself to the mind. The lake, then, must have retired 1230 feet in 750 years. This granted, M. Gilliéron easily calculated the time which would be taken for a retreat of 11,072 feet, this number representing the distance from the present shore to the entrance of the defile which contains the settlement of the bridge of Thièle. He found by this means that the settlement is at least 6750 years old, a figure which confirms those of Morlot.

The preceding calculations assign to the Stone Age in Switzerland an antiquity of 6000 to 7000 years before the Christian era, and to the bronze epoch an antiquity of 4000 years before the same era. There is still much uncertainty in the figures thus given to satisfy public curiosity; but there is at least one fact which is altogether unquestionable—that these calculations have dealt a fatal blow to recognised chronology.

FOOTNOTE:

[38] 'Le Danemark à l'Exposition Universelle de 1867, by Valdemar Schmidt,' vol. i. pp. 60-64. Paris, 1868.

II.
The Iron Epoch.

CHAPTER I.

Essential Characteristics of the Iron Epoch—Preparation of Iron in Prehistoric Times—Discovery of Silver and Lead—Earthenware made on the Potter's Wheel—Invention of Coined Money.

WITHOUT metals, as we have said in one of the preceding chapters, man must have remained for ever in a state of barbarism. To this we must add, that the civilisation of man has made progress just in proportion to the degree of perfection he has arrived at in the working of the metals and alloys which he has had at his disposal. The knowledge and use of bronze communicated a strong impulse to nascent civilisation, and was the means of founding the first human communities. But bronze is far from possessing all the qualities which ought to belong to metals when applied to various industrial purposes. This alloy is neither hard nor elastic enough to make good tools; and, in addition to this, it is composed of metals which in a natural state are very scarce. Man requires a metal which is cheap, hard, easy to work, and adapted to all the requirements which are exacted by industrial skill, which is so manifold in its works and wants.

A metal of this sort was at length discovered, and a new era opened for the future of men. They learned how to extract from its ore iron—the true king of metals, as it may well be called—on account of its inestimable qualities. From the day when iron was first placed at man's disposal civilisation began to make its longest strides, and as the working of this metal improved, so the dominion of man—his faculties and his intellectual activity—likewise enlarged in the same proportion.

It is, therefore, with good reason that the name of *Iron Epoch* has been given to the latest period of the development of primitive man, and it is not surprising that the last portion of the iron epoch formed the commencement of historical times. After this period, in fact, man ceased to live in that half-savage state, the most striking features of which we have endeavoured to portray.

As the use of iron essentially characterises this epoch in the history of mankind, we ought to give an account of the processes of manufacture employed by the primitive metallurgists, that is to say, we should inquire how they proceeded at this epoch to extract iron from its native ore.

The art of metallurgy had made great progress during the bronze epoch. There were at that time considerable workshops for the preparation of bronze, and small foundries for melting and casting this alloy. When once formed into weapons, instruments, and tools, bronze objects were fashioned by artisans of various professions. The moulder's art had already attained to a high degree of perfection, a fact which is proved by the gigantic bronze objects which we have already mentioned, as well as the castings, so many of which have been represented in the preceding pages. The phenomenon of *tempering* was well known, that is the principal modifications which are experienced by bronze in its cooling, whether slow or sudden. It was well known how to vary the proportions of the tin and copper so as to obtain bronze of different degrees of hardness. All the means of soldering were also familiarly known. Damascening was introduced in order to diversify the appearance of wrought metallic objects. The cutting qualities of instruments were increased by forging them and consolidating them by hammering. They had even gone so far as to discover the utility of the addition of certain mineral salts in the founder's crucible in order to facilitate the fusion of the bronze.

Thus at the end of the bronze epoch the knowledge of metals had attained to a comparatively considerable development. Hence we may conclude that the substitution of iron for bronze took place without any great difficulty. Owing to the natural progress and successive improvements made in metallurgic art, the blacksmith made his appearance on the scene and took the place of the bronze-moulder.

What, however, was the process which enabled our earliest metallurgists to extract iron from its native ore?

Native iron, that is metallic iron in a natural state, is eminently rare; except in aërolites it is scarcely ever found. According to Pallas, the Russian naturalist, certain Siberian tribes have succeeded, with a great amount of labour, in obtaining from the aërolites which have been met with in their country small quantities of iron, which they have made into knives. The same practice existed among the Laplanders. Lastly, we are told by Amerigo Vespucci that in the fifteenth century the Indians at the mouth of the La Plata river were in the habit of making arrow-heads and other instruments with iron extracted from aërolites.[39]

But, as we hardly need observe, stones of this kind do not often drop down from the skies, and their employment is of too accidental a character ever to have suggested to men the right mode of the extraction of iron. It is, therefore, almost certain that the first iron used was extracted from its ore just like copper and tin, that is, by the reduction of its oxide under the influence of heat and charcoal. In opposition to this explanation, some bring forward as an objection the prodigiously high temperature which is required for the fusion of iron, or, in fact, the almost impossibility of melting iron in the primitive furnaces. But the fusion of iron was in no way necessary for the extraction of this metal; and if it had been requisite to procure liquid iron, primitive industrial skill would never have succeeded in doing it. All that was necessary was so to reduce the oxide of iron as to obtain the metal in a spongy state without any fusion. The hammering of this spongy mass when in a red-hot state soon converted it into a real bar of iron.

If we cast a glance on the metallurgic industry of some of the semi-barbarous nations of ancient times, we shall find, as regards the extraction of iron, a process in use among them which will fully justify the idea we have formed of the way in which iron must have been obtained in primitive times. Gmelin, the naturalist, during his travels in Tartary, was a witness of the elementary process which was employed by these northern tribes in procuring iron. There, every one prepares his own iron just as every household might make its own bread. The furnace for the extraction of iron is placed in the kitchen, and is nothing but a mere cavity, 9 inches cube, which is filled up with iron-ore; the furnace is surmounted by an earthen chimney, and there is a door in front of the furnace for introducing the ore, this door being kept closed during the smelting process. In an orifice at the side the nozzle of a pair of bellows is inserted, which are blown by one man whilst another introduces the ore and charcoal in successive layers. The furnace never holds more than 3½ lbs. of ore for each operation. When this quantity has been placed in the furnace, in small pieces one after the other, all that is done is keeping up the action of the bellows for some minutes. Lastly, the door of the furnace is opened, and the ashes and other products of combustion having been drawn out, a small mass of spongy iron is found, which proceeds from the reduction of the oxide of iron by means of the charcoal, without the metal being in a state of fusion, properly so called. This small lump of iron was cleaned with a piece of wood, and was put on one side to be subsequently welded to others, and hammered several times when in a red-hot state; and by means of several forgings the whole mass was converted into a single bar.

This same process for the extraction of iron from its natural oxide, without fusion, is practised by the negroes of Fouta-Djallon, in Senegal.

After having become acquainted with the elementary process which is practised by the semi-barbarous tribes of the present day, we shall find but little difficulty in understanding all that Morlot, the Swiss naturalist, has said as to the iron-furnaces of pre-historic man, and shall probably agree in his opinions on the subject. Morlot, in his 'Mémoires sur l'Archéologie de la Suisse,' has described the vestiges of the pre-historic furnaces intended for the preparation of iron, which were found by him in Carinthia (Austria).

According to M. Morlot, the plan adopted for extracting iron from its oxide in pre-historic times was as follows:—On the side of a slope exposed to the wind, a hole was hollowed out. The bottom of this hole was filled up with a heap of wood, on which was placed a layer of ore. This layer of ore was covered by a second heap of wood; then, taking advantage of a strong breeze rising, which had to perform the functions of the bellows, the lowest pile of wood was kindled at its base. The wood by its combustion was converted into charcoal, and this charcoal, under the influence of heat, soon reduced the iron oxide to a metallic state. When the combustion had come to an end, a few pieces of iron were found among the ashes.

By increasing the size of the apparatus used, far more considerable results were of course obtained. In Dalecarlia (Sweden), M. Morlot found smelting-houses, so to speak, in which the original hole, of which we have just been speaking, is surrounded with stones so as to form a sort of circular receptacle. In this rough stone crucible layers of charcoal and iron-ore were placed in succession. After having burnt for some hours, the heap was searched over and the spongy iron was found mixed with the ashes at the bottom of the furnace.

The slowness of the operation and the inconsiderable metallic result induced them to increase the size of the stone receptacle. They first gave to it a depth of 7 feet and then of 13 feet, and, at the same time, coated the walls of it with clay. They thus had at their disposal a kind of vast circular crucible, in which they placed successive layers of iron-ore and wood or charcoal.

In this altogether elementary arrangement no use was made, as it seems, of the bellows. This amounts to stating that the primitive method of smelting iron was not, as is commonly thought, an adaptation of the *Catalan furnace*. This latter process, which, even in the present time, is made use of in the Pyrenean smelting works, does not date back further than the times of the Roman empire. It is based on the continual action of the bellows; whilst in the pre-historic furnaces this instrument, we will again repeat, was never employed.

These primitive furnaces applied to the reduction of iron-ore, traces of which had been recognised by Morlot, the naturalist, in Austria and Sweden, have lately been discovered in considerable numbers in the canton of Berne by M. Quiquerez, a scientific mining engineer. They consist of cylindrical excavations, of no great depth, dug out on the side of a hill and surmounted by a clay funnel of conical form. Wood-charcoal was the fuel employed for charging the furnaces, for stores of this combustible are always found lying round the ancient smelting works.

In an extremely curious memoir, which was published in 1866 by the Jura Society of Emulation, under the title of 'Recherches sur les anciennes Forges du Jura Bernois,' M. Quiquerez summed up the results of his protracted and minute investigations. A few extracts from this valuable work will bring to our knowledge the real construction of the furnaces used by pre-historic man; 400 of these furnaces having been discovered by M. Quiquerez in the district of the Bernese Jura.

We will, however, previously mention that M. Quiquerez had represented, or materialised, as it were, the results of his interesting labours, by constructing a model in miniature of a siderurgical establishment belonging to the earliest iron epoch. This curious specimen of workmanship showed the clay-furnace placed against the side of a hill, the heaps of charcoal, the scoriæ, the hut used as a dwelling by the workmen, the furnace-implements—in short, all the details which formed the result of the patient researches of the learned Swiss engineer.

M. Quiquerez had prepared this interesting model of the ancient industrial pursuits of man with a view of exhibiting it in the *Exposition Universelle* of 1867, together with the very substances, productions, and implements which he had found in his explorations in the Jura. But the commission appointed for selecting objects for admission refused to grant him the modest square yard of area which he required for placing his model. How ridiculous it seems! In the immense Champ de Mars in which so many useless and absurd objects perfectly swarmed, one square yard of space was refused for one of the most curious productions which was ever turned out by the skilful hands of any *savant*!

The result of this unintelligent refusal was that M. Quiquerez' model did not make its appearance in the *Exposition Universelle* in the Champ de Mars, and that it was missing from the curious Gallery of the History of Labour, which called forth so much of the attention of the public. For our readers, however, it will not be altogether lost. M. Quiquerez has been good enough to forward to us from Bellerive, where he resides (near Délémont, canton of Basle, Switzerland) a photograph of his curious model of a pre-historic workshop for the preparation of iron. From this photograph we have designed the annexed plate, representing a *primitive furnace for the extraction of iron*.

Fig. 231.—Primitive Furnace for Smelting Iron.

This composition reproduces with tolerable accuracy the model in relief constructed by the author. The furnace is shown; it is nothing but a simple cavity surmounted by a conical chimney-funnel, and placed against the side of a hill. Steps made of rough stone, placed on each side of the mound, enable the workmen to mount to the summit. The height of the funnel is about 9 feet. At the side of the furnace stands the hut for the labourers, constructed of a number of round poles placed side by side; for centuries past huts of this kind have been erected in almost every country.

On the right, in the foreground, we may notice a heap of charcoal intended to be placed in the furnace in order to reduce the ore; on the left, there is the store of ore called in the ironworks the *ore-pen*. The provision of iron-ore is enclosed between four wooden slabs, forming a quadrangular space. In the centre are the scoriæ which result from the operations carried on. A workman is extracting the cake of spongy iron from the ashes of the furnace; another is hammering on the anvil a piece of iron drawn from the furnace in order to forge it into a bar. Round the furnace various implements are scattered about, such as the anvil, the pincers, the hammer, &c. All the instruments are designed from various specimens found by the author.

After these explanations, we may now give some extracts from M. Quiquerez' work, and we trust our readers will find no difficulty in comprehending the details given by the learned engineer, describing the primitive furnaces for the extraction of iron which he discovered in the Bernese Jura.

M. Quiquerez has remarked two kinds of primitive furnaces for the fabrication of iron, or, rather, two stages of improvement in their construction. The first sort, that which the author considers as dating back to the most remote antiquity, is not so numerous as the others; the second kind form the largest number of those which he has explored.

"Furnaces of the first kind," says M. Quiquerez, "consisted of nothing but a small cylindrical excavation of no great regularity in shape, with a cup-shaped bottom, hollowed out in the side of a hill so as to give more natural height on one side; the front of the furnace was closed up by fire-proof clay, supported with stones. This cavity was plastered over with 4 to 6 inches of clay, generally of a whitish colour, which became red after coming in contact with the fire. These smelting-furnaces were not more than 12 to 18 inches in depth, as seemed to be shown by the upper edges being rounded and more or less scoriated. The front, which was always more or less broken, had an opening at its base to admit a current of air, and to allow the workmen to deal with the melted material; but this opening seems to show that the piece of metal which had been formed during the operation must have been extracted by breaking in the front.

"The second kind of furnace, which is by far the most numerously found and widely distributed, is, in fact, nothing but an improvement of that which preceded it, the edges of the furnace or crucible being considerably raised in height. They vary in depth from $7\frac{1}{2}$ to 8 feet, with a diameter of most irregular dimensions, from 18 inches upwards, and a thickness of 12 inches to 7 feet. They are likewise formed of fire-proof clay, and their average capacity is about 25 gallons.

"The constructor, having dug out in the side of the hill an opening circular, or rather semi-circular, at the base, with a diameter nearly three times as wide as the future furnace, arranged in the centre of this hole a kind of furnace-bed made of plastic clay at bottom, and covered with a layer of fire-proof clay on the top of it. The bed of the furnace, which lies on the natural and hardly levelled earth, is, generally speaking, not so thick as the side walls, which are formed of sandy or siliceous clay, always fire-proof on the inside, but sometimes of a more plastic nature on the exterior; the empty space left between the walls of the furnace and the solid ground round it was filled up with earth and other material. In front the furnace was enclosed by a rough wall, sometimes straight and sometimes curving, built, without mortar, of rough limestone, and dressed with earth to fill up the gaps. In front of the furnace an opening was made in this wall, taking its rise a few inches above the bottom of the furnace, and increasing in size in an outward direction, so as to enable the workmen to see into, and work in, the furnace.

"The work thus commenced was carried up to the requisite height; and when the excavation in the side of the hill was not lofty enough, the dome of the furnace was raised by placing buttresses against the fire-clay, so as to prevent the earth falling in. When these furnaces were established on almost level ground, as is sometimes the case, they form a truncated cone, with a base varying in size according to the height of the apparatus.

"The furnace was not always built upright; it often deviated from the perpendicular, leaning to one side or the other to an extent as considerable as its own diameter, but no constant rule as to this can be recognised. The internal shape was just as irregular, changing from circular to oval, without any apparent motive beyond want of care in the workman. The crucibles or furnaces are sometimes larger at the top than at the bottom, and sometimes these proportions are reversed, but always with extreme irregularity. We have noticed some which at a point 10 or 12 inches above the crucible were perceptibly contracted on three sides, thus representing the first rudiments of the appearance of our modern furnaces. But this, perhaps, was nothing but a caprice on the part of the builder.

"The furnace thus being established, the wood was withdrawn which had formed the cone, if, indeed, any had been used, and at the hole made at the base of the crucible a clod of fire-clay some inches in height was placed, so as to form a dam, and to confine in the crucible the molten or soft metal; the scoriæ, being of a lighter nature and floating at the top, made their escape over the top of the dam. As the latter were not very liquid, their issue was promoted by means of pokers or wooden poles, perhaps damped, with which also the metal was stirred in the crucible.

"In neither of these two kinds of furnaces do we find any trace of bellows, and a more or less strong draught must have been procured through the opening made for the escape of the scoriæ, according to the elevation of the dome of the furnace. The limestones which have been found in certain furnaces were probably employed with a view of increasing the draught; they doubtless belonged to the upper part of the furnace, where they had been fixed so as to add height to the orifice. This rudimentary plan must have been likewise used in the earliest crucibles. The mode of obtaining a draught which we have just pointed out is indicated most plainly by the scorification of the walls of the furnace on the side opposite to the air-passage; this side has evidently experienced a more intense heat, whilst on the other the walls are much less affected by the fire, and in some cases pieces of the mineral still remain in a pasty or semi-molten state, just as they were when the work of the furnace ceased....

"The absence of any machine in the shape of bellows in the ancient metal works of the Jura appears all the more remarkable as these implements were known both to the Greeks and Romans; hence we may at least infer, not only that these nations did not introduce the art of iron-working into the Jura, but that it must have existed at a much earlier period. It must also be remarked that the openings in the furnaces are not placed in the direction of the winds prevailing in the country—a plan which might have increased the draught—but are made quite at hazard, just as the nature of the spot rendered the construction of the furnace more easy.

" ... In respect to fuel it must be remarked that in all the siderurgical establishments which we have discovered, certain features indicate that wood carbonised in a stack was exclusively used as fuel. The furnaces are too small for the employment of rough wood; added to this, charcoal stores are placed near the furnaces; and charcoal burnt in a stack is constantly met with all round the sites, in the scoriæ, and all the *débris*. We must, besides, mention the discovery, at Bellelay, of a charcoal store 8 feet in diameter, situated under a compact bed of peat 20 feet in thickness. It was established on the solid earth, anterior to the formation of the peat. Now from this very peat a parcel of coins belonging to the fifteenth century was recovered, over which only 2 feet of peat had grown in a period of 400 years. There, too, at a depth of 9 feet, were found the scattered bones of a horse, with the foot still shod with those undulating edged shoes with elongated and strongly punched holes, in which were fitted the ends of nails of the shape of a T, the heads of which were conical. This kind of shoe is found in the Celtic settlements, the villages, habitations, and ironworks, also in the pasturages and forests of the country, but rarely in the Roman camps; in the latter they are always in less number than the wider metallic shoes, which are larger, and furnished with a groove indicating the line in which the nail-holes were punched. The calculations which have been made from the discovery of the coins of the fifteenth century (A.D. 1478) would give an antiquity of at least twenty to twenty-four centuries to the horse-shoe we have just mentioned, for the animal must have died and been devoured on the then existing surface of the ground, and could not have been buried in the peat, as the bones, instead of lying grouped together, were dispersed in every direction. These same calculations would carry back the date of the charcoal-store to an era 4000 years ago.

"Owing to the imperfection of the furnaces, the quantity of charcoal used must have been quadruple the present consumption for the same results. The metal, as it was extracted from the ore, fell down into the bottom of the crucible. In proportion as the mass of metal increased, a workman, with a poker made of damp green wood, brought out the scoriæ which floated on the top, and stirred the metal so as to fine it. It is proved that these wooden pokers or poles were made use of in all the furnace-works. A quantity of morsels of scoriæ is found which, having been in a soft state when extracted, have retained the imprint of the piece of wood, the end of which was evidently charred. M. Morlot, in his article on the Roman ironworks at Wocheim, in Upper Carniola, has also noticed the existence, in the scoriæ, of frequent traces of pokers, sometimes round and sometimes three-cornered in shape, but all of them must have been made of iron, whilst throughout the whole of the Jura we have never recognised the traces of any but wooden implements of this kind.

"Owing to the imperfection of the furnaces, and especially, the deficiency in the draught caused by the want of bellows, the metal contained in the ore could be but very imperfectly extracted; the scoriæ are therefore still so very rich in iron that, about twenty years ago, the manager of the ironworks at Untervelier tried to use them over again as ore. Accumulations of this dross, measuring from 100 to 200 yards square, may be seen near certain furnaces-a fact which would infer a somewhat considerable production of iron. The examination of these scoriæ proves that iron was then made by one single operation, and not liquid pigs fit for casting, or to be converted into iron by a second series of operations.

"The iron produced was introduced into commerce in large blocks, shaped like two quadrangular pyramids joined at the base, weighing from 12 to 16 lbs. One of these pieces was found near a furnace which had been demolished in order to establish a charcoal furnace, in the commune of Untervelier, and another in one of the furnaces of Boécourt.

"All round the furnaces there have been found numerous remains of rough pottery; it is badly baked, and made without the help of the wheel, from clay which is mingled with grains of quartz—the pottery, in fact, which is called Celtic. Pieces of stag's horn have also been discovered, which must have been used for the handles of tools; also iron hatchets. One of them has a socket at the end made in a line with the length of the implement; it is an instrument belonging to the most remote period of the iron age. The others have transversal sockets like our present hatchets. One of the latter was made of steel so hard that it could not be touched with the file. With regard to coins, both Gallic and Roman were found, and some of the latter were of as late a date as that of the Constantines. The persistence in practising the routine of all the most ancient processes may be explained by the monopoly of the iron-working trade being retained in the same families. We have the less need to be surprised at this, because we may notice that the wood-cutters and charcoal-burners of our own days, when they have to take up their abode in a locality for any length of time, and to carry on their trade there, always make certain arrangements which have doubtless been handed down from the most primitive times. In order to protect their beds from the damp, they make a kind of shelf of fir-poles which is used as a bedstead. Some of them have two stories; the under-one intended for the children, and the one above for the parents. Moss, ferns, and dried grass form the mattress. Coverlets impossible to describe were made good use of, and some were even made of branches of fir-trees. These bedsteads take the place both of benches and chairs. A stone fire-place, roughly arranged in the centre of the hut, fills the double function of warming in winter and cooking the food all the year round. We may also add, that the fire, which is almost always kept lighted, and the ashes spread over the floor all round, preserve the hut from certain troublesome insects, which lose their lives by jumping imprudently into this unknown trap. The smoke finds no other issue but through a hole made in the roof."[40]

Such is the description given by M. Quiquerez of the iron furnaces of a really pre-historic character, those, namely, which are characterised by the absence of bellows. We think, however, that there must have been holes below the hearth which afforded access to currents of air, and, by being alternately open or closed, served either to increase or diminish the intensity of the draught. But bellows, properly so called, intended to promote the combustion and chemical reaction between the oxide of iron and the charcoal did not then exist.

The addition of the bellows to iron-furnaces brought an essential improvement to the art of the manufacture of iron.

Another improvement consisted in making, at the bottom of the stone receptacle where the fuel and the ore were burnt together, a door composed of several bricks which could be readily moved. At the completion of each operation they drew out, through this door, the cake of iron, which could not be so conveniently extracted at the upper part of the furnace, on account of its height. The hammering, assisted by several heatings, finally cleared the iron, in the usual way, from all extraneous matter, consolidated it, and converted it into the state of bar-iron fit for the blacksmith's use, and for the fabrication of utensils and tools.

These improved primitive furnaces are well-known to German miners under the name of *Stucköfen* ("fragment-furnaces"). They are modified in different ways in different countries; and according to the arrangement of the furnace, and especially according to the nature of the ferruginous ores, certain methods or manipulations of the iron have been introduced, which are nowadays known under the names of the Swedish, German, Styrian, Carinthian, Corsican, and Catalan methods.

The ancient furnaces for the extraction of iron may be combined under the name of *smelting-forges* or *bloomeries*.

The invention of siliceous fluxes as applied to the extraction of iron, and facilitating the production of a liquid scoria which could flow out in the form of a stream of fire, put the finishing stroke to the preparation of iron. The constructors next considerably increased the height of the stone crucible in which the fuel and the ore, now mingled with a siliceous flux, were placed, and the *blast furnace*, that is, the present system of the preparation of iron, soon came into existence.

But, there may be reason to think, neither of these two kinds of furnaces belongs to the primitive ages of mankind which are the object of this work. In the iron epoch—that we are considering—the furnace without bellows was possibly the only one known; the iron was prepared in very small quantities at a time, and the meagre metallic cake, the result from each operation, had to be picked out from among the ashes drawn from the stone receptacle.

Gold, as we have already said, was known to the men of the bronze epoch. Silver, on the contrary, did not come into use until the iron epoch.

Another characteristic of the epoch we are now studying is the appearance of pottery made on the potter's wheel, and baked in an improved kind of furnace. Up to that time, pottery had been moulded by the hand, and merely burnt in the open air. In the iron epoch, the potter's wheel came into use, and articles of earthenware were manufactured on this wheel, and baked in an unexceptionable way in an oven especially constructed for the purpose.

There is another fact which likewise characterises the iron epoch; this was the appearance of coined money. The earliest known coins belong to this period; they are made of bronze, and bear a figure or effigy not stamped, but obtained by melting and casting.

The most ancient coins that are known are Greek, and date back to the eighth century before Christ. These are the coins of Ægina, Athens, and Cyzicum, such as were found many years ago in the duchy of Posen. In the lacustrine settlement of Neuchâtel, coins of a remote antiquity have also been found. We here represent in its natural size (fig. 232), taken from M. Desor's work, a bronze coin found in the settlement of La Tène in the lake of Neuchâtel. But these coins are not more ancient than the Greek specimens that we have before named. They are shown to be Gallic by the horned horse, which is a Gallic emblem.

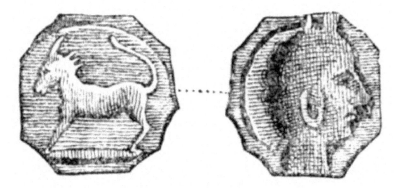

Fig. 232.—Bronze Coin, from the Lake of Neuchâtel.

At Tiefenau, near Berne, coins have been found of a nearly similar character associated with others having on them the effigy of Apollo, and bearing an imprint of *Massilia* (Marseilles). As the foundation of this Phocæan colony dates back to the sixth century before Christ, these coins may be said to be among the most ancient which exist.

Glass became known, as we have before stated, in the bronze epoch.

In short, the essential features which distinguish the iron epoch are, iron instruments, and implements combining with those of bronze to replace stone in all the uses for which it was anciently employed—the knowledge of silver and lead, the improvement of pottery, and the introduction of coined money. With regard to its chronological date we should adopt that of about 2000 years before the Christian era, thus agreeing with the generality of authors—the date of the bronze epoch being fixed about 4000 years before Christ.

After these general considerations, we shall pass on to give some account of the manners and customs of man during the iron epoch, or, at least, during the earlier portion of this period, which ere long became blended with historic ages.

When we have completed our study of man in the earlier period of the iron epoch, we shall have terminated the rapid sketch which we have intended to trace out of primitive man and his labours. This period commenced, as we have just stated, about 2000 years before Christ, and ultimately merged into the earliest glimmer of historical records. Our task now is to describe all we know about man at this date of nascent civilisation. Afterwards, the earliest historians—and among them, Herodotus, the father of history—are the authorities whom we must consult for an account of the actions and exploits of the human race in Europe.

FOOTNOTES:

[39] Details as to the relation of the Stone Age to the Bronze and Iron Ages may be found in 'Researches into the Early History of Mankind,' by Edward B. Tylor. Chap. VIII., 'Pre-Historic Times,' by Sir J. Lubbock, Chaps. I. and II.

[40] 'De l'Age du Fer, Recherches sur les anciennes Forges du Jura Bernois,' by A. Quiquerez, Engineer of the Jura Mines. Porrentruy, 1866; pp. 35-39, 77-80. Also, 'Matériaux pour l'Histoire positif de l'Homme,' by G. de Mortillet, vol. ii. pp. 505-510.

CHAPTER II.

Weapons—Tools, Instruments, Utensils, and Pottery—The Tombs of Hallstadt and the Plateau of La Somma—The Lake-Settlements of Switzerland—Human Sacrifices—Type of Man during the Iron Epoch—Commencement of the Historic Era.

THE most valuable traces of the manners and customs of man during the earlier period of the iron epoch have been furnished by the vast burial-ground discovered recently at Hallstadt, near Salzburg in Austria. M. Ramsauer, Director of the salt-mines of Salzburg, has explored more than 1000 tombs in this locality, and has described them in a work full of interest, a manuscript copy of which we have consulted in the Archæological Museum of Saint-Germain.

As the tombs at Hallstadt belong to the earlier period of the iron epoch, they represent to us the natural transition from the epoch of bronze to that of iron. In fact, in a great number of objects contained in these tombs—such as daggers, swords and various ornaments—bronze and iron are combined. One sword, for instance, is formed of a bronze hilt and an iron blade. This is represented in figures 233, 234, 235 and 236, drawn from the sketches in M. Ramsauer's manuscript work entitled 'Les Tombes de Hallstadt,' in which this combination of the two metals is remarked upon; the sword-hilts being formed of one metal and the blades of another.

Fig. 233.—Sword, from the Tombs of Hallstadt (with a Bronze Hilt and Iron Blade).

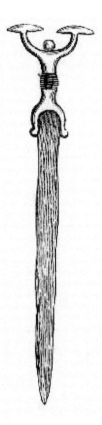

Fig. 234.—Sword, from the Tombs of Hallstadt (with a Bronze Hilt and Iron Blade).

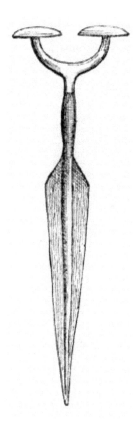

Fig. 235.—Dagger, from the Tombs of Hallstadt (Bronze Handle and Iron Blade).

Fig. 236.—Dagger, from the Tombs of Hallstadt (Bronze Handle and Iron Blade).

By taking a rapid survey of the objects found in the tombs of Hallstadt, we can form a somewhat accurate idea of the first outset of the iron age.

The first point which strikes us in this period, is the utter change which had taken place in the interment of the dead.

During the Stone Age, the dead were placed in small subterranean crypts, that is in *dolmens* or *tumuli*. During the Bronze Age it became to a great extent customary for men to burn the dead bodies of their friends.

This custom was destined to become more and more prevalent century after century, and during historic times it became universal among a great many nations.

In fact, in the tombs of Hallstadt, several little earthen vessels containing ashes may be seen. Sometimes only part of the body was burnt, so that a portion of a skeleton was found in these tombs, and near it the ashes of the parts which the fire had consumed.

The remains found in the tombs of Hallstadt are almost equally divided between these two modes of inhumation. About half of the tombs contain nothing but ashes; in the other half, corpses are laid extended, according to the custom which was most prevalent in the iron age. Lastly, as we have just stated, some of them contained skeletons which were partially burnt. Sometimes it was the head, sometimes the whole bust, or sometimes the lower limbs which were consumed, the ashes being deposited by the side of the intact portions of the skeleton. Fig. 238, which is designed from one of the illustrations in M. Ramsauer's manuscript work 'Les Tombes de Hallstadt,' in the Museum of Saint-Germain, represents a skeleton, part of which (the chest) has been consumed. The ashes are contained in small earthen vessels which are seen near the corpse.

Fig. 237.—Funeral Ceremonies during the Iron Epoch.

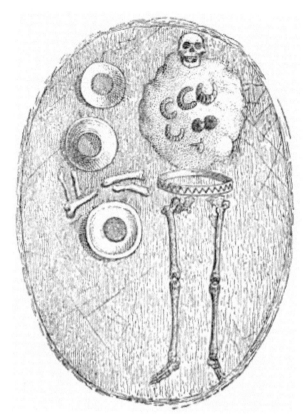

Fig. 238.—A Skeleton, portions of which have been burnt, from the Tombs of Hallstadt.

From the *data* which we have acquired as to this custom of burning dead bodies during the iron epoch, we have been able to represent *the funeral ceremonies of the iron epoch* in the preceding figure.

The corpse is placed on a funeral pile, and the stone door of the tumulus is raised in order to deposit in it the cinerary urn. The relations of the deceased accompany the procession clothed in their handsomest garments and adorned with the bronze and iron ornaments which were then in vogue. One of those present may be seen throwing some precious objects into the flames of the funeral pile in honour of the deceased.

The tombs of Hallstadt are the locality in which the largest number of objects, such as weapons, instruments and implements, have been met with, which have tended to throw a light upon the history of the transition from the bronze to the iron epoch. All these objects are either of bronze or iron; but in the weapons the latter predominates. Swords, spear-heads, daggers, knives, socketed hatchets and winged hatchets form the catalogue of the sharp instruments. In the preceding pages (figs. 233, 234, 235 and 236) we have given representations of swords and daggers designed from the specimens in the Museum of Saint-Germain. In all these weapons the handle is made of bronze and the blade of iron. Warriors' sword-belts are frequently formed of plates of bronze, and are embellished with a *repoussé* ornamentation executed by the hammer.

In fig. 239 we give a representation of a necklace with pendants which is most remarkable in its workmanship. It may be readily seen that art had now attained some degree of maturity. This necklace was a prelude to the marvellous works of art which were about to be brought to light under the skies of Greece.

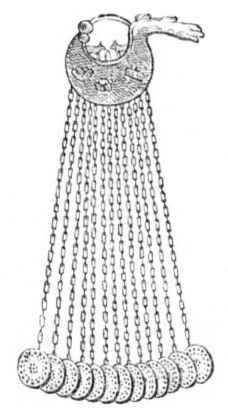

Fig. 239.—A Necklace with Pendants, from the Tombs of Hallstadt.

The bracelets which have been met with by hundreds, hair pins and bronze fibulæ are all wrought with taste, and are often adorned with very elegant pendants. In figs. 240 and 241 we show two bracelets, the sketches for which were taken from the designs in the manuscript of the 'Tombes de Hallstadt.'

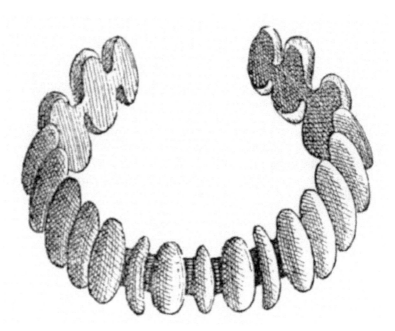

Fig. 240.—Bracelet, from the Tombs of Hallstadt.

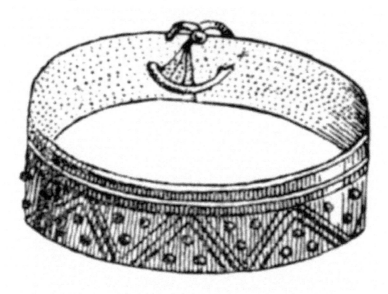

Fig. 241.—Bracelet, from the Tombs of Hallstadt.

We may add a few amber necklace-beads and some of enamel, and we have then concluded the series of personal ornaments.

In the tombs of Hallstadt, nearly 200 bronze vessels have been discovered, some of which are as much as 36 inches in height. These bronze vessels were composed of several pieces skilfully riveted but not soldered. Plates 242 and 243 are reproduced from the same beautiful manuscript.

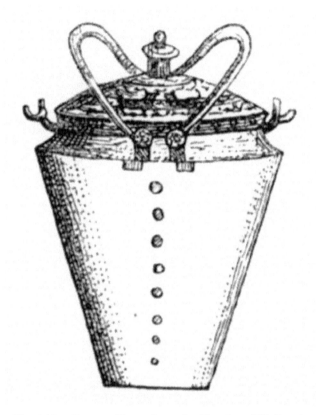

Fig. 242.—Bronze Vase, from the Tombs of Hallstadt.

Fig. 243.—Bronze Vase, from the Tombs of Hallstadt.

In the tombs of Hallstadt some small glass vessels have also been discovered.

Remains of pottery are very plentiful, and a decided improvement is shown in their workmanship. Some gold trinkets were also met with in these tombs. The gold was, doubtless, obtained from the mines of Transylvania.

African ivory abounds in these graves—a fact which indicates commercial intercourse with very distant countries. This product, as well as the glass, was introduced into Europe by the Phœnicians. The inhabitants of central Europe obtained ivory from Tyre and Sidon by means of barter.

The ivory objects which were found at Hallstadt consisted of the heads of hair-pins and the pommels of swords.

There were no traces whatever of money, the use of it not being then established in that part of Europe.

The population which lived in the vicinity of the Salzburg mines were in reality rich; for the salt-mines were a source of great wealth to them at a period when the deposits of rock-salt in Poland, being still buried in the depths of the earth, were as yet unknown or inaccessible. In this way, we may account for the general opulence of these commercial nations, and for the elegance and taste displayed in the objects which have been found in the tombs of Hallstadt.

Guided by these various remains, it is not difficult to reproduce an ideal picture of *the warriors of the iron epoch*, a representation of which we have endeavoured to give in fig. 244. The different pieces of the ornaments observed on the horseman, on the foot-soldier, and also on the horse, are drawn from specimens exhibited in the Museum of Saint-Germain which were modelled at Hallstadt. The helmet is in perfect preservation and resembles those which, shortly after, were worn by the Gallic soldiers. The bosses, also, on the horse's harness, ere long came into use both among the Gauls and also the Romans.

Fig. 244.—Warriors of the Iron Epoch.

Next to the tombs of Hallstadt, we must mention the tombs discovered on the plateau of La Somma, in Lombardy, which have contributed a valuable addition to the history of the earliest period of the iron epoch.

On this plateau there were discovered certain tombs, composed of rough stones of a rectangular form. In the interior there were some vases of a shape suited to the purpose, containing ashes. The material of which they were made was fine clay; they had been wrought by means of the potter's wheel, were ornamented with various designs, and also provided with encircling projections. On some of them, representations of animals may be seen which indicate a considerable progress in the province of art. The historic date of these urns is pointed out by *fibulæ* (clasps for cloaks), iron rings and bracelets, sword-belts partly bronze and partly iron, and small bronze chains. The tombs of La Somma belong, therefore, to a period of transition between the bronze and iron epochs. According to M. Mortillet, they date back to the seventh century before Christ.

Under the same head we will class the tombs of Saint-Jean de Belleville, in Savoy. At this spot several tombs belonging to the commencement of the iron epoch have been explored by MM. Borel and Costa de Beauregard. The latter, in a splendid work published in Savoy, has given a detailed description of these tombs.[41]

Some of the skeletons are extended on their backs, others have been consumed, but only partially, like those which we have already mentioned in the tombs of Hallstadt. Various objects, consisting chiefly of trinkets and ornaments, have been met with in these tombs. We will mention in particular the *fibulæ*, bracelets and necklaces made of amber, enamelled glass, &c.

In figs. 245 and 246 we give a representation of two skeleton arms, which are encircled with several bracelets just as they were found in these tombs.

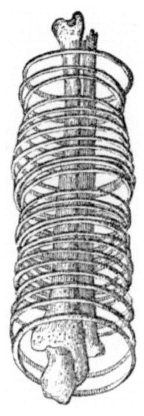

Fig. 245.—Fore-arm, encircled with Bracelets, found in the Tombs of Belleville (Savoy).

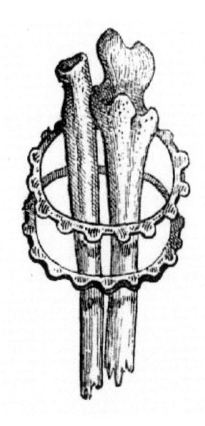

Fig. 246.—Fore-arm, encircled with Bracelets, found in the Tombs of Belleville (Savoy).

The lacustrine settlements of Switzerland have contributed a valuable element towards the historic reconstruction of the iron epoch.

In different parts of the lakes of Bienne and Neuchâtel there are pile-works which contain iron objects intermingled with the remains of preceding ages. But there is only one lacustrine settlement in Switzerland which belongs exclusively to the earliest period of the Iron Age—that of La Tène on the Lake of Neuchâtel.

Most of the objects which have been met with in this lacustrine settlement have been recovered from the mud in which they had been so remarkably preserved, being sheltered from any contact with the outer air. There are, however, many spots in which piles may be seen, where objects of this kind have not been found; but if subsequent researches are attended with any results, we shall be forced to attribute to the settlement of La Tène a considerable degree of importance, for the piles there extend over an area of 37 acres.

The remains of all kinds which have been found in this settlement are evidently of Gallic origin. It is an easy matter to prove this by comparing the weapons found in this settlement with those which were discovered in the trenches of Alise-Sainte-Reine, the ancient *Alesia*, where, in its last contest against Cæsar, the independence of ancient Gaul came to an end.

M. de Rougemont has called attention to the fact that these weapons correspond very exactly to the description given by Diodorus Siculus of the Gallic weapons. Switzerland thus seems to have been inhabited in the earliest iron epoch by Gallic tribes, that is to say, by a different race from that which occupied it during the stone and bronze epochs; and it was this race which introduced into Switzerland the use of iron.

Among the objects collected in the lake settlement of La Tène, weapons are the most numerous; they consist of swords and the heads of spears and javelins. Most of them have been kept from oxidation by the peaty mud which entirely covered them, and they are, consequently, in a state of perfect preservation.

The swords are all straight, of no very great thickness, and perfectly flat. The blade is from 31 to 35 inches in length, and is terminated by a handle about 6 inches long. They have neither guards nor crosspieces. Several of them were still in their sheaths, from which many of them have been drawn out in a state of perfect preservation, and even tolerably sharp.

Fig. 247 represents one of the iron swords from the Swiss lakes, which are depicted in M. Desor's memoir.

Fig. 247.—Iron Sword, found in one of the Swiss Lakes.

On another sword, of which we also give a representation (fig. 248), a sort of damascening work extends over almost the whole surface, leaving the edges alone entirely smooth.

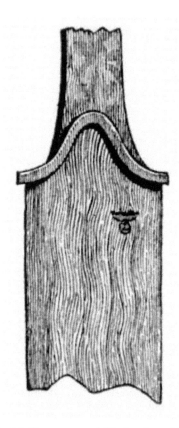

Fig. 248.—Sword with Damascened Blade, found in one of the Swiss Lakes.

M. de Reffye, the archæologist, accounts for this fact in the following way:—He is of opinion that the body of the blade is made of very hard unyielding iron, whilst the edges are made of small strips of mellower iron which have been subsequently welded and wrought by the hammer. This mode of manufacture enabled the soldier, when his sword was notched, to repair it by means of hammering. This was a most valuable resource during an epoch in which armies did not convey stores along with them, and when the soldier's baggage was reduced to very little more than he could personally carry. Several of these damascened blades have been found in the trenches of Alise.

The sheaths, the existence of which now for the first time comes under our notice, are of great importance on account of the designs with which they are ornamented. Most of these designs are engraved with a tool, others are executed in *repoussé* work. All of them show great originality and peculiar characteristics, which prevent them from being confounded with works of

Roman art. One of these sheaths (fig. 249), which belongs to M. Desor's collection and is depicted in his memoir, represents the "horned horse," the emblem of Gaul, which is sufficient proof of the Gallic origin of the weapons found in the Lake of La Tène. Below this emblem, there is a kind of granulated surface which bears some resemblance to shagreen.

Fig 249.—Sheath of a Sword, found in one of the Swiss Lakes.

This sheath is composed of two very thin plates of wrought iron laid one upon the other, except at the base, where they are united by means of a cleverly-wrought band of iron. At its upper extremity there is a plate, on one side of which may be seen the designs which we have already described, and on the other a ring, intended to suspend the weapon to the belt.

The lance-heads are very remarkable on account of their extraordinary shape and large size. They measure as much as 16 inches long, by 2 to 4 inches wide, and are double-edged and twisted into very diversified shapes. Some are winged, and others are irregularly indented. Some have perforations in the shape of a half-moon (fig. 250). The halberd of the middle ages was, very probably, nothing but an improvement on, or a deviation from, these singular blades.

Fig. 250.—Lance-head, found in one of the Swiss Lakes.

Fragments of wooden staves have been met with which had been fitted into these spear-heads; they are slender, and shod with iron at one end.

The care with which these instruments are wrought proves that they are lance-heads, and not mere darts or javelins intended to be thrown to a distance and consequently lost. They certainly would not have taken so much pains with the manufacture of a weapon which would be used only once.

It is altogether a different matter with respect to the javelins, a tolerably large number of which have been found in the lacustrine settlements of La Tène. They are simple socketed heads (fig. 251), terminating in a laurel-leaf shape, about 4 to 5 inches in length.

Fig. 251.—Head of a Javelin, found in the Lacustrine Settlement of La Tène (Neuchâtel).

It appears from experiments ordered by the Emperor of the French, that these javelins could only have been used as missile weapons, and that they were thrown, not by the hand merely grasping the shaft (which would be impossible to do effectually on account of their light weight), but by means of a cord or thong, which was designated among the Romans by the name of *amentum*. These experiments have shown that a dart which could be thrown only 65 feet with the hand, might be cast four times that distance by the aid of the *amentum*. There probably existed among the Gauls certain military corps who practised the use of the *amentum*, that is to say, the management of *thonged javelins*, and threw this javelin in the same way as other warriors threw stones by means of a sling. This conclusion, which has been drawn by M. Desor, seems to us a very just one.

Javelins of the preceding type are very common in the trenches of Alise. In this neighbourhood a large number of iron arrows have also been found which have never been met with in the lacustrine settlement of La Tène.

War was not the only purpose for which these javelins were used by the men of the iron epoch. Hunting, too, was carried on by means of these missile weapons. The bow and the thonged javelin constituted the hunting weapons of this epoch. We have depicted this in the accompanying plate, which represents *the chase during the iron epoch*.

Fig. 252.—The Chase during the Iron Epoch.

Next to the weapons come the implements. We will, in the first place, mention the hatchets (fig. 253). They are larger, more solid, and have a wider cutting edge than those used in the bronze epoch; wings were no longer in use, only a square-shaped socket into which was fitted a wooden handle, probably made with an elbow.

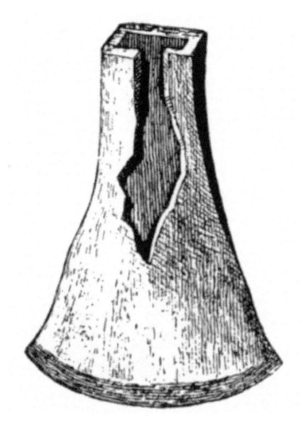

Fig. 253.—Square-socketed Iron Hatchet, found in one of the Lakes of Switzerland.

The sickles (fig. 254) are likewise larger and also more simple than those of the bronze epoch; there are neither designs nor ornaments of any kind on them.

Fig. 254.—Sickle.

With the pruning-bills or sickles we must class the regular scythes (fig. 255) with stems for handling, two specimens of which have been discovered in the lake settlement of the Tène. Their length is about 14 inches, that is, about one-third as large as the scythes used by the Swiss harvest-men of the present day. One important inference is drawn from the existence of these scythes; it is, that at the commencement of the iron epoch men were in the habit of storing up a provision of hay, and must consequently have reared cattle.

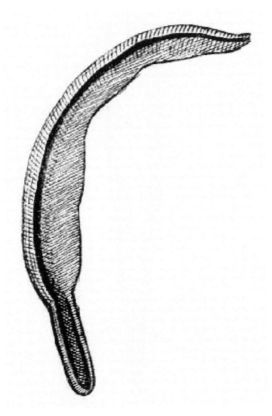

Fig. 255.—Scythe, from the Lacustrine Settlements of Switzerland.

The iron fittings at the ends of the boat-hooks used by the boatmen on the lake are frequently found at La Tène; they terminate in a quadrangular pyramid or in a cone (fig. 256). Some still contain the end of the wooden pole, which was attached to it by means of a nail.

Fig. 256.—Iron Point of Boat-hook, used by the Swiss Boatmen during the Iron Epoch.

Next in order to these objects, we must mention the horses' bits and shoes; the first being very simply constructed so as to last for a very long period of time. They were composed of a short piece of iron chain (fig. 257), which was placed in the horse's mouth, and terminated at each end in a ring to which the reins were attached.

Fig. 257.—Horse's Bit, found in the Lake of Neuchâtel.

The *fibulæ* (fig. 258), or clasps for cloaks, are especially calculated to attract attention in the class of ornamental objects; they are very elegant and diversified in their shapes, their dimensions varying from 2½ to 5 inches. They are all formed of a pin in communication with a twisted spring bent in various ways. They are provided with a sheath to hold the end of the brooch pin, so as to avoid any danger of pricking. A large number of them are in an excellent state of preservation, and might well be used at the present day.

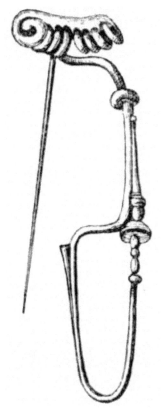

Fig. 258.—*Fibula*, or Iron Brooch, found in the Lake of Neuchâtel.

These brooches, which we have already called attention to when speaking of the tombs of Hallstadt, were also used by the Etruscans and the Romans; their existence in the pre-historic tombs tends to prove that, like the above-named nations, the Swiss and Germans wore the toga or mantle. These *fibulæ* have a peculiar character, and it is impossible to confuse them with the Roman *fibulæ*. They are, however, similar in every way to those which have been found at Alise.

There have also been found in the Swiss lakes, along with the *fibulæ*, a number of rings, the use of which is still problematical. Some are flat and others chiselled in various ways. It is thought that some of them must have been used as buckles for soldiers' sword-belts (fig. 259); but there are others which do not afford any countenance to this explanation. Neither can they be looked on as bracelets; for most of them are too small for any such purpose. Some show numerous cuts at regular intervals all round their circumference; this fact has given rise to the supposition that they might perhaps have served as a kind of money.

Fig. 259.—Iron Buckle for a Sword-belt, found in the Lake of Neuchâtel.

In the lake-settlement of La Tène (Lake of Neuchâtel), iron pincers have also been found (fig. 260), which were doubtless used for pulling out hair, and are of very perfect workmanship; also scissors with a spring (fig. 261), the two legs being made in one piece, and some very thin blades (fig. 262), which must have been razors.

Fig. 260.—Iron Pincers, found in the Lake of Neuchâtel.

Fig. 261.—Iron Spring-Scissors, found in the Lake of Neuchâtel.

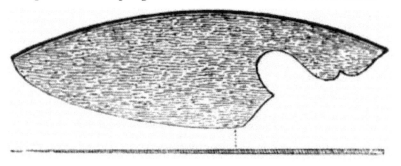

Fig. 262.—Razor.

The specimens of pottery belonging to this date do not testify to any real progress having been made beyond the workmanship of the bronze epoch; the clay is still badly baked, and of a darkish colour. It certainly is the case, that along with these remains a quantity of fragments of vessels have been picked up, and even entire vessels, which have been made by the help of the potter's wheel and baked in an oven, and consequently present the red colour usual in modern earthenware. But archæologists are of opinion that this class of pottery does not date back beyond the Roman epoch; and this opinion would seem to be confirmed by the existence, in the midst of the piles at the settlement of La Tène, of a mass of tiles, evidently of Roman origin. The conclusion to be drawn from these facts is, that many of the pile-works in the Swiss lakes continued to be occupied when the country was under the Roman rule.

One of the characteristics of the iron epoch is, as we have before stated, the appearance of coin or money. In 1864, M. Desor recovered from the Lake of La Tène five coins of unquestionable Gallic origin. They are of bronze, and bear on one side the figure of the horned horse, and on the other a human profile. In fig. 232, we gave a representation of these curious specimens of coin found by M. Desor in the lacustrine settlements of the Lake of Neuchâtel. The marks of the mould still existing on each side show that these coins were cast in a series, and that after the casting the coins were separated from one another by means of the file.

Coins of a similar character have been discovered, as we before observed, at Tiefenau, near Berne, with others bearing the effigy of Diana and Apollo, and the imprint of *Massilia*, The latter date from the foundation of Marseilles, and could not, therefore, be anterior to the sixth century before the Christian era; it is probable that those discovered along with them must be referred to nearly the same epoch.

Such are the relics of instruments, tools, weapons, &c., made of iron and recovered from the lacustrine settlement of La Tène, that is, from the Lake of Neuchâtel. We must add that, near Berne, at a spot which is designated by the name of the "Battle-field of Tiefenau," because it appears to have been the theatre of a great conflict between the Helvetians and the Gauls, a hundred swords and spear-heads have been picked up, similar to those found at La Tène; also fragments of coats of mail, rings, *fibulæ*, the tires of chariot-wheels, horses' bits, and lastly, Gallic and Marseillaise coins in gold, silver, and bronze. This field of battle appears, therefore, to have been contemporary with the settlement at La Tène.

In addition to these valuable sources of information—La Tène and Tiefenau—Switzerland also possesses *tumuli* and simple tombs, both constituting records useful to consult in respect to the iron epoch. But on this point, it must be remarked that it is often difficult, with any degree of security, to connect them with the two preceding sites; and that considerable reserve is recommended in attempting any kind of identification.

Upon the whole, the Iron Age, looking even only to its earliest period, is the date of the beginning of real civilisation among European nations.

Their industrial skill, exercised on the earliest-used materials, such as iron and textile products, furnished all that was required by the usages of life. Commerce was already in a flourishing state, for it was no longer carried on by the process of barter only. Money, in the shape of coin, the conventional symbol of wealth, came into use during this epoch, and must have singularly facilitated the operations of trade. Agriculture, too, had advanced as much as it could at this earliest dawn of civilisation. The remains of cereals found in the lake-settlements of Switzerland, added to the iron instruments intended to secure the products of the cultivation of the ground, such as the scythes and sickles which we have previously depicted (figs. 254 and 255), are sufficient to show us that agriculture constituted at that time the chief wealth of nations. The horse, the ass, the dog, the ox, and the pig, had for long time back been devoted to the service of man, either as auxiliaries in his field-labours, or as additions to his resources in the article of food. Fruit-trees, too, were cultivated in great numbers.

Fig. 263.—Agriculture during the Iron Epoch.

As a matter of fact, we have no acquaintance with any of the iron and bronze instruments which were used by men of the iron epoch in cultivation of the ground. Scythes and sickles are the only agricultural implements which have been discovered. But even these instruments, added to a quantity of remains of the bones of cattle which have been found in the lacustrine and palustrine settlements, are sufficient to prove that the art of cultivating the earth and of extracting produce from its bosom, rendered fertile by practices sanctioned by experience, existed in full vigour among the men who lived during the period immediately preceding historic times.

The plate which accompanies this page is intended to represent in a material form the state of agriculture during the iron epoch. We may notice the corn-harvest being carried on by means of sickles, like those found in the lacustrine settlements of Switzerland. A man is engaged in beating out, with a mere stick, the wheatsheaves in order to thrash out the grain. The grain is then ground in a circular mill, worked by a horizontal handle. This mill is composed of two stones revolving one above the other, and was the substitute for the rough primitive corn-mill; it subsequently became the mill used by the Romans—the *pistrinum*—at which the slaves were condemned to work.

Indications of an unequivocal character have enabled us to recognise as a fact, that human sacrifices took place among the Helvetians during this period. It is, however, well known, from the accounts of ancient historians, that this barbarous custom existed among the Gauls and various nations in the north of Europe. In a *tumulus* situated near Lausanne, which contained four cinerary urns, there were also found the skeletons of four young females. Their broken bones testified but too surely to the tortures which had terminated their existence. The remains of their ornaments lay scattered about in every direction, and everything was calculated to lead to the belief that they had been crushed under the mass of stones which formed the *tumulus*—unhappy victims of a cruel superstition. Not far from this spot, another *tumulus* contained twelve skeletons lying in all kinds of unusual postures. It is but too probable that these were the remains of individuals who had all been immolated together on the altar of some supposed implacable divinity.

What was the character of the type of the human race during the iron epoch? It must evidently have been that of the present era. Both the skulls and the bodies of the skeletons found in the tombs of this epoch point to a race of men entirely identical with that of our own days.

We shall not carry on our study of pre-historic mankind to any later date. We have now arrived at an epoch upon which sufficient light has been thrown by oral tradition combined with historical records. The task of the historian begins at the point where the naturalist's investigations come to an end.

FOOTNOTE:

[41] 'Les Sépultures de Saint-Jean de Belleville,' with lithographed plates.

PRIMITIVE MAN IN AMERICA.

THE development of mankind has, doubtless, been of much the same character in all parts of the world, so that, in whatever quarter of the world man may come under our consideration, he must have passed through the same phases of progress ere he arrived at his present state. Everywhere, man must have had his Stone Age, his Bronze Epoch, and his Iron Epoch, succeeding one another in the same order which we have ascertained to have existed in Europe. In the sketch which we have drawn of primitive man we have devoted our attention almost entirely to Europe; but the cause simply is, that this part of the world has, up to the present day, been the principal subject of special and attentive studies in this respect. Asia, Africa, and America can scarcely be said to have been explored in reference to the antiquity of our species; but it is probable that the facts which have been brought to light in Europe, would be almost identically reproduced in other parts of the world.

This is a fact which, as regards *dolmens*, has been already verified. The sepulchral monuments of the Stone Age, which were at first believed to be peculiar to France, and, indeed, to one province of France, namely Brittany, have since been met with in almost every part of the world. Not only have they been discovered all over Europe, but even the coasts of Africa bring to our notice numerous relics of them; also, through the whole extent of Asia, and even in the interior of India, this same form of sepulchre, bearing witness to a well determined epoch in man's history, have been pointed out and described by recent travellers.

Thus, the information which we possess on these points as regards Europe, may well be generalised and applied to the other quarters of the world—to Asia, Africa, America, and Oceania.

America, however, has been the scene of certain investigations concerning primitive man which have not been without fertile results; we shall, therefore, devote the last few pages of our work to a consideration of the pre-historic remains of America, and to giving an account of the probable conditions of man's existence there, as they have been revealed to us by these relics.

The information which has been made public on these points concerns North America only.

It would be useless to dwell on the stone and bone instruments of the New World; in their shape they differ but little from those of Europe. They were applied to the same uses, and the only perceptible difference in them is in the substance of which they were made. We find there hatchets, knives, arrow-heads, &c., but these instruments are not so almost universally made from flint, which is to a considerable extent replaced by obsidian and other hard stones.

In the history of primitive man in North America, we shall have to invent another age of a special character; this is the *Age of Copper*. In America, the use of copper seems to have preceded the use of bronze; native metallic copper having been largely in use among certain races. On the shores of Lake Superior there are some very important mines of native copper, which must have been worked by the Indians at a very early date; in fact, the traces of the ancient workings have been distinctly recognised by various travellers.

Mr. Knapp, the agent of the Minnesota Mining Company, was the first to point out these pre-historic mines. In 1847, his researches having led him into a cavern much frequented by porcupines, he discovered, under an accumulation of heaped-up earth, a vein of native copper, containing a great number of stone hammers. A short time afterwards, some other excavations 25 to 35 feet in depth, and stretching over an extent of several miles, came under his notice. The earth dug out had been thrown on each side of the excavations; and mighty forest-trees had taken root and grown there. In the trunk of a hemlock-tree growing in this "made ground," Mr. Knapp counted 395 rings of growth, and this tree had probably been preceded by other forest-giants no less venerable. In the trenches themselves, which had been gradually filled up by vegetable *débris*, trees had formerly grown which, after having lived for hundreds of years, had succumbed and decayed; being then replaced by other generations of vegetation, the duration of which had been quite as long. When, therefore, we consider these workings of the native copper-mines of Lake Superior, we are compelled to ascribe the above-named excavations to a considerable antiquity.

In many of these ancient diggings stone hammers have been found, sometimes in large quantities. One of the diggings contained some great diorite hatchets which were worked by the aid of a handle, and also large cylindrical masses of the same substance hollowed out to receive a handle. These sledges, which are too heavy to be lifted by one man alone, were doubtless used for breaking off lumps of copper, and then reducing them to fragments of a size which could easily be carried away. If we may put faith in Professor Mather, who explored these ancient mines, some of the rocks still bore the mark of the blow they had received from these granite rollers.

The work employed in adapting the native copper was of the most simple character. The Indians hammered it cold, and, taking into account its malleable character, they were enabled with tolerable facility to give it any shape that they wished.

In America, just as in Europe, a great number of specimens of pre-historic pottery have been collected. They are, it must be confessed, superior to most of those found in the ancient world. The material of which they were made is very fine, excepting in the case of the vessels of every-day use, in which the clay is mixed with quartz reduced to powder; the shapes of the vessels are of the purest character, and the utmost care has been devoted to the workmanship. They do not appear to have been constructed by the aid of the potter's wheel; but Messrs. Squier and Davis, very competent American archæologists, are of opinion that the Indians, in doing this kind of work, made use of a stick held in the middle. The workman turned this stick round and round inside the mass of clay, which an assistant kept on adding to all round the circumference.

In regard to pottery, the most interesting specimens are the pipes, which we should, indeed, expect to meet with in the native country of the tobacco plant and the classic calumet. Many of these pipes are carved in the shape of animals, which are very faithfully represented. These figures are very various in character, including quadrupeds and birds of all kinds. Indeed, in the state of Ohio seven pipes were found on each of which the manatee was so plainly depicted that it is impossible to mistake the sculptor's intention. This discovery is a curious one, from the fact that at the present day the manatee is not met with except in localities 300 or 400 leagues distant, as in Florida.

The pre-historic ornaments and trinkets found in North America consist of bracelets, necklaces, earrings, &c. The bracelets are copper rings bent by hammering, so that the two ends meet. The necklaces are composed of shell beads (of which considerable quantities have been collected) shells, animals' teeth, and small flakes of mica, all perforated by a hole so as to be strung on a thread. The earrings also are made of the same material.

All these objects—weapons, implements, pottery, and ornaments—have been derived from certain gigantic works which exhibit some similarity, and occasionally even a striking resemblance, to the great earthwork constructions of the Old World. American archæologists have arranged these works in various classes according to the probable purpose for which they were intended; we shall now dwell for a short time on these divisions.

In the first place, we have the *sepulchral mounds* or *tumuli*, the numbers of which may be reckoned by tens of thousands. They vary in height from 6 feet to 80 feet, and are generally of a circular form; being found either separately or in groups. Most frequently only one skeleton is found in them, either reduced almost to ashes, or—which is more rare—in its ordinary condition, and in a crouching posture. By the side of the corpse are deposited trinkets, and, in a few cases, weapons. A practice the very contrary to this now obtains in America; and from this we may conclude that a profound modification of their ideas has taken place among the Indians since the pre-historic epochs.

It is now almost a certain fact that some of the small *tumuli* are nothing but the remains of mud-huts, especially as they do not contain either ashes or bones. Others, on the contrary, and some of the largest, contain a quantity of bones; the latter must be allied with the *ossuaries* or bone-pits, some of which contain the remains of several thousand individuals.

It would be difficult to explain the existence of accumulations of this kind if we did not know from the accounts of ancient authors that the Indians were in the habit of assembling every eight or ten years in some appointed spot to inter all together in one mass the bones of their dead friends, which had been previously exhumed. This singular ceremony was called "the feast of the dead."

We shall not say much here as to the *sacrificial mounds*, because no very precise agreement has yet been arrived at as to their exact signification. Their chief characteristics are, that, in the first place, they are nearly always found within certain sacred enclosures of which we shall have more to say further on, and also that they cover a sort of altar placed on the surface of the ground, and made of stone or baked clay. In the opinion of certain archæologists, this supposed altar is nothing but the site of a former fire-hearth, and the mound itself a habitation converted into a tomb after the death of its proprietor. It will therefore be best to reserve our judgment as to the existence of the human sacrifices of which these places might have been the scene, until we obtain some more complete knowledge of the matter.

The *Temple-Mounds* are hillocks in the shape of a truncated pyramid, with paths or steps leading to the summit, and sometimes with terraces at different heights. They invariably terminate in a platform of varying extent, but sometimes reaching very considerable dimensions. That of Cahokia, in Illinois, is about 100 feet in height, and at the base is 700 feet long and 500 feet wide. There is no doubt that these mounds were not exclusively used as temples, and, adopting as our authority several instances taken from Indian history, we may be permitted to think that on this upper terrace they were in the habit of building the dwelling of their chief.

The most curious of these earthworks are, beyond question, those which the American archæologists have designated by the name of *animal-mounds*.

They consist of gigantic bas-reliefs formed on the surface of the ground, and representing men, mammals, birds, reptiles, and even inanimate objects, such as crosses, pipes, &c. They exist in thousands in Wisconsin, being chiefly found between the Mississippi and Lake Michigan, and along the war-path of the Indians. Their height is never very considerable, and it is but seldom that they reach so much as 6 feet; but their length and breadth is sometimes enormously developed. Many of these figures are copied very exactly from Nature; but there are, on the other hand, some the meaning of which it is very difficult to discover, because they have been injured by the influence of atmospheric action during a long course of ages.

In Dale county there is an interesting group composed of a man with extended arms, six quadrupeds, a simple *tumulus*, and seven mounds without any artistic pretensions. The man measured 125 feet long, and nearly 140 feet from the end of one arm to the other. The quadrupeds are from 100 to 120 feet long.

The representation of lizards and tortoises are frequently recognised in these monstrous figures. A group of mounds, situate near the village of Pewaukee, included when it was discovered two lizards and seven tortoises. One of these tortoises measured 470 feet. At Waukesha there was found a monstrous "turtle" admirably executed, the tail of which stretched over an extent of 250 feet.

On a high hill near Granville, in the state of Ohio, a representation is sculptured of the reptile which is now known under the name of alligator. Its paws are 40 feet long, and its total length exceeds 250 feet. In the same state there exists the figure of a vast serpent, the most remarkable work of its kind; its head occupies the summit of a hill, round which the body extends for about 800 feet, forming graceful coils and undulations; the mouth is opened wide, as if the monster was swallowing its prey. The prey is represented by an oval-shaped mass of earth, part of which lies in the creature's jaws. This mass of earth is about 160 feet long and 80 feet wide, and its height is about 4 feet. In some localities excavations are substituted for these raised figures; that is to say, that the delineations of the animals are sunk instead of being in relief-a strange variety in these strange works.

The mind may readily be perplexed when endeavouring to trace out the origin and purpose of works of this kind. They do not, in a general way, contain any human remains, and consequently could not have been intended to be used as sepulchres. Up to the present time, therefore, the circumstances which have accompanied the construction of these eminently remarkable pre-historic monuments are veiled in the darkest mystery.

We now have to speak of those enclosures which are divided by American archæologists into the classes of *defensive* and *sacred*. This distinction is, however, based on very uncertain data, and it is probable that a large portion of the so-called *sacred* enclosures were in the first place constructed for a simply *defensive* purpose. They were, in general, composed of a wall made of stones, and an internal or external ditch. They often assumed the form of a parallelogram, and even of a perfect square or circle, from which it has been inferred that the ancient Indians must have possessed an unit of measurement, and some means of determining angles. These walls sometimes embraced a considerable area, and not unfrequently inside the principal enclosure there were other smaller enclosures, flanked with defensive mounds performing the service of bastions. In some cases enclosures of different shapes are grouped side by side, either joined by avenues or entirely independent of one another.

The most important of these groups is that at Newark, in the Valley of Scioto; it covers an area of 4 square miles, and is composed of an octagon, a square, and two large circles. The external wall of one of these circles is even at the present day 50 feet in width at the base, and 13 feet high; there are several doorways in it, near which the height of the wall is increased about 3 feet. Inside there is a ditch 6 feet in depth, and 13 feet in the vicinity of the doors, its width being about 40 feet. The whole enclosure is now covered by gigantic trees, perhaps 500 or 600 years old—a fact which points to a considerable antiquity for the date of its construction.

When we reflect on the almost countless multitude, and the magnificent proportions of the monuments we have just described, we are compelled to recognise the fact that the American valleys must at some early date have been much more densely populated than at the time when Europeans first made their way thither. These peoples must have formed considerable communities, and have attained to a somewhat high state of civilisation—at all events a state very superior to that which is at present the attribute of the Indian tribes.

Tribes which were compelled to seek in hunting their means of every-day existence, could never have succeeded in raising constructions of this kind. They must therefore necessarily have found other resources in agricultural pursuits.

This inference is moreover confirmed by facts. In several localities in the United States the ground is covered with small elevations known under the name of *Indian corn-hills*; they take their rise from the fact that the maize, having been planted every year in the same spot, has ultimately, after a long course of time, formed rising grounds. The traces of ancient corn-patches have also been discovered symmetrically arranged in regular beds and parallel rows.

Can any date be assigned to this period of semi-civilisation which, instead of improving more and more like civilisation in Europe, became suddenly eclipsed, owing to causes which are unknown to us? This question must be answered in the negative, if we are called upon to fix any settled and definite date. Nevertheless, the conclusion to which American archæologists have arrived is, that the history of the New World must be divided into four definite periods.

The first period includes the rise of agriculture and industrial skill; the second, the construction of mounds and inclosures; the third, the formation of the "garden beds." In the last period, the American nation again relapsed into savage life and to the free occupation of the spots which had been devoted to agriculture.

In his work on 'Pre-historic Times' Sir John Lubbock, who has furnished us with most of these details, estimates that this course of events would not necessarily have required a duration of time of more than 3000 years, although he confesses that this figure might be much more considerable. But Dr. Douler, another *savant*, regards this subject in a very different way. Near New Orleans he discovered a human skeleton and the remains of a fire, to which, basing his calculations on more or less admissible *data*, he attributes an antiquity of 500 centuries! Young America would thus be very ancient indeed!

By this instance we may see how much uncertainty surrounds the history of primitive man in America; and it may be readily understood why we have thought it necessary to adhere closely to scientific ideas and to limit ourselves to those facts which are peculiar to Europe. To apply to the whole world the results which have been verified in Europe is a much surer course of procedure than describing local and imperfectly studied phenomena, which, in their interpretation, lead to differences in the estimate of time, such as that between 3000 and 50,000 years!

CONCLUSION.

BEFORE bringing our work to a close we may be permitted to retrace the path we have trod, and to embrace in one rapid glance the immense space we have traversed.

We have now arrived at a point of time very far removed from that of the dweller in caves, the man who was contemporary with the great bear and the mammoth! Scarcely, perhaps, have we preserved a reminiscence of those mighty quadrupeds whose broad shadows seem to flit indistinctly across the dim light of the quaternary epoch. Face to face with these gigantic creatures, which have definitively disappeared from the surface of our globe, there were, as we have seen, beings of a human aspect who, dwelling in caves and hollows of the earth, clothed themselves in the skins of beasts and cleft flakes of stone in order to form their weapons and implements. We can hardly have failed to feel a certain interest in and sympathy with them, when tracing out the dim vestiges of their progress; for, in spite of their rude appearance, in spite of their coarse customs and their rough mode of life, they were our brethren, our ancestors, and the far-distant precursors of modern civilisation.

We have given due commendation to their efforts and to their progress. After a protracted use of weapons and implements simply chipped out of the rough flint, we have seen them adopt weapons and instruments of polished stone, that is, objects which had undergone that material preparation which is the germ of the industrial skill of primitive nations.

Aided by these polished-stone instruments, added to those of bone and reindeer's or stag's horn, they did not fear to enter into a conflict—which every day became more and more successful—with all the external forces which menaced them. As we have seen, they brought under the yoke of servitude various kinds of animals; they made the dog and the horse the companion and the auxiliary of their labour. The sheep, the ox, and other ruminants were converted into domesticated cattle, capable of insuring a constant supply of food.

After the lapse of ages metals made their appearance!—metals, the most precious acquisition of all, the pledge of the advent of a new era, replete with power and activity, to primitive man. Instruments made of stone, bone, reindeer or stag's horn, were replaced by those composed of metal. In all the communities of man civilisation and metals seem to be constant companions. Though bronze may have served for the forging of swords and spears, it also provides the material for implements of peaceful labour.

Owing to the efforts of continuous toil, owing also to the development of intelligence which is its natural consequence, the empire of man over the world of nature is still increasing, and man's moral improvement follows the same law of progression. But who shall enumerate the ages which have elapsed whilst these achievements have been realised?

But thy task is not yet terminated! Onward, and still onward, brave pioneer of progress! The path is a long one and the goal is not yet attained! Once thou wert contented with bronze, now thou hast iron—iron, that terrible power, whose function is to mangle and to kill—the cause of so much blood and so many bitter tears; but also the beneficent metal which fertilises and gives life, affording nutriment to the body as well as to the mind. The Romans applied the name of *ferrum* to the blade of their swords; but in after times *ferrum* was also the term for the peaceful ploughshare. The metal which had brought with it terror, devastation, and death, erelong introduced among nations peace, wealth and happiness.

And now, O man, thy work is nearly done! The mighty conflicts against nature are consummated, and thy universal empire is for ever sure! Animals are subject to thy will and even to thy fancies. At thy command, the obedient earth opens its bosom and unfolds the riches it contains. Thou hast turned the course of rivers, cleared the mountain sides of the forests which covered them, and cultivated the plains and valleys; by thy culture the earth has become a verdant and fruitful garden. Thou hast changed the whole aspect of the globe, and mayst well call thyself the lord of creation!

Doubtless the expanding circle of thy peaceful conquests will not stop here, and who can tell how far thy sway may extend? Onward then! still onward! proud and unfettered in thy vigilant and active course towards new and unknown destinies!

But look to it, lest thy pride lead thee to forget thy origin. However great may be thy moral grandeur, and however complete thy empire over a docile nature, confess and acknowledge every hour the Almighty Power of the great Creator. Submit thyself before thy Lord and Master, the God of goodness and of love, the Author of thy existence, who has reserved for thee still higher destinies in another life. Learn to show thyself worthy of the supreme blessing—the happy immortality which awaits thee in a world above, if thou hast merited it by a worship conceived in spirit and in truth, and by the fulfilment of thy duty both towards God and towards thy neighbour!

Milton Keynes UK
Ingram Content Group UK Ltd.
UKHW052106300624
444882UK00004B/315